New Technologies at Work

New Technologies At Work
People, Screens and Social Virtuality

Edited by Christina Garsten and Helena Wulff

Oxford • New York

First published in 2003 by
Berg
Editorial offices:
First Floor, Angel Court, 81 St Clements Street, Oxford OX4 1AW, UK
838 Broadway, Third Floor, New York, NY 10003–4812, USA

Berg is the imprint of Oxford International Publishers Ltd.

Library of Congress Cataloging-in-Publication Data
New technologies at work : people, screens, and social virtuality/edited by Christina
Garsten and Helena Wulff.
    p. cm.
Includes bibliographical references and index.
    ISBN 1-85973-644-0 (Cloth) – ISBN 1-85973-649-1 (Paper)
    1. Employees–Effect of technological innovations on–United States–Case studies.
2. Electronic data processing personnel–Supply and demand–United States. 3.
Internet–Economic aspects–United States. 4. Information technology–Economic
aspects–United States. 5. Telecommuting–United States. 6. Information society–United
States. I. Garsten, Christina. II. Wulff, Helena.
HD6331.2.U5N49 2003
331.25–dc22

                                                                        2003017015

British Library Cataloguing-in-Publication Data
A catalogue record for this book is available from the British Library.

ISBN   1 85973 644 0 (Cloth)
        1 85973 649 1 (Paper)

Typeset by Avocet Typeset, Chilton, Aylesbury, Bucks.
Printed in the United Kingdom by Biddles Ltd, Guildford and King's Lynn.

www.bergpublishers.com

Contents

Acknowledgements   vii

Notes on Contributors   ix

Introduction: From People of the Book to People of the Screen   1
Christina Garsten and Helena Wulff

1. Living with New (Ideals of) Technology   7
Daniel Miller

2. The Computer as a Focus of Inattention: Five
Scenarios concerning Hospital Porters   25
Nigel Rapport

3. Digital Ditches: Working in the Virtual Grass Roots   45
Sarah Green

4. Real-time, Real-place Market: Transnational
Connections and Disconnections in Financial Markets   69
Anna Hasselström

5. Mobile Workplacing: Office Design, Space and Technology   91
Heinrich Schwarz

6. Claiming the Future: Speed, Business Rhetoric and
Computer Practice   119
Robert Willim

7. Networking as a Form of Life: The Transnational
Movement of Internet Pioneers   145
Paula Uimonen

8. Mainstream Rebels: Informalization and Regulation
in a Virtual World   165
Christina Garsten and David Lerdell

9. Steps on Screen: Technoscapes, Visualization and
Globalization in Dance   187
Helena Wulff

**10. Screening the Classroom: Students, Teachers and
Computers in an Urban American School**   205
*William Washabaugh, Catherine Washabaugh, Mary Roffers
and Kira Kaufmann*

**11. Open-Source Software Development as Gift Culture:
Work and Identity Formation in an Internet Community**   223
Magnus Bergquist

Index   243

Acknowledgements

The idea for this volume on technology and work practice springs out of the academic context in which we work. It merges a long-standing interest in technology and culture on one hand and work practice on the other in the Department of Social Anthropology at Stockholm University. It is a great privilege to have been socialized into anthropology in such an inspiring milieu. We are grateful for the intellectual rigour and creative climate in our department. For early support of this volume, we would also like to thank Keith Hart very much.

Danny Miller has been an important advisor and collaborator from beginning to end with the volume. It has been a real pleasure to work with him. *New Technologies at Work* would, however, not have been completed without Kathryn Earle's careful persistence. It is because of her unique combination of warmth, wit and cunning that this volume is now ready.

Christina Garsten and Helena Wulff

Notes on Contributors

Magnus Bergquist is Associate Professor of Cultural Anthropology and researcher at the Viktoria Institute, Gothenburg, Sweden. He is also senior faculty member of the Department of Informatics, Gothenburg University. His research focuses on cultural aspects of information technology in organizations, both on and off the Internet. Special interests are open source, virtual communities, organizational knowledge sharing and cooperation and methodological aspects of Internet research. He has published his work in e.g. *Journal of Information Systems, Journal of Information Technology* and *AI and Society*.

Christina Garsten is Associate Professor at the Department of Social Anthropology (Stockholm University) and Research Director at Score (Stockholm Center for Organizational Research, Stockholm University and Stockholm School of Economics). Her general research interests are in the anthropology of organizations and markets. She has done research on organizational culture and globalization in a high-tech company (*Apple World: Core and Periphery in a Transnational Organizational Culture*, Almquist & Wiksell, 1994). Later research has focused on the flexibilization of employment, emerging forms of regulation, and their impacts on the formation of work-related identities in the temporary-staffing sector (*Learning to be Employable: New Agendas on Work, Responsibility and Learning in a Globalising World*, co-edited with Kerstin Jacobsson, Palgrave, 2003). Current interests are orientated toward the anthropology of markets, with a particular view to issues of social accountability in the corporate world ('Risky business: Risk and (ir)responsibility in globalizing markets', with Anna Hasselström, *Ethnos*, 2, 2003).

Sarah Green is a Senior Lecturer in Social Anthropology at the University of Manchester. She has carried out ethnographic research on feminist separatism in London; concepts of place, landscape and the Balkans on the Greek-Albanian border; environmental problems among citrus farmers in the Peloponnese (southern Greece); and the introduction of high bandwidth information and communications technologies in Manchester, the latter as part of the ESRC's 'Virtual Society?' programme, with Penny Harvey and Jon Agar. She has published *Urban Amazons* (1997, Macmillan) and is currently completing two book manuscripts on her work in Greece and Manchester. Her key interests include concepts of the person and the anthropology of bodies; the anthropology of place, space and borders; gender and sexuality; the ethnography of Greece and the Balkans; and new information and communications technologies.

Anna Hasselström is a PhD student at the Department of Social Anthropology, Stockholm University. Her dissertation focuses on the production, distribution and organization of financial-market knowledge in financial markets. Her area of interest is the fashioning of contemporary markets. She has written articles on the relation between business and friendship, and co-authored with Christina Garsten 'Risky Business: Discourses of Risk and (Ir)responsibility in Globalizing Markets', *Ethnos*, 2, 2003.

David Lerdell currently holds a PhD candidate position for research on 'Information Technology, Law, Power and Ethics' funded by the Swedish Research Council and based at the Stockholm Center for Organizational Research (SCORE), Stockholm University and Stockholm School of Economics. He is working on a dissertation with the preliminary title *Organizing the Internet*. It focuses on the development of the Internet, aiming for an understanding of the initial organizing of the network, the organizational structure surrounding the Internet and the critical process in organizational terms, namely the transition of the system for names and numbers, the so-called Domain Name System (DNS). His publications include articles on the Internet and security, and OECD collaboration and organization.

Kira Kaufmann has a Master's degree in Anthropology from Florida State University and more than 20 years of anthropological and archaeological experience. She is currently in her fourth year of doctoral study at the University of Wisconsin-Milwaukee (UWM). Although she is now undertaking her dissertation work in archaeological studies of Southeastern Wisconsin, she is also pursuing studies of pedagogical methods, and serving a second year as a research assistant in the collaborative project at Riverside University High School under the auspices of the Cultures and Communities Program at UWM.

Daniel Miller is Professor of Material Culture at the Department of Anthropology, University College London. His previous publications range from three books on the topic of shopping to three based on fieldwork in Trinidad. Recent work in material culture include an edited collection about the car (*Car Cultures*) and one on the home (*Home Possessions*). With Don Slater he published *The Internet: An Ethnographic Approach*, which is an examination of the impact of the Internet in one region. Currently he is working with Mukulika Banerjee on a book about *The Sari* in India, and in the longer term he is working on a project to rethink the concept of value, which has so far included fieldwork on the process of audit in local government and will next turn to the world of finance.

Nigel Rapport holds a Chair in Anthropological and Philosophical Studies in the Department of Social Anthropology at the University of St Andrews. He is also Adjunct Professor at the Norwegian University of Science and Technology, Trondheim. He has conducted participant-observation research in England, Israel and Canada as well as in Scotland. His theoretical interests revolve around individuality and social complexity, and their representation. Among his recent publications are: *Transcendent Individual* (1997), *Migrants of Identity* (1998), *Social and Cultural Anthropology: The Key Concepts* (2000), *British Subjects* (2002), and *The Trouble with Community* (2002).

Mary Roffers has worked in schools and in other educational programmes serving youth over the past two decades. She served as a school board member for a private Montessori school for eight years, worked as a teaching assistant in three Montessori programmes, co-ordinated an Odyssey of the Mind programme, led a Junior Great Books programme for ten years, mentored high school students, and served on programme-evaluation teams for a Wisconsin school district. Currently, she is an anthropology Master's student at Univeristy of Wisconsin-Milwaukee.

Heinrich Schwarz, a recent graduate from MIT's Program in Science, Technology and Society, is Assistant Professor at the Department of Communication, University of Colorado, Boulder. His research investigates information and communication technologies in their everyday, social, organizational and cultural context. He recently finished his dissertation that explores the spatial, technological and social reorganization of information-based work toward more mobile, flexible and virtual forms. Currently, he studies changes in advertising firms in work practices and professional identities brought about by new digital and network technologies.

Paula Uimonen, PhD, specializes in Internet development in developing countries. Based on fieldwork in Southeast Asia, her dissertation *Transnational. Dynamics@Development.Net* (2001) discusses the Internet, globalization and modernization (see http://www.i-connect.ch/uimonen). She is currently working as a consultant, developing strategies for ICT for development. Her clients include the Swedish International Development Cooperation Agency (Sida) and various United Nations agencies. Her recent research interest has to do with the Internet and tourism in developing countries. Born in Finland, she grew up in Sweden and is currently living in Switzerland.

William Washabaugh is Professor of Anthropology at the University of Wisconsin-Milwaukee, and author of *Five Fingers for Survival: A Caribbean Sign Language* (1986), *Speak Into the Mirror: A Story of Linguistic Anthropology* (1988), *Flamenco: Passion Politics and Popular Culture* (1994), and *Deep Trout: Angling in Popular Culture* (2000).

Catherine Washabaugh has served as a public educator for 30 years. After graduating from the University of Connecticut, she taught in middle schools and high schools in Connecticut, Michigan and Wisconsin. She earned a Master's degree in Educational Administration at the University of Wisconsin-Milwaukee, thereafter serving as a principal in the Milwaukee Public Schools for five years. Currently, she teaches English and supervises the school newspaper at Riverside University High School.

Robert Willim, PhD, is a researcher in the Department of European Ethnology and the Department of Service Management at Lund University. During the last few years he has been studying cultural dimensions of digital media. He wrote his doctoral dissertation about rhetorics and practices within the IT business and the new economy (see www.framtid.nu). Currently he is working on a research project on digital media and music. He is also a producer of electronic music and is involved in several IT-related art projects.

Helena Wulff is Associate Professor in the Department of Social Anthropology, Stockholm University. Her English-language publications include *Twenty Girls: Growing Up, Ethnicity and Excitement in a South London Microculture* (Almqvist & Wiksell International, 1988) and *Ballet across Borders: Career and Culture in the World of Dancers* (Berg, 1998), as well as journal and volume articles. She has also co-edited the volume *Youth Cultures: A Cross-Cultural Perspective* (with Vered Amit-Talai, Routledge, 1995). Her research interests have revolved around youth culture and ethnicity, and currently around the anthropology of dance, the arts, and aesthetics, visualization, information technology and transnationality. She is now engaged in a study of dance and culture in Ireland and questions of social memory, modernity and place ('Yo-yo Fieldwork: Time and Mobility in a Multi-Local Study of Dance in Ireland', *Anthropological Journal on European Cultures*, 11, 2002).

Introduction: From People of the Book to People of the Screen

Christina Garsten and Helena Wulff

'Will we still turn pages?' was the headline of a Time article (Kelly 2000) discussing People of the Book[1] versus People of the Screen in terms of a cultural battle. People of the Book are portrayed as text-centred adhering to the authority of authors, while People of the Screen keep up with the constant flux and speed of screens such as movie, television, computer and telephone screens. People of the Book are worried that the page, as well as reading and writing, will become obsolete. This is unlikely to happen, according to the author of the article, Kevin Kelly, who points at the possibility to write with digital ink on thin plastic sheets. Such 'paper screens' can be put together into a book. Readers will thus continue to turn pages whether they are digital or classic paper pages.

On the following paper pages, anthropologists and European ethnologists investigate the recent impact of information and communication technologies on work practices and organizational culture. For information and communication technologies have become a part of everyday life and work. There is no doubt that these technologies have had a major impact on many work practices and career patterns, including changes in professional identities. They have made some work routines obsolete and added new ones. They have increased the speed, precision and safety with which certain tasks can be performed. The accessibility of employees has expanded considerably: employees are expected to be reachable through mobile phones and modems when they are not in the office but working from home or while travelling. All this also feeds into wider discussions on the role of information technologies in driving globalization.

Renegotiations of space, mobility, time and home have become central in contemporary work practices, making it easier to switch back and forth between work and leisure, as well as planning working hours more freely, which often means working longer hours than before, but also that certain groups of people such as the disabled or women in religious seclusion are able to work at all since they can do it from home.

With previous research from the 1980s and early 1990s on computerization and the workplace by Kidder (1981), Traweek (1988), Dubinskas (1988), Pfaffenberger (1990), Kunda (1992), Hakken (1993), Garsten (1994, 2001) among others as a point of departure, this volume aims to discuss, not so much the advent of information and communication technologies at workplaces, but changing work practices brought about by these technologies, which connect to emerging wider lines of inquiry on dualisms such as locality and globality. As Donna Haraway (1991) reminded us some time ago, dualisms including body and mind, culture and nature, and male and female have traditionally been the basis for much Western thought and related to power. Haraway put forward the idea that high technology is going to change these dualisms, especially the one between male and female: through connections between human and machine these dualisms will take on new forms. In this volume, we discuss new dualisms that have been produced by working on-line, in particular the relationship between virtuality and social life.

We pursue an ethnographic approach which includes social life in the form of work practice around technologies such as the Internet, which will uncover the interaction between on-line and off-line worlds (cf. Miller and Slater 2000). Arguing against Manuel Castells's (1996: 358–75) division of the real and the virtual as separate units and a 'culture of real virtuality', Miller and Slater (2000: 6–8) point out that the two are integrated. Virtuality is 'not a new reality' but '*part* of everyday life', they say (see also Pfaffenberger 1992). So virtuality is social, and should be thought of in terms of *social virtuality*, we suggest, and anchored – more or less and in new ways – in places. Even 'practices and relationships that only exist online' are connected to everyday life, according to Miller and Slater (2000: 7), which does not make the exploration of how the particular format of the Internet, for example, influences its content less urgent, especially when it comes to work practices of occupational virtual communities.

It was in the 1980s, in line with the growth of technological development in society in general, that an orientation toward the study of new technologies became evident in anthropology. Socio-technical systems were identified in order to accentuate the social meaning of human technological activity. The social organization of technology is now often positioned as a branch of comparative cultural studies. Because of the transnational nature of technology this volume ties in with theoretical work on globalization and transnational cultural processes which has been formulated by anthropologists such as Arjun Appadurai (1996) and Ulf Hannerz (1992, 1996). There is also the volume *Cyborgs and Citadels*, edited by Downey and Dumit (1997). They identify the so-called citadel problem, i.e. how technological aspects tend to overshadow social and cultural aspects in popular discourse about science, technology and medicine. Downey's (1998) ethnography at the body/machine interface among computer engineers is another point of reference for this volume, as is the recent *The Internet* by Daniel Miller and Don Slater (2000).

Despite the fact that information and communication technologies are now everywhere and that we consequently often take them for granted, they continue to generate strong feelings for or against – sometimes expressed in terms of 'techno euphoria' versus 'techno fright'. The opening reference to the clash between People of the Book and People of the Screen is an example of this. Euphoric moments may occur both in connection with the learning process which includes discovery of the scope of extension and combinations of tasks that can be executed on the Internet, for example, and during an intense work phase when a piece of missing information might be found just in time through an exchange on e-mail. Techno fright, on the other hand, is produced by an awareness that information on the Internet is impossible to protect and might be of a subversive nature, as well as that there may be a risk of health problems for computer and mobile-phone users. An awareness of the vulnerability of the Internet also belongs here: a virus can shut down systems on a global level within seconds. (In Sweden, there are now special clinics treating patients with Internet addiction who are unable to stop surfing on the Internet, a condition which is comparable to gambling or drug addiction.)

A dichotomy between techno euphoria and techno fright can be traced back to Raymond Williams's (1975) path-breaking work on the revolutionary possibilities of television for education and democracy as well as the risk that it will manipulate the masses.

Already in the 1930s, Walter Benjamin (1969) had written his classic article 'The Work of Art in the Age of Mechanical Reproduction' where he celebrates mass media as a potentially liberating force (for the suppressed masses). This was later critiqued not least by other scholars from the Frankfurt School who argued that mass media suppress, stupefy and manipulate people. But this was before new forms of media and technology emerged, such as grass-roots media that to a certain extent can be controlled by people themselves. Writing about cassette culture in India, Manuel (1993) shows how political agendas can be furthered through underground press, posters, pirate radio stations, videos and cassettes. Also the Internet can be utilized as a grass-roots medium or technology in this sense.

Most people seem to be neither incessantly celebratory nor sceptical about working with new technologies, however. They have learnt to use them and like them, and it may in fact not be until their computer breaks down that that they realize how dependent they have become on it. This is true both of those who work *on* technology by developing computer software programmes or designing web pages, and that vast majority of people who work *through* technology, mostly the Internet, by getting and exchanging information there.

There is an imagery of unlimited flow of global business on the Internet, or e-commerce, that recent ethnographic studies are beginning to challenge. In a study of the Internet in Trinidad, Miller and Slater (2000) conclude, for instance, that although the Trinidadians have embraced the Internet as a useful way to communicate with their diaspora, their attempts to do business such as advertising on-line, had failed because they had not learnt the conventions of this technology. This is thus one case when the economic world system of centres and peripheries is duplicated on the Internet. In this volume, we seek to highlight the social embeddedness of information technologies. Following Miller and Slater (ibid.) we argue that conventions of communication on the Internet reflect already existing social norms of communication.

A central part of working with information and communication technologies consists of watching, an activity which lately has attracted an analytical interest formulated in terms of visualization or an awareness of the cultural meaning of the visual. Coming out of the subfield of visual anthropology, this new anthropology of 'the visual' is defined by Marcus Banks and Howard Morphy (1997: 5) as 'the anthropology of visual systems or, more broadly, visible cultural forms'. This includes the visual in cultural process, indigenous ways of seeing, and visual representations. This volume addresses the growing impact of the visual in connection with work practices.

In an age of changing ethnographic practice, this volume also contributes to the expanding discussions on new methods in anthropology by reporting on multiple methodological approaches to the study of technologies and work. This includes transnational, mobile and multi-sited field studies as discussed by Garsten (1994), Marcus (1995), Clifford (1997), Wulff (1998, 2002), Hannerz (1998), as well as a range of techniques complementing traditional participant observation and interviews which Gusterson (1997) has termed 'polymorphous engagement'. When it comes to the ethnographic study of information and communication technologies and work this includes spending time with people while they work with technology, but also using the Internet as a research tool by logging onto web sites, taking part in discussion groups and chat rooms, and investigating e-mails (cf. Hakken 1999, Bull 2000, Miller and Slater 2000), even conducting additional interviews on e-mail or presenting the study on a homepage (Uimonen 1999).

Finally, we would like to add a note on the prominence of the inherent future-orientation both in a general discourse on technologies and in studies of technologies which relates to the topic of time in the volume. Hakken's (1999) book is subtitled *An Ethnographer Looks to the Future*, and he argues that the computer revolution has not really occurred yet, even that 'it is too early to conclude that new forms of labor like virtual work or telecommunicating constitute a new mode of employment society' (ibid.: 214). In their analysis of the

Internet, Miller and Slater (2000: 14) identify 'its very novelty that makes it an ideal idiom for imagining the future'. This volume explores work practices in the recent past and the present, and to some extent ideas about future ones. All these work practices are instances of social virtuality.

Note

1. Originally, the Book referred to in this expression was the Bible.

References

Appadurai, A. (1996), *Modernity at Large: Cultural Dimensions of Globalization*, Minneapolis: University of Minnesota Press.
Banks, M. and Morphy, H. (1997), 'Introduction: Rethinking Visual Anthropology', in M. Banks and H. Morphy (eds), *Rethinking Visual Anthropology*, New Haven: Yale University Press.
Benjamin, W. (1969 [1936]), 'The Work of Art in the Age of Mechanical Reproduction', in *Illuminations,* New York: Shocken.
Bull, M. (2000), *Sounding the City*, Oxford: Berg.
Castells, M. (1996), *The Rise of the Network Society*, Oxford: Blackwell.
Clifford, J. (1997), *Routes: Travel and Translation in the Late Twentieth Century*, Cambridge, MA: Harvard University Press.
Downey, G.L. (1998), *The Machine in Me: an Anthropologist Sits among Computer Engineers*, New York and London: Routledge.
Downey, G.L. and Dumit, J. (eds) (1997), *Cyborgs and Citadels: Anthropological Interventions in Emerging Sciences and Technologies*, Santa Fe, NM: School of American Research Press.
Dubinskas, F. (ed.) (1988), *Making Time*, Philadelphia: Temple University Press.
Garsten, C. (1994), *Apple World: Core and Periphery in a Transnational Organizational Culture*, Stockholm Studies in Social Anthropology, 33, Stockholm: Almqvist & Wiksell.
—— (2001), 'Play at Work: Contested Frames of Hacking', *Focaal*, 37: 89–101.
Gusterson, H. (1997), 'Studying Up Revisited', *Political and Legal Anthropology Review*, 20(1): 114–19.
Hakken, D. (1993), 'Computing and Social Change: New Technology and Workplace Transformation, 1980–1990', *Annual Review of Anthropology*, 22: 107–32.
—— (1999), *Cyborgs@Cyberspace?* New York: Routledge.
Hannerz, U. (1992), *Cultural Complexity: Studies in the Social Organization of Meaning*, New York: Columbia University Press.
—— (1996), *Transnational Connections*, London: Routledge.

—— (1998), 'Transnational Research', in H.R. Bernard (ed.), *Handbook of Methods in Cultural Anthropology*, Walnut Creek: Altamira.

Haraway, D.J. (1991), 'A Cyborg Manifesto: Science, Technology, and Socialist-Feminism in the Late Twentieth Century', in *Simians, Cyborgs, and Women*, London: Free Association Books.

Kelly, K. (2000), 'Will we still turn pages?', *Time*, 3 July.

Kidder, T. (1981), *The Soul of a New Machine*, New York: Avon Books.

Kunda, G. (1992), *Engineering Culture*, Philadelphia: Temple University Press.

Manuel, P. (1993), *Cassette Culture*, Chicago: Chicago University Press.

Marcus, G.E. (1995), 'Ethnography in/of the World System: the Emergence of Multi-Sited Ethnography', *Annual Review of Anthropology*, 24: 95–117.

Miller, D. and Slater, D. (2000), *The Internet: an Ethnographic Approach*, Oxford: Berg.

Pfaffenberger, B. (1990), *Democratizing Information*, Boston: G.K. Hall.

—— (1992), 'The Social Anthropology of Technology', *Annual Review of Anthropology*, 21: 491–516.

Thomas, N. (1997), 'Collectivity and Nationality in the Anthropology of Art', in M. Banks and H. Morphy (eds), *Rethinking Visual Anthropology*, New Haven: Yale University Press.

Traweek, S. (1988), *Beamtimes and Lifetimes*, Cambridge, MA: Harvard University Press.

Uimonen, P. (1999) '"Technology, Modernity and Globalization": Some Social Aspects of Internet Development', *Antropologiska Studier*, 62–63: 7–15.

Williams, R. (1975), *Television*, New York: Schocken Books.

Wulff, H. (1998), *Ballet across Borders: Career and Culture in the World of Dancers*, Oxford: Berg.

—— (2002), 'Yo-yo Fieldwork: Mobility and Time in a Multi-Local Study of Dance in Ireland', *Anthropological Journal on European Cultures*, issue on Shifting Grounds: Experiments in Doing Ethnography, vol. 11: 117–36.

–1–

Living with New (Ideals of) Technology

Daniel Miller

Introduction: the Virtual Life of Ideals

It is no coincidence that the fundamental challenge posed by this book turns out to be the problematic reification of ideals of new technology separated out from its practice. After all, this is largely the work of sustained ethnographic encounter, and the result is a remarkably clear and diverse picture of new technologies as the practice of work. As such the authors of this volume do something that is very rare within the writings of practitioners themselves. They try to soberly assess what is actually happening in the day-to-day life of working activity, without using this in order to establish these new practices as some kind of ideal. Most of those who work in the industry are, by contrast, clearly trying to sell something, whether it is the potential commodification of the technology or designs that they have created, or the idea that what they are doing now is inevitably going to become standard practice in the future, since they are aware that belief in this trajectory as inevitable will help ensure its coming to be.

Indeed one of the clearest lessons of the last decade has been that the myths and ideals of new technology have had at least as much an impact as their practice, which is why there has been a premium on abstracting these ideals and focusing upon them. This book highlights the danger in this separation, in this creation of the virtual ideal. It demonstrates at a more mundane level something that has already been made very clear at a macro level in the dot.com fiasco itself. In brief, this consisted of the articulation of new techniques of finance with new forms of technology. Central to modern finance are forms of derivatives and the mechanisms of leverage. These devices capitalize on the assumed potential of some new asset to eventually be worth a considerable amount, and allow that future value to be played with and invested as though it were already realized. Leverage is the extra amount of value that is created by speculating upon the potential of these new developments. The bubble effect of the dot.com episode was entirely dependent upon being able to separate out an ideal or promise of such future developments and fetishize this as though it were a concrete asset and thereby already a form of value.

Within finance this virtualism of the promise of new technology is made explicit and clear. I want to argue that the common theme throughout this book follows the same fundamental logic, but as it can be demonstrated to exist within the actual usage and effects of new technology in the workplace, without the independent effects of finance. In every single one of the chapters in this volume we start with the problem of how an ideal or promise seen to be intrinsic to the new technology reveals this potential for reification – that is, to be abstracted from the practice of people and their labour. This is not necessarily a negative effect. We would be a poorer population if we never sought to construct ideals and then live up to them. But the abstraction of ideals has its inherent dangers. It can become part of what I would call a 'virtualism' (Miller 1998) when it loses touch with its source in a practice that people can work with, absorb and relate directly to. This is the virtualism of the ideal. Curiously the concept of virtual as the site of communication technology is probably rather more spurious (see various discussions in Woolgar 2002). Yet ultimately it is not virtual cyberspace but virtual ideals that can become destructive, when potentially positive uses of technology become sacrificed upon the alter of an untenable or in some cases actually less-than-ideal ideal. What this volume offers as a collection is not just the unprecedented insights given by its own close adherence to the observation of practice, but also a wide range of examples. This provides a kind of spectrum that allows us to ask important questions, which a single case study could not answer. In this instance I want to suggest that it allows us to think about the nature of ideals themselves, and to try to come to some kind of formulation of what actually is an ideal ideal.

The chapters of the book may therefore be separated out along such a spectrum. We start with some examples of rather unedifying ideals, that is to say ideals that are anything but ideal since we do not actually desire them (though others do). From there we can move to examples where the ideal is problematic precisely because it has been abstracted so far from any link with ordinary practice and then fetishized as a thing in and of itself to be lived up to that it becomes oppressive even though it is considered to be beneficial and to represent a true ideal. The third stage in this process is to consider ideals which are held as ambivalent because they lie closer to practice and because those involved are thereby more conscious of the negative effects that now appear to be inseparable from the perceived benefits of these new technologies. Interestingly they clearly remain ideals, but they are tempered by experience. Finally we can move to the end of such an investigation by considering whether by exploring all these case studies we have come any closer to what might be termed an ideal ideal.

Unedifying Ideals

The first three chapters concern ideals which are not likely to be shared by anthropologists, partly on political grounds but partly because they seem so narrowly conceived and so far from what we might regard as lessons from history. For this reason the authors of the first two examples are mainly concerned with how the populations they studied thwart or subvert or survive those ideals. The primary ideal is couched largely in a model of the market, one that seems to assert its own inevitability. This rests in turn upon the way it is supported by an abiding myth about new technologies in general. When school-children were taught history at schools in Britain, there was always a rather strange break at the point at which one stopped being taught about kings, queens and politics and started learning about new technologies, devices such as the 'Spinning Jenny' and 'Arkwright's Mule'. These were the harbingers of the industrial revolution and it is instructive that rather than being explicitly about the development of capitalism, it is the technology itself that was foregrounded. It was new machines that industrialized cotton-cloth production, from which somehow all sorts of elements of modern life 'naturally' followed.

As taught in schools, new technologies caused the industrial revolution and that in turn caused capitalism, under which people become subject to the deter-minants of commerce and capital as in effect commodified wage labour. There is a direct line between this mythic origin of modern life and the dot.com bubble. Our most recent fiasco was quite dependent upon a continued adherence to this myth of origin. It too presupposed that technological development would in and of itself move industrial capitalism forward to a distinctive new phase. Essentially it had to suppose that new technologies create new ways of control-ling the world, and that includes the control of people through work and the creation of value through new forms of capitalism. The implication always seems to be that this is the intrinsic quality of the technology itself. The effect would be greater profitability that could be turned through instruments of finance into speculative investments. New technology was thus a boost to the economy that could be leveraged as the share value of the firms that were associated with it. Downstream from this was the belief by the public and by governments that we would all become new kinds of workers – 'information workers'. We must learn the new skills and knowledges that would allow us to keep up with a history that has accelerated on the back of this new technology.

In different ways Rapport and Green focus upon people and institutions that are potentially oppressed by this myth and the idealized and simplified concept of economy that develops in its wake. In both cases they start with institutions of government that turn this myth into an ideal of new technology creating a more successful economy through this same sequence by which labour is increasingly commodified. Instructively, Rapport shows that hospital managers assume that all new technologies have this capacity, legitimated by this origin myth of modern life. The telephone and the computer are part of the hospital regime, that which makes it work efficiently and cost effectively. The purpose of the porter is to be a cog in that machine, which reduces to their function as wage labour. As such the development of technology is the development of their commoditization as labour. But by starting his chapter with the telephone rather than the computer, Rapport effectively reveals what is evident to the porters themselves. A technology that can be used as an instrument of control is just as easily used as part of their everyday lives at home where it is an instrument of communication and leisure. The telephone thereby provides their route to the colonization of the computer, since having seen the absurdity and blinkered way the telephone is presented to them at work, it doesn't take much of an analogy to see the same potential for the computer – and they clearly do follow this analogy. So although the computer is first introduced as a machine which is going to pinpoint their exact position at any time and thus control them, they quickly see all sorts of other possibilities for subverting this process which would otherwise reduce them to mere commodity forms.

My favourite image from Rapport's Chapter 2 is of the individual who is a porter at work, but a football 'manager' thanks to his console at home. But the most telling materials are the various strategies by which we start with a machine that is supposed to turn porters into a commodity, and end up with porters who find ways to turn the machine back into a commodity for their own purposes. This includes making copies of CDs, buying and selling consoles from notice boards, or ultimately by stealing and then selling the machines themselves. In all these ways the porters effectively reverse the original logic of the origin myth.

This is very familiar to me from Trinidad (Miller and Slater 2000). Albert, for example, has an attitude that in Trinidad is not peripheral but mainstream. The first thing one looks for in any new technology is based upon what it enables you to get for free that you couldn't get for free before. In one of the first cybercafés that Don Slater and I went into, the main notice on the wall was a list of everything one could get for free. Indeed from the point of view of this perspective the very logic of their masters is reversed. Trinidadians feel that other people are stupid, precisely because they don't see that this search for free stuff is the first use of a technology. For them, as probably for Albert, this is blindingly obvious as the proper attitude for an intelligent person to take. Their distance from the others allows them to create their own world as inverse. It is not a world without its own order. They may look like the extreme opposite of the order that would impose itself upon them, but as Rapport makes clear even their use of pornography has its own morality and codes, something that emerges clearly from Slater's work (Slater 1998, 2000).

It is not that they don't know the dominant discourse or its power. They too believe that if they want to progress to a better job they have to rethink these things as skills for which they gain qualifications. But what they cannot do is be in the state of 'denial' where the fact that a phone is something you used to ask a woman to go out on a date with is completely excluded when the phone is presented to you in the workplace. At one level, then, the porters simply occupy a reality, obvious to them but denied by a dominant discourse true to its own origin myth about the role of new technologies.

What emerges from Green's Chapter 3, and indeed from most of the chapters in this volume, is the extent to which the discourse created by this myth of origin is itself what determines the history of institutions. The problem that her chapter outlines is that the British government does have some sense of the wider potential of computing, and even manages to conceive of it in relation to social welfare and the reduction of inequalities. But it can only imagine this happening in one way – that is, by skilling the workforce and thus developing the economy. 'It seems appropriate that the Internet should be used to address the perceived need for "lifelong learning": a need to generate a flexible workforce able to continually absorb new information and develop new skills to go with the flexible (information-based) economy with which we now live.' Actually we should be very concerned with the narrowness of the government's conception of what is going on. If life-long learning is only there to create skills for the workplace, then it follows that the government has lost any rationalization of its own purposes, compatible with an ideal that values lifelong learning in its own right. It implies once again that all of us who work in education do so ultimately only to somehow enhance shareholder value.

Smaller organizations, however, being often marginal to the state, may have a rather broader view. For example, the sense of empowerment of women's groups may not be limited to the idea that one has to be skilled for purely entrepreneurial purposes. The dot.com fiasco allowed this contradiction to be avoided for a while. This was because it seemed as though giving money for general education was assumed to be a vital part of creating an information-technology-savvy population. As such this investment in people's welfare would one day 'pay dividends' (pun intended). Later on as the dot.com bubble starts to burst, Green makes clear that the contradictions in legitimacy come to the fore. 'What this experience makes clear is that despite the apparent commitment to "social exclusion" in public funding for ICTs, the message voluntary organizations were getting was that commitment was not guided by a commitment to social welfare, but by a determination to get people "on-line" so that they could remove their own "social exclusion" through the economic opportunities offered by ICTs. The skills required were "business" skills; and the world in which these skills would be used was a different one from that in which the earlier voluntary organizations had been formed.' What Green's discussion makes frighteningly clear is that notwithstanding all the evidence for what computers actually can do, the government simply has no language, no means for expressing the legitimacy of these advances, other than that of business, and skills for business. Government even when it 'sort of' knows it is there to enhance the welfare of the population that voted for it, has lost its voice, and this is partly because of the origin myth that technology has only one aim and consequence, and that social evolution passes through this alone.

The irony that the anthropology of business constantly exposes is that this pure notion of how business creates profits is one held far more strongly by government and the public sector than it is within the private sector of business itself, where a greater realism about the inefficiencies and ineffectiveness of commerce cannot be ignored. So the contradictions that Green points out with respect to government are equally apparent within the world of finance itself, as demonstrated by Hasselström in Chapter 4. Most of the popular – in the sense of journalistic – books about how capitalism actually works, books such as *Liar's Poker* (Lewis 1989) or *Barbarians at the Gate* (Burrough and Helyar 1990), show how much social networks and competition and culture intersect with the effects of technology, or of new financial instruments.

At one level it is easy to see high finance as a screen-based workplace in which information can be simultaneous, in a global sense, and thus timeless and placeless. So at this level technology dominates the flow of information. But there is a critical factor here that contextualizes this and negates its apparent effects. The people who work in this sector are in competition with each other. They only make money if they can offer something before or beyond what their competitors can. So the irony is that all this screen information, by virtue of the fact that it is global and simultaneous, is in and of itself worthless as a means to make money. Of course you have to be able to afford it and become part of the exclusive group that does so. But once you are perched at this level you are all equal. So what becomes clear in Hasselström's Chapter 4 is that it is precisely the other kinds of information that come to have the potential to create financial value. That is to say, the more that new technology creates a sameness the greater is the premium upon difference. The brokers are constantly going back to various forms of social interaction, in the hope that they will hear something different or first (See also Leyshon and Thrift 1997 on the City of London). As they keep saying quite explicitly, only information that they can't get on the screen or that they get before the other brokers actually 'adds value' since value here is always defined by their competition with others.

So the paradox is that the more information arrives by the screen the more valuable it makes other information that does not, since screen information cannot give competitive advantage. Only with placed and timed contextualiza-

tion, combined with well-informed interpreters that have been specifically cultivated as friends for that purpose, can one turn the sameness of this information
into difference. So once again, though for different reasons, control by the
machine and commodification by the machine turns into its opposite. As the
author says, the effect of this is that 'information technology provides an important backdrop for the organization, production and distribution of financial flows
as argued by Castells (1996, 1997, 1998). But the seemingly hypermobile, placeless and timeless financial flows of information-technology-based financial
markets are in fact deeply intertwined with certain shared place-bound, time-
bound and social practices of trading.'

I have called the myth of origin an unedifying ideal, because I can't imagine
many social scientists supporting the idea that the intrinsic quality of new technology is always to increase commodification including the commodification of
labour. What these three chapters demonstrate is the degree to which new technologies also contain quite the opposite potential, the potential to turn commodified labour back into 'people'. At this level Hasselström is really making the
same point as Rapport and Green. Working with this new technology forces
dealers to focus upon the human aspect of other people as the basis for difference. In Rapport it is the porters themselves, and in Green the values held by
organizations such as women's groups who assert this other potential. We should
not romanticize technology by fetishizing this other process of decommodification; rather, the lesson is surely that both possibilities lie inherent in new technology, and which of them is fostered will depend upon factors other than those
embedded in the technology itself.

The Ideal as Fetish

If Rapport, Green and Hasselström start us off with the unedifying ideal of the
pure market, in which technology is valued only for its capacity to create
commodification, then four further chapters clarify what might be taken to the
central problem exposed by this collection. This is the tendency for an ideal to
become virtual, that is to say to shift from being a formulation of the positive
potential of new technology to becoming itself an oppressive force that clearly
mitigates against such positive effects. This amounts to what we may call a
fetishism of ideals. What ought to be a movement forward and upward for the
experience and condition of labour, as involved in the new technologies,
becomes instead an abstraction that is held against them. In varying ways this
was true for the chapters already discussed also.

A particularly clear instance of this process of fetishism is found in Schwarz's
Chapter 5, since architecture has an evident tendency to fetishize ideals, in the
sense of rendering them object-like. It literally renders them 'concrete'. An ideal

here becomes material ideology. This occurs when people imagine a potential new social order based on the imminent possibilities of these technologies, and have the power to construct a material world that manifests this ideal irrespective of the actual practice under which such technologies are employed. In effect this comes close to the traditional concept of ideology in Marxist theory, where certain groups have the power to remake the world in their image and interest. In this case we are not talking about a whole capitalist class but rather a partnership between designers and owners. This is especially evident because the basis of Schwarz's chapter is an ethnography of production but not of consumption.

Architecture, and most of all modernism, as Frampton (1992), Wigley (1996) and many other architectural historians have shown, is in many ways a history of the fetishism of untenable ideals. For architects and designers the seating arrangement of a room is a potential open to the expression of an ideal such as 'most effective and efficient usage'. This blissfully refuses to know what 'everyone knows,' which is that people soon have favourite chairs, or that we prefer to have much of our mundane decision-making established in routines that we don't have to think about. This kind of knowledge designers and architects prefer not to know. Actually the situation is rather worse. The designers wanted to unknow how people operate with things, in order to teach them ultra-'modern' relationships. So when it is said 'It was felt that giving everyone a dedicated desk that would be empty for a large part of the time was not an effective use of space', it means that they wanted to develop what is in effect a changed collo-quial concept of property and rights. With the new technologies come all sorts of academic language about placelessness and spacelessness, so that designers believe they can utilize these to give workers a new sense of flexibility and freedom. It is very hard to read this account without constantly reflecting upon its absurdity. Constantly coming to mind is the life of a 'real' office, where typically there are several workers and managers who are not on speaking terms, and do not trust each other, and have developed routines of avoidance that at least save other managers from having to spend most of their time sorting out such petty quarrelling and rivalry. But for designers and architects managers are not allowed to 'not' see each other.

In effect then this is a study of a new materiality that is intended to reflect a vision of an ideal future. As such it is likely to prove no more successful than open-plan architecture had already been as a short-term fashion in domestic architecture. Already it was becoming evident that instead of an ideal new centralized electronic 'filing cabinet', new forms of private-information property had developed in highly dispersed personal laptops. So Schwarz's Chapter 5 has the merit of showing us what happens when ideal is fetishized outside of any contextualization by practice. What an ethnography of consumption might have shown is how often such intentions are contradicted by their effects.

A close companion to Schwarz's chapter is Willim's Chapter 6. Indeed, at the end of his discussion Willim introduces the idea of 'conceptual congruity' which helps us to further understand Schwarz's material. This is the idea that in order to both envisage and then inhabit the future, various orders must be rendered compatible. The phrase is remarkably similar to Bourdieu's (1977) notion of 'habitus', except that while Bourdieu is looking at structural homology between different domains developed from socialisation and history, this concept is like a deliberate attempt to develop an inhabitable habitus for the future. In this case we see compatibility not just between furnishing and machines, as was the case with Schwarz's, but also between ways of thinking. Indeed as Willim convincingly argues, this amounts to an aesthetic ideal in which, along with the modern art that no doubt ornaments such modern offices, we try to conceive of the 'shape of the future'.

Overall Willim's chapter charts a trajectory from a phenomenology of waiting to a fetishism of the future itself. He examines how our sense of time may be based on a relativism of expectations. Fast companies are impatient companies. When you are used to a certain speed of connection or boot-up time for your computer, then home connections look slow, and you are reluctant to work from home. It is part of the company's task as a 'fast company' to help employers 'feel' how time will feel in the future, since the very term future has the ring of inevitability about it. If one is not already there one is doomed. This phenomenological sensibility leads to a fetishism, then, of the future itself as the only place to be. The task was simply to find the visual model, in this case the S-curve and language, that could live up to this vision of the future. Willim presents the wonderful image of vapourware as a means for conjuring up a future, what he calls 'strategic invocations.' It is hard to imagine a term so redolent of the sense that the future has become a fetish.

The reason why the future in Willim's chapter is no more an ideal ideal than was the office in Schwarz's, is again the narrowness of the conception and most especially the failure to properly envisage the future user. A proper phenomenology of time, a study of relative expectations, would have to consider the relationship to the computer relative to other experiences of time. A boot-up time that is quick relative to the previous boot-up time seems like inevitable progress. But if the already present boot-up time is roughly that which it takes to sort out our papers and chairs and be ready for work, then it can be placed comfortably 'in the scheme of things' which makes any further speed of little value. But this only appears in relation to a wider view of computer use, the kind of study Lally (2002) has recently produced of computer use in the home. Two years ago it seemed that increases in speed would inevitably lead to increases in sales as they had done for many years. Today, however, we find that this was only because increase in speed led to a commensurate increase in the effectiveness of the main software packages used. Today, an increase in computer speed doesn't appear to make a whole lot of difference to the way we use a program such as Microsoft Word, so for the user there is no great desire to upgrade one's computer. This may come as a shock to the company employees who have fetishized the future in the form of speed in and of itself as part of their aesthetics of how life must be. Indeed in some ways these workers' relationship to their machines evokes a very ancient relationship to the material world. They peer into the machines like omen takers or soothsayers trying to forecast the future.

In these chapters by Schwarz and Willim we see a process of objectification in which the imagination of the future is realized through the images directly based upon the technologies themselves and their associated material culture. They thereby contrast with the next pair of chapters, those by Uimonen (Chapter 7) and by Garsten and Lerdell (Chapter 8). In both these chapters the process of objectification under scrutiny is as much one of personification, since it is the people themselves and their image of themselves that are used to directly embody the ideal of the future. Furthermore, both chapters bring out important questions regarding the relationship between on-line and off-line worlds. Most of the more substantive recent studies of how new technologies are actually used (e.g. Miller and Slater 2000, Woolgar 2002) emphasize the degree to which on-line activity and off-line activity have major, often unexpected, effects upon each other. What we find in their two discussions, however, is an added twist. It is that new-technology practitioners are extremely concerned that there SHOULD be consequences for off-line life. This is because off-line life really ought to become the key testimony to the importance of what they claim to have achieved in on-line practice. In both chapters the pressure is on people to live up to a fetishized ideal that now regulates off-line as well as on-line actions.

Not surprisingly the practitioners and pioneers of these new technologies have their own missionary tendencies, which come to the fore when they meet for the kind of convention studied by Uimonen in Chapter 7. In this case what emerges is the importance for these missionaries to feel that something about themselves and their practice really does live up to the ideal that they have as their mission. For them this is achieved in the ideal of the cosmopolitan. The new globalization and placelessness that is supposed to be delivered by the technology is manifested in their own lives. Its positive nature is evident in that there are people represented from all over the world and they have thereby transcended traditional forms of regionalism and parochialism. This is an ideal, but not an ideal ideal, because it fixes upon the image of pure cosmopolitanism as the future of the world. It is reminiscent of all those science-fiction portrayals that show spaceships full of people that once had disparate origins but here are all united in wearing the same silver suits. But this is really a failure of imagination. First, it refuses to reflect on the negative side of the cosmopolitanism of Internet-mediated communication. People do not regard sending an e-mail greeting card as satisfactory as being there when one's child blows out the candles. Nor do they (usually) regard the mutual masturbation of cybersex as being as satisfactory as sleeping with one's partner. They do, however, understand that an animated and personalized egreeting card is much better than no card at all because of slow postal services. Cybersex with a partner might be imagined as better than using the hotel pay-per-view pornography. But a better class of substitution is not an ideal ideal. As Uimonen suggests, to focus simply upon the inclusory nature of one's social relations under cosmopolitanism may also be a denial of its exclusionary nature, such as the absence of one's partner and children. Curiously, the image conjured by Uimonen's chapter is rather like an off-line attempt to realize status that follows the game plan of certain on-line pursuits. To gain status and to respect people seem to be goals rather like those of computer-game players who must locate and master various new skills and pick up hard-to-locate jewels that grant you an extension of 'life' or the ability to move up to the next level of the game.

Garsten and Lerdell in Chapter 8 also investigate a complex and constant interplay between living up to certain ideals off-line and on-line that is created by the commandment to personify an ideal supposedly inherent in new technology. In their case this revolves around the apparent paradox they identify as the formal requirement to appear informal. This representation of informality applies equally to the 'netiquette' of appearance in on-screen communication as it does to the sartorial commandment not to wear suits to meetings. There are many fine examples in their chapter that beautifully illustrate this paradox, but the chapter itself is concerned with the deeper contradictions that are thereby revealed. Some of the reasons are more contingent and particular. Informality is almost part of the 'brand recognition' of Apple as against IBM, and the one story almost everyone seems to know of Bill Gates is that he supposedly wears GAP clothing. Much deeper than this is the paradox of libertarian ideals. In his classic commentary 'A Rape in Cyberspace', Dibbell (1999: 11–30) showed how a similar group of libertarian netplayers suddenly discovered the 'virtues' of regulation and censorship when their on-line roles are taken over and attacked. The logic revealed by Garsten and Lerdell is one in which the 'hippie' originators of this philosophy of freedom either come to terms with such regulation or continue to refuse these consequences of growth and turn to what might be seen as the more negative connotation of the term Luddite, the anarchic destructive power of the hacker who unleashes a virus.

Indeed in some ways this brief history is a kind of quick replay of the philosophical understanding of freedom itself. We start with the pure liberationist ideals of the French Revolution and will probably end in the realization (of Hegel and others) that the true foundation of freedom must reside in institutionalized law. At this current juncture what we find is the anxiety of those who only see the contradictions of what appears as a form of regulated informality. The contradiction is expressed by the phase 'Normative Freedom' (Miller and Slater 2000). Groups espouse these new ideals of freedom which they see as inherent in the technology, but they want adherence to them to be normative rather than based on formal regulation. Without regulation or normative adherence these freedoms tend to create considerable anxiety, as these authors reveal, over what we should wear (see also Clarke and Miller 2002), and how we should act while on-line. On the other hand, they can generate a certain amount of playful freedom and, as Danet (2001) has shown, a kind of on-line folk art.

In conclusion, these four chapters amount to an important contribution to our sense of how ideals become fetishized. In each case what seems like a positive potential ends up as an oppressive measure that constrains workers under the guise of liberating them. In the case of Schwarz this happens when an ideal of new free relationships is constructed as the material environment within which workers are forced to operate. In Willim we see this in the fetishization of on-screen information such as to deny the reality of off-screen encounters and knowledge as the true basis of competitive difference. Both Uimonen and Garsten and Lerdell demonstrate that this fetishism is equally powerful if it is objectified in the bodies and practices of workers, the way they are supposed to behave, whether it is in typing messages, relating to their laptops, wearing the right clothing or generally embodying this ideal of placeless, libertarian and informal relationships.

The Ambivalent Ideal

In the next pair of chapters, by Wulff (Chapter 9) and by Washabaugh, Washabaugh, Roffers and Kaufmann (Chapter 10), we examine a mid-way position between the four cases just described and some sense of an ideal ideal, since these two chapters are concerned principally with the contradictions involved in this interaction with new technology as an image of the future. Willim argued quite explicitly in Chapter 6 for the aesthetic nature of this envisaging the future, and so it is not that surprising that when we turn to a self-designated aesthetic medium such as dance, the first people we meet are those who are interested in very much the same thing. Though in their case it is the question of how to dance the future. As Wulff points out, the fact that this is done through both the means of and the idiom of the latest technology is itself nothing new. All media have at some time in the past been 'new media' and dance has responded to the possibilities of each in turn. But what Wulff's material adds significantly, thereby creating a distinction from the four preceeding chapters, is that this is not a group of people who are wedded to the embodiment of modernity. On the contrary, they have rather more invested in their ability to embody the past, especially in those areas that might be labeled 'classical' dance. Indeed, an effect of this relationship to tradition is that we forget that the relationship to an audience mediated by a theatre and its seating plan is quite remarkably artificial, which allows us to imagine it as some kind of ideal of authenticity and immediacy against which the new technologies are judged with suspicion.

Wulff presents us with a picture of sustained ambivalence that properly represents actual contradictions emergent from changes in technology. Is one 'closer' to a dancer when seen from a hundred metres away as a seated audience but with no intervening technology, or when one is viewing through a screen in such a way that every gesture and grimace of the dancer's face can be seen? As Goffman (1975) famously argued, the theatre is a prime example of 'frame analysis' where, as in all the arts, we agree to abide by certain conventions of illusion, so that a new space of performance needs new conventions. A person tries to put his or her body into virtual space only to find that an interactive viewer now feels free to kick the first person's virtual head in. By the same token an aesthetic vanguard sees the creative possibilities inherent in this transitional period before new conventions of viewing and performing become established. Overall there is a sense of a balance of gain and loss. That the fact that one has to dance in a manner determined by the camera and associated technology is a constraint but one that may be acceptable because of the audience it brings both on television and then in turn as live audience. Some dance (it's hard not to think of Fred Astaire) seems made for the screen, because that's how we encountered it, other dance seems betrayed by it. After a while the divisions of live and mediated themselves become ambiguous. This appears particularly to be the case in more commercial dance where, as in the *Riverdance* example, dancers have microphones in their shoes, and performance, video and CD all work together to produce what is experienced as the 'phenomenon' that is Riverdance. But then, as is clear in Wulff's conclusion, a simple notion of reality was never going to fare very well in consideration of a genre such as dance.

One reason the two chapters being considered in this section are stronger on ambivalence than on fetishism is the emphasis upon the consumption of new technologies. While for Wulff this is the consumption by dance practice, for Washabaugh, Washabaugh, Roffers and Kaufmann consumption is centre stage since they are themselves the practitioners that are being investigated here. Indeed, any reader would sympathize with the complexity and difficulty of such a context as an underperforming high school. Personally I still think we are better served by ethnographic appraisals that are carried out by those who are participant observers but not the actual practitioners, as in the case of the other chapters in this volume, and who may therefore be able to demonstrate the failings through analysis of structural contradictions without any implication of person failings in such ventures. Clearly the authors think otherwise and I suspect most people will agree with them.

The considerable advantage of such a practitioner's point of view of the school itself, however, can be seen in contrast with circumstances in other chapters. For example, it is hard to imagine the hospital managers in Rapport's paper sympathetically working with and through their knowledge of the various subversive possibilities operated by the porters. By contrast, these teachers need to be fully aware of the 'downside' of computers, the problematic material that the Internet contains, and the obvious desire to play games or use the technology to detract from, rather than enhance, processes of learning. They talk about 'disciplinary integration' and a collaborative version of 'project-based learning'. The sense one has from the detail of the chapter is of an attempt, then, to take this contextualization a stage further both through learning from the experience of using computers as it progressed and by showing sensitivity to the particular nature and tendencies of particular students rather than assuming a one-size-fits-all solution. Certainly one of the things that makes an ideal more ideal is the way in which it manages this balance between its status as an ideal and the compromises made in manifesting this ideal as a practice.

What is more difficult to evaluate, when this close to the 'coalface', is the contradictory impact of the technology itself: for example, whether it is possible to prevent the fetishism of image and speed, where homework in so many schools now consists of quickly finding and downloading the photos that fit the homework project rather than understanding the project's aim and content. As the authors note in their conclusion, Internet-based learning is paradoxically a good deal slower. So many liberal ideas of schooling have sacrificed learning for the apparent advantages of freedom. This may well come down to a discussion about whether teaching children how to buy a cheaper car part (which ones suspects is the actual skill retained) is in fact a better (in the sense of more appropriate) form of 'education' in some cases than learning the names of Greek gods. This depends on concept of choice, which are properly raised by the chapter, but cannot be fully debated in this particular context.

The Ideal Ideal

So what, then, comes across as an ideal ideal? Bergquist chooses to hang his Chapter 11 on a discussion of the anthropological concept of the gift (often with analogies such as the potlatch which to my mind don't work). I feel this is a pity since actually the chapter's material goes rather beyond this narrow academic debate. Instead it provides a vital contrast with the four chapters on the fetishism of ideals. Open-source technology is different from any of the other examples studied in this book (though clearly closest to those of the two chapters just discussed) because it is one in which there is relatively little separation between ideal and practice. At one level open source technology is just as idealized, or indeed utopian, as the topic of those other chapters. If anything it is even more closely meshed with the new potentials of new technologies. The critical difference is that it is an ideal that is largely being formulated and advanced as a practice and not only as an abstracted discourse about that practice. It doesn't really need to know where it is going, so much as knowing how to manage the process of movement forward. As such we can see several problems explored in the previous chapters being resolved. First, there is considerable regulation involved in open source, but this works not by forcing people to represent an ideal of informality, or placelessness, but rather through the practice itself. Basically those who work according to the ideals to produce useful new developments find that these are taken up while others are simply ignored and therefore never come to form part of this process of development.

Unlike the pure liberationist ideals of informality, these practices are highly conditioned by the regulation inherent in the machine codes themselves. They simply have to work well. A claim or ideal in and of itself is worthless. Furthermore, they are not particularly individualistic. Developments are commonly made by teams, and in any case contributions often end up as anonymous and unacknowledged. There is merely the authors' private satisfaction in seeing their work adopted. We should not be carried away by an idea that 'everyone' is involved in its development. Actually the main progress is made by a tightly woven network of experts and professionals. But since this is essentially run by emulation – i.e., accepting what seems to work – it can be genuinely meritocratic rather than autocratic. This is the opposite end of the spectrum from discussions in those chapters dominated by ideology where what is supposed to be meritocratic usually ends up as autocratic.

There are other important conclusions here. The simplistic reading of these chapters would be to assume that everyone who works in open source is modest and generous, while say the designers studied by Schwarz or Uimonen's new-technology missionaries are personally ambitious and arrogant. Actually there is a much more complex implication to this comparative set of studies. The reason for the differences in the appearances of the people involved has more to do with the nature and structure of the work they are involved in. Open source is a process whereby survival is only through adoption and adoption is best fostered through giving away one's innovations as widely as possible. Bergquist shows how 'newbies' learn to become gift-givers. In the same way that academics (some of whom we might consider personally anything but generous) become involved in the operation of peer review knowing that the way they treat others is likely to eventually come back to them in the way they are treated. So we should not romanticize open-source technocrats any more than we should romanticize Rapport's porters as subversive heroes, and for the same reason we should be careful of any self-congratulatory tone taken by practitioners in the chapter by Washabaugh et al. What these chapters separate out are not so much the goodies and baddies but the way in which certain kinds of structure facilitate more or less ideal ideals and in which these become embodied and manifested by those who happen to have jobs in the relevant sectors. In some ways also the final example returns us to the first chapter considered. Open source as a case study is as destructive of the myth of origin of modernity through new technologies as are the first three chapters considered. Open source may lead to commodification as in paying for services and repairs, but clearly has inherent tendencies to decommodification. Indeed, this is perhaps the clearest example of the general argument that new technologies generally contain both tendencies.

There is one final ideal ideal that has been revealed by this collection. It concerns the potential for ethnography in the study of the topic in question; new technologies within the workplace. As I suggested in my introduction to this chapter, it is no coincidence that one can locate a constant theme throughout this volume around the discrepancy between ideal and practice. This emerges because of the commitment made to ethnography itself. Every one of these chapters is based on the scholarship involved in participant observation, in following through the day-to-day activities of work. Ethnography involves, among many pursuits, listening to the people involved and observing what they are doing. I would suggest that what emerges most positively from this collection is the latter. It is not listening to people but the observation of practice which is the unique feature of ethnography, since other approaches also may include interviews or focus groups. But language tends to foster the expression of ideals, whether or not they are manifested in practice. While what these chapters show is that the central component of action is normativity, the moral framework expressed in what it is considered appropriate to do and inappropriate to do. Normativity is best studied through the close observation of practice and sensitivity to any discrepancy between practice and the claims people make in legitimating themselves. It is this sensitivity to practice that is remarkable in all the chapters of this volume. It is this above all which makes the volume as a whole a unique contribution to understanding the real consequences of new technologies for people's working lives.

References

Bourdieu, P. (1977), *Outline of a Theory of Practice*, Cambridge: Cambridge University Press.

Burrough, B. and Helyar, J. (1990), *Barbarians at the Gate*, London: Arrow.

Castells, M. (1996), *The Rise of the Network Society*, Oxford: Blackwell.

—— (1997), *The Power of Identity*, Oxford: Blackwell.

—— (1998), *End of Millennium*, Oxford: Blackwell.

Clarke, A. and Miller, D. (2002), Fashion and Anxiety, *Fashion Theory*, 6: 191–213.

Danet, B. (2001), *Cyberpl@y*, Oxford: Berg.

Dibbell, J. (1999), *My Tiny Life*, London: Fourth Estate.

Frampton, K. (1992), *Modern Architecture: a Critical History*, London: Thames & Hudson.

Goffman, E. (1975), *Frame Analysis*, Harmondsworth: Penguin.

Lally, E. (2002), *At Home with Computers*, Oxford: Berg.

Lewis, M. (1989), *Liar's Poker*, London: Hodder & Stoughton.

Leyshon, A. and Thrift, N. (1997), *Money/Space: Geographies of Monetary Tranformation*, London: Routledge.

Miller, D. (1998) 'A Theory of Viritualism', in J. Carrier and D. Miller (eds), *Virtualism: a New Political Economy*, Oxford: Berg.

Miller, D. and Slater, D. (2000), *The Internet: an Ethnographic Approach*, Oxford: Berg.

Slater, D. (1998), 'Trading Sexpics on IRC: Embodiment and Authenticity on the Internet', *Body and Society*, 4: 91–117.

—— (2000), 'Consumption without Scarcity: Exchange and Normativity in an Internet Setting', in P. Jackson, M. Lowe, D. Miller and F. Mort (eds), *Commercial Cultures*, Oxford: Berg.

Wigley, M. (1996), *White Walls, Designer Dresses: the Fashioning of Modern Architecture*, Cambridge, MA: MIT Press.

Woolgar, S. (ed.) (2002), *Virtual Society? Technology, Cyberbole, Reality*, Oxford: Oxford University Press.

The Computer as a Focus of Inattention: Five Scenarios concerning Hospital Porters

Nigel Rapport

Introduction

In Constance Hospital, Easterneuk, Scotland, porters do not use computers. Doctors and managers use computers, as do nurses, laboratory technicians and clerks; but porters, like domestics, do not. This chapter explores the ways and extent to which hospital porters might be described, nonetheless, as 'people of the screen'. For while porters are not called upon to make use of computers as part of their work practices, computers (and other advances in information and communication technology such as mobile phones and the Internet) do still figure in individual porters' lives.

In particular, this chapter seeks to examine the place which porters make for computers, their feelings toward them, as route to and manifestation of identities and routines beyond the hospital, its distinctions, hierarchies and rules. In five scenarios, encountered during my employment as a hospital porter while under-taking participant-observation research, we meet computers as porters do use them: making them parts of their worlds of (i) genealogy, (ii) marketing, (iii) black-marketing, (iv) the uncivil and uncouth, and (v) thieving. Here are computer technologies as arenas of inattention within the work environment. A concluding discussion shifts the focus from the ethnography, and ends by considering whether the appropriation by the hospital porters of these new technologies represents a departure from other behaviours and attitudes of 'personalization' which they might manifest in the work-place.

Induction

Information and communication technologies punctuated the 75-minute induction lecture which I and five other male neophytes were given, by a portering submanager, in subtle but significant ways. Seated in silence facing 'Pat' in his office, we were instructed, for instance, in how the telephone was to become part of the controlling regime of the hospital. It was our responsibility, if we were unable to come to work due to sickness, to phone in and tell our supervisor; if we did not we would be docked a day's pay. (As the period of absence escalated, so did the requisite response: from phone message to sick note to doctor's note to an appointment with the Department of Occupational Health.) If using telephones inside the hospital, receiving messages of jobs that needed doing, a similar etiquette applied: we were to say things such as 'This is the porters'', 'Hello', 'Bye', and not simply 'Piss off!' – Pat's choice of this colloquialism bringing titters from us lads. Next, Pat showed us how a pager worked, in case we were issued with one, by demonstrating with his own. Dialling the number of his pager into the phone in his office he was, however, embarrassed to find that nothing happened. Angrily he phoned the hospital switchboard: 'Did he not ask for his pager to be switched on at 9 a.m.?!'. Shortly afterward his pager produced the proper bleeps and Pat warned us about the dangers of being incommunicado in the hospital due to the switchboard's mistakes.

After more than an hour of this lecturing and hectoring, and then a trip to the Laundry to collect our new portering uniforms of blue polo-shirt and trousers, I was left in no doubt about the disciplinary and hierarchical regime into which I was being initiated; also about the agonistic stance it was anticipated, as member of a group of porters, I would adopt within it. 'You might think porters are a small cog in a large machine', Pat said at one point, 'but don't think you're nothing just because people say you are. People might say you're "just a porter" but it's not true; no part of the hospital could run without you (the same with Domestics).'

Part of what made the hospital environment mechanistic ('industrial') and coercive, I would suggest, concerned these communication technologies by means of which the hospital regime was to be maintained. And significantly it was by openly defying hospital regulations in these areas – grabbing one's pager from one's belt and hurling it away; hurling abuse at the telephone just before or after answering it and not seriously minding if one's 'Fuck Off!' had been caught by the person on the other end of the line – that I would find my portering co-workers showing their contempt for and dismissal of the disciplinary culture.

But no mention of computers or other advanced telecommunications, such as mobile phones, had graced Pat's induction lecture. And this was to prove significant. For while such technologies might be directly associated with the hospital regimen by others of its employees (doctors and nurses, and so on) who, as I have said, used them as routine parts of their work duties, the fact that porters did not use them made their references to them, in words and behaviour, characteristically positive and hopeful, if not wistful. There was talk among the porters on one occasion about how, according to one union shop-steward, the hospital planned to introduce a computer system which would locate where the porter was on the hospital site at any one time, what job he had been allocated and how long he had been engaged with it; for the present, however, this 'Day of Judgement' was a future threat. For the present, computers etc. remained what I would describe as 'foci of inattention' in portering practice: means and medium by which porters would bring the rest of their lives into the workplace, resist its strictures and transcend its boundaries.

While imbued with a characteristically positive tone, however, I want also to convey the range of reference to computing technologies that porters make, the diversity of ways in which they profit by them – literally as well as metaphorically. I offer the following ethnographic scenarios, then, as a sample.[1]

Five Scenarios

The Genealogy of Computing

Some 137 porters work at Constance Hospital. All but two are male, while they range in age from 17 to 64. This spread tends to reflect the 'genealogical' connection between porters and computing know-how. Almost all the porters will have some information to do with computing to share, but what precisely will differ genealogically – according to their relationship to it.

In a windowless locker room of male ancillary staff, in the bowels of Constance near the mortuary and the loading bay, Luke and I arrive at work together. Luke, in his forties, unpacks his rucksack and, in a gesture of comradeship, itemizes its contents for me: one bread roll; one Celtic Football Club sticker that his son has given him for the inside of his locker door; a container of white sugar; some tea bags; new leather boots bought from a cut-price store in Carlisle where his wife comes from; and a computerized 'data organizer' in yellow plastic that his son used to use. Luke lets me touch it, and explains that they (he and his wife) got his son a new organizer, and having erased the data from the old one, made it over to Luke (although Luke is unsure what he will use it for).

It is quite common for fathers to talk, as Luke did, proudly if also uncomprehendingly, about their sons' habitualities (and it is always sons') with the new information technologies. The accounts elucidate their sons' computer know-how, their fetish for 'gadgets', but also how this ties in with other, more traditional accomplishments of theirs. Fred, for instance, explains to me how his sons are both hard workers, and in university, while the younger one, who wants to be a graphic artist, is particularly 'good with computers':

> And they're both quiet lads, thank goodness. Not like the ones you get here [among the porters]. Aren't they terrible, Nigel? Imagine having kids like the ones who work here! Mine just come in and go upstairs to their computers and work away for hours. And that's also educational, isn't it, playing computer games? Like playing 'Football

Manager' teaches you all about doing numbers in y' head ... They'll say 'Look at this, Dad', and show me something on the computer [Fred mimes looking over someone's shoulder], and I don't know what's going on! So I just look and say: 'Oh yes. How did you do that!' ... Sometimes the computer foxes them too, and that really fires them up! But the kids working here in the hospital just wanna smoke dope; it's amazing what you see here ... But I know I'm just old-fashioned.

The generational distance between such mature, adult egos and computer know-how does not always hold true. But when age difference does not explain the difference in accomplishment, another obvious factor often replaces it. Such as gender: if it is not sons who possess the knowledge of computers that their fathers do not, then it might be wives. Thus, Martin tells me that although he can play Playstation all evening with his brother (especially if he wants to get out of the house and away from his wife's female friends for an evening) he's 'no computer man': he 'can't work a PC [personal computer]. But my wife can; she uses one on her [nursing] course'. Or again, Kevin tells me that while he 'would not even know how to turn a computer on', his wife 'is better at those things: mobile phones, computers, e-mail and things'. They have e-mail at home, as part of their SKY TV package, and he can type in the code and get it open, but it is his wife who sends the mail. He imagines it might be different if he ran his own business and always needed to stay in contact but in his job, as a porter, he does not.

Then again, when an incontrovertible factor such as age or gender does not account for differences in computing accomplishment between *ego* and *alter*, a special contingent factor might be introduced. Bill, for instance, reveals that Graham, who used to porter, now has a job in computer graphics 'or something'; but then Graham had such a 'genius' for drawing that some of his daubings can still be found, un-defaced, around 'Pipe Street' (the name the porters give to the extensive 'backstage' area of heating and ventilation pipes that fill the basements of the hospital). While Martin, envious that a little boy in the hospital has been given a £3000 computer to learn and play on – as well as an all-expenses-paid trip to Florida for two weeks with all his family, and having his photograph in the paper – accounts for it by adding that the boy does have cancer and also real behavioural problems:

He's a real wild one – cos of his illness and what he's been through. He 'f's and 'c's all over the place ... His sister's friend was in here once and said: 'Look! He's got no hair'; and he replied: 'Cos I've been having fucking radiotherapy!'! ... Imagine the pilots having him for nine hours in the plane to the States; they'd have felt like letting him get out part-way across!

For many of the younger porters, meanwhile, the topic of computing know-how is broached by way of first-hand experience. Bill, for instance, in his early twenties, is on a '0.25 contract' at the hospital, working as a porter in between studying Computer Arts and Japanese at a local university. It is a four-year course, and Bill is only in his first year but he is definite he will see it through:

It's what I want to do ... When I left school I did not think I'd go to Uni. Not like my brother and sister ... I worked for a year doing shitty jobs. And then I felt ready for Uni; I did not want to go on doing shitty jobs for the rest of my life! Like portering!! [We are near the porter's lodge, and within earshot.] I could've gone straight into the second year at Uni, but I'm happy where I am. The class is a good one, and I'm enjoying the course. It's only been going two years so they're still sorting it out; I probably know more about the computer package we're using than the tutor! ... But I'd still like to go away to Uni, you know. There is a college in Savannah, Georgia, that does a famous computing course I'd like to go to next year – for a semester or a year – if I can arrange it and get on it.

Bill's immersion in his computing course and the future translocal possibilities it holds out to him appear correlative with his distance from the 'shittiness' of portering; he is as much a computer student, he claims, as he is not a mere porter. And this equation, 'computing versus portering' (a different version of the relation we found above between porter-parents and computing ignorance), seems to hold true for other younger porters. Roger has just completed a four-year course in Computing and Physical Education (the latter, admittedly, being the part he liked best), but now feels he 'needs something different'; making money (i.e., portering) must, he feels, come first: 'College is okay when you're young but in your twenties you wanna have a wage at the end of the week.'

Finally, it should be said that the connection between computing and enrolling in a college or university course is not exclusive to the younger porter. Andrew, in his fifties, tells me he also undertook one, but significantly, in his case too, the temporal and substantive differences between computing and portering still are made to apply. As he recalls with some nostalgia, he managed a supermarket for 20 years, before he was made redundant:

Then I managed a computerized brick kiln in a factory for seven years. Till that was hit by the recession of 1989 ... They sent me to university for a year for that, you know. Paid for it too! ... Aye, I've done lots of things, Nigel.

In short, computing know-how seems to relate to a certain otherness which is distinct from the portering present; it bespeaks a past or possible future, and a world away from the mundane worldliness of 'shitty' or gritty wage-earning.

This first scenario has identified the various 'genealogical' links by which many porters would claim some relationship to computer know-how, but a relationship characterized at the same time by a certain distance; the porter does not himself possess the know-how to any degree, it is his son who does, or his wife, or his exceptional acquaintance. Even when *ego's* relationship to computing is one of personal expertise, this often pertains to a past time when the rigours of earning a living through portering did not apply; or else computing know-how is laying foundations whereby the lowliness of portering will not delimit job horizons in the future.

The Marketing of Computing

If, however, in the role of 'hospital porter', individuals claim some dislocation from computing know-how, this does not mean that they are not at the same time interested and canny consumers of computer products. Indeed, they buy and sell in the hospital, scanning, for instance, the many noticeboards where doctors, nurses and laboratory technicians put up items for sale. Martin's wife is in the market for a computer table, he tells me as he jots down a phone number from a 'For Sale' notice in the laboratory block:

> And that's a good price! Lots of these notices you see are from doctors, selling cos they've been posted elsewhere, or abroad. Or students, who move on to another placement and sell the contents of their flats.

In market terms, 'doctors' and 'students' become 'sellers' who, whatever might be their elevated statuses and easy lifestyles in comparison to those of the porters, have a need to off-load computing possessions when they too are shifted by the medical regime. They become just 'men' and 'women' who can be bargained down to a good price; as when Bill appears in the porter's lodge (or 'buckie' in local parlance) on his day off, having just popped into work and 'bought a computer off a woman in Photobiology who had one or two adverts up'. 'A Dreamcast and console and some games', Bill explains to me, 'in good condition'; new they would cost between £140 and £150, and he paid £100 – for his mum's Christmas present.

Porters also buy and sell computing *matériel* among themselves, displaying a fine knowledge of brand names and an awareness of the latter's profitability. It is with no change in demeanour, then, that Lee, a portering chargehand (a sub-submanager, dressed in white shirt and tie, who allocates tasks throughout the day to the porters around him in the buckie) accosts me as I return from a job with the abrupt: 'Wanna buy an Ericsson mobile phone, Nige? For 30 quid?' He holds it up toward me, and grins. I grin back, guessing his offer cannot be great. My suspicion is confirmed when Dave, another chargehand, butts in with the news that 'Ericsson are going down the tubes'. A discussion follows, in which

Lee, Dave and Michael (another porter) agree that it is Vodaphone who have just announced profits, while Michael knows that Ericsson and Nokia plan to merge; Lee concludes by expressing his confidence in Motorola's future, whatever the newspapers' gloomy predictions.

It is in terms of the Internet, however, that porters seem most aware of the marketing of computing, its opportunities and pleasures. They tell one another tales of what they have found there for sale or already successfully acquired at cut-price: car valves, vegetation for home aquariums, the latest Ducatti motor-bikes.

Dave, the chargehand, seemed particularly taken by this mode of buying and selling, and would often lead conversations along this path, as the following two extracts indicate. In the first, Dave is explaining to an audience in the buckie how he and his wife plan to have a holiday in London at the end of February:

Dave:	Just three to five days, you know. So last night we looked on the computer for possible hotels.
Tracy:	(*a nurse and the wife of another porter, Steve*): Aren't you TGWU (*members of the Transport and General Workers' Union*)?
Dave:	Aye.
Tracy:	Well they have a special hotel, by Lancaster Gate (*in London*), where you get good rates.
Dave:	(*gives a sceptical look*) No … it's fine by World Wide Web. And they have photos so you can see what you're getting.
Tracy:	You know Trevor, the ambulance driver? (*Dave nods*) Well, he went to Lancaster Gate and said it was fine … I'd not go to London without going somewhere that someone else had been already. There are so many dodgy hotels there, and you don't know till you see it … And this one's convenient.
Dave:	(*still looking sceptical*) No. We enjoy playing with the computer; and this has photos so you can see exactly what you're getting.

It is significant how confident Dave is in the Internet, and his and his wife's computing skills in accessing what they perceive as trustworthy information by way of it. He is prepared to stick by it over and against the more traditional route to surety that the Union might be seen to represent, and to register that loyalty openly, even at the expense of querying or negating the freely proffered advice of a colleague's wife. He finds the Internet fun – taking him beyond the norms of Easterneuk, hospital and Union life – and he seems excited by the horizons it gives onto.

This is equally apparent in a second conversational extract. Here, again in the buckie, Dave engages with Ian. As well as being a porter, Ian is a semi-professional footballer, and as such is something of an icon and hero to the others, the younger porters in particular. With his name and photograph episodically appearing in the local paper, it is clearly the portering that is to be regarded as his part-time occupation, and when he is on site, he holds court in the buckie with the latest news and tales from his more glamorous life. On this particular day, Ian has been napping in the buckie after lunch and after a hard evening's training the day before; his name had again appeared in the paper with news of a goal he had made. Hearing Ian complaining about the perennial heat in the buckie, Dave jokes that he will have to make sure Ian is out on jobs all afternoon (and hence away from the buckie). The five or so other porters then in the buckie laugh, and Dave continues:

>   I wonder where you'll be playing next season, Ian?
> *Ian*:   Well I don't fancy Arbroath: playing in a gale-force wind all the time!
> *Dave*:   So what about Hong Kong? You really should get yourself over there! Have you heard anything yet?
> *Ian*:   No; my man (*agent*) has said nothing more about it. But lots of Italians get over there now, so ...
> *Dave*:   You should just get on the Internet yourself and get yourself over there. Put an ad in.
> *Arthur*: And you'd not be short for a Chinky, either! You'd be tall over there. You could be a centre half! ...

Clearly, for Dave and others the world of computing, of the Internet and mobile phones, is viewed as a site of entrepreneurial possibility, one in which they are happy to be active. And although this takes place for them against the backdrop of the hospital – something discussed and partaken of during work hours – the latter becomes something of an irrelevancy. Accessing the Internet may not occur on site but text messaging on mobile phones does, and so does the buying and selling of computing *matériel*. The world of computing, it might be said, flattens the hospital hierarchy of skilled grades into buyers and sellers and, by putting the porters in touch with London hotels, Italian motorbikes and Hong Kong football agents, transcends its borders.

The Black-marketing of Computing

The buckie is the institutional (as well as the social) centre of portering activities in the hospital. It is here that the chargehands sit, at a desk with four telephones, receiving jobs from around the hospital, writing each in the task-book, and apportioning them. It is here that porters clock in and out of work, and here, in between jobs or over a meal break, that many gather to chat, drink tea and coffee, make toast and microwaveable food. It is also here that Albert bases his business in the sale of pirated video tapes and compact discs ('CDs'). Nor is he alone in this among the porters: a number of price-lists of available material for sale circulates discreetly, each the initiative of a different porter-salesman, and many porters will have their regular man to whom they go: Albert, or Roy, say, or 'a man in Clinical Measurement who sells CDs more cheaply than Roy', as Roger once excitedly informed me. And Roy himself concurs:

> It's a regular knocking-shop here, Nigel! Everything gets sold: CDs, tapes, booze, cigarettes! I mean, you've got to make a bit extra to survive, right?

If computing-marketing emphasizes above all porters in the role of consumers of *matériel* such as the Internet, then their black-marketing finds them essentially as producers.

When among porters, Albert is quite open about his black-market business. His black hold-all, packed tight with tapes and CDs, goes with him everywhere round the hospital, and when in the buckie Albert makes frequent trips each day to where it sits under a chair to retrieve an order for a porter-customer; when he is away on a job, other porters or the chargehand keep an eye on it for him. Nurses and domestics buy from Albert too; thus, when the chargehand was busy and I once answered a phonecall with the message that Albert should 'call the supervisor when he comes on shift', those around me all knew, since it was a female voice, that it must be the Domestics' Supervisor wanting her videos and CDs. 'Its like Global Video in here!', Oliver cackled, nicely clothing Albert's side-deals in the success and respectability of a High Street vendor.

Porters' attitudes to Albert, nevertheless, are often ambivalent. In his late forties, Albert is teased about the ponytail he still nurtures (tied back for work). Why does he not cut it off 'for charity?', Donald jokes; because 'it's a disgrace', Martin adds, 'makes him look like a woman!'. Albert is also teased about the time he wastes standing outside the door of the hospital smoking cigarettes and drinking coffee. As other porters watch Albert engaging in his underhand doings in the buckie throughout the day, the exchanged looks veer from the conspiratorial to the supercilious. For while he is offering a service that many profit from – while Albert is the porters' 'tame' wide-boy – he is also making more money than they while ostensibly working the same hours at the same job (by using the time for his own purposes, and perhaps at their expense).

Albert's reaction to this commentary is a mixed one. When, as a new porter, I first asked him about his business – how much the cost, how good the quality – teasing comments were made around us about 'shady deals' being afoot. At which Albert, loudly responding to them through me, became defensive and sounded hurt:

What do they mean 'shady deals'?! Why do they say that? They ask me for something and I get it; and then they say that! No, the videos are pirates, Nigel, good quality. £6 each. I'll get you a list. If you order one I should have it tomorrow … And I can get most new CDs. £5.50 for singles and £8.50 for doubles. I've got no list with me but I'll try to remember to bring one in for you.

I never do get a list, because as Albert explains to me on another occasion, he is too busy copying CDs to photocopy his CD-list, since the photocopying takes him longer than the CD-copying: 'four minutes, unless there is visual material on the CD too, and depending on the speed of the machine'. However, I purchase from Albert and he drops his suspicions. Once 'on board', Albert is pleased to tell me about his business practices and how seriously he takes his responsibility to his customers – getting their orders back before Christmas, for instance, so that gifts are not late:

> Everyone orders just before Christmas, see Nige, and they don't realize how hard it is. Last year, I remember, I was on an early shift about this time [i.e. starting work at 6 a.m.] and I would finish at 2.30 [p.m.] and then work solidly on videos and that till 1, then go to bed for a few hours, then start my shift! After 10 days or so I was completely exhausted and I said 'never again'. I mean I don't need the money: my wife [a nurse] is in a good paying job. But people just don't appreciate how busy I am: I've got computers going all the time at home: 2 PCs, a video, DVD.

Seemingly, Albert has as much business as he can handle, although he is also always quick to play down how seriously he takes the venture and how much he earns; the video sales are on commission, he will explain, and he gets far more from portering. Or:

> Business is a bit slow this week, Nige, but that's okay; I don't push it. Some weeks just are. And I don't mind. I'm only in it for beer-money. And petrol perhaps.

Nevertheless, the venture is an important one, and reciprocally regarded as such by buyers too. Porters show a seriousness about their purchases and their speedy arrival; they also recognize the specialness of their relationship to their black-market supplier, the importance of showing loyalty to him for the supply not to dry up, and the way the risks he takes means it is not like a normal market transaction. As Dwayne explains to Henry one day:

> If you bought that computer game from Roy and it does not work it's probably cos your computer hasn't got the right chip inside it or the box is different … But it's a problem for Roy, you know, cos he can't take it back to his friend: cos he works with him. So he ends up out of pocket.

It is Dwayne I also ask about buying CDs from Roy; his prices seem competitive and his list long. We are in the buckie at the time and Dwayne quickly mimes to me 'Be Quiet', and then mimes a 'mouth' sign; I am to understand that this is Albert's patch and that, anyway, Roy does not want loose talk about his business. Outside the buckie, Dwayne directs me to the Operating Theatres where Roy is an orderly.

When I meet Roy at the Theatres he whisks me into his locker room as if for a secret assignation; he explains how, even here among other porters, his locker keeps getting broken into. The main reason for the secrecy surrounding Roy's operation, however, besides its possibly more illegal nature, is, I feel, the impreciseness of the boundaries of Albert's patch – and Albert's pre-eminence as the porters' oldest and original wide-boy – and the duty porters feel to be loyal to their main supplier. Those who work with Roy in the Theatres may buy from him routinely, as may particular friends – Roger, for instance, commending Roy to me as someone who is not only cheap but also a 'real laugh' and who 'used to be a roadie with a local rock-band' – but most porters seem to be clients of Albert's. It is likely that clienteles overlap but there is a sensitivity, especially on Roy's part (as the newcomer), not to push the issue or bring it into the open. As Martin explains to me one day, while picking up a photocopy of a list of Playstation games (that Roy has left for him inside the transportation box containing sealed, post-operation body-parts being sent to the laboratories for analysis):

> Yes, Roy's price-list is great ... But don't show it to Albert Forrester ... I think Albert knows someone else sells them but he's not sure who ... Or he may know who the competition is but not the prices.

When Martin once noticed me in the locker room carrying CDs I had just purchased from Roy, he teased me with the over-loud exclamation: 'I hope those are not pirate CDs, in a hospital!' What is significant in the black-marketing of computing in which porters engage, in sum, is how many and contradictory are the responses they manage to maintain in relation to it. The practice may be wrong but it is also financially appropriate, even necessary. Hence, it is an open secret. Likewise the probable source of the *matériel*. (Roger informs me that Albert and Roy probably access the music CDs on the Internet, and then photocopy the graphics; Martin informs me he does not know how expensive the copying machine is, but the blank CDs, if they are the same as those you use for Playstation games, cost about £1 each.) There might therefore be some teasing of the black-marketeers – how they do not conform to the standards of others in terms of their personal demeanour or their being overtly focused at work – but their status as black-marketeers is not threatened. To the contrary, a special loyalty attaches itself to them from their clients such that they take on something

of the character of group totems; the overt inattention they practice is an embodiment of that to which all may aspire.

Hence, there is a mutuality between porters as a group, or groups, and 'their'
black-marketeer(s); the porters make the black-marketeer wealthier while his
legally marginal activities makes him socially marginal and special in the
hospital. He is a focal figure who brokers anti-institutional borderlands on behalf
of those he represents. Through his ministrations, moreover, many can benefit
from the financial savings which computing technologies can provide; together
they are 'cottagers' in the larger medical-industrial complex.

The Computing of Uncivility and the Uncouth

'Am you married?', Bob asks me one day in the buckie, a broad grin over his face
and a large plastic bag held ostentatiously in his hand – even though he already
knew the answer. 'Do you have a wife?', he redundantly adds, drawing out the
suspense still further, 'because he will only show me what's in the bag if I am'.
Once he has my repeated assurances – and he seems serious about extracting
them (and suddenly unsure about my reaction) – Bob pulls out a photocopied
sheet of paper; 'Muffdiver Gold Medal' it is entitled, and purports to show a man
with his entire head inside a woman's vagina. Bob garners laughs from me and
others as he shows it around, and gasps of amazement and horror; he got it from
the Web, Bob explains, and he is going to take it home. He wonders whether the
picture can be real: 'that woman must have had a few babies!', he concludes with
a smirk.

Two aspects of the above are particularly noteworthy. While talk of their
wished-for, past and present sexual exploits with women is a common form of
bantering and boasting among the porters, the World Wide Web ('Web') is the
source here of sexual *matériel* which is extraordinary and beyond the norm. It is
beyond the norm, too, in terms of the kinds of teasing and the trading of insults
that otherwise go on regarding one another's sexual practices; one ordinarily
claims that others are homosexual or virgin or impotent or poorly endowed but
not that they have, for instance, freakish bodies. Bob's picture, of a seeming
human impossibility, instantiates the Web as home to human sexual exceptionalism.

But then also significant is the way that Bob insists on trying to domesticate
this exceptionalism, bringing it into the buckie initially hidden and then with a
claim that it was only for the morally mature and sexually initiated. The bag and
the extracted promises of adulthood were liminal devices by which the shocking
nature of the picture could be more slowly and safely brought home (as well as
its effect being heightened). And while it worked out satisfactorily for Bob in the
end – he was congratulated by others' laughter and could repackage his wonder
for the journey home (and further unveilings) – there was still that moment when

Bob was unsure of my reaction and, beneath his opening banter, wondered whether after all he was doing the right thing. For this kind of uncouth exchange was not normal fare in our relationship and Bob did not seem to want to threaten that. The sexual exceptionalism and uncivility that the Web gave onto, in other words, followed regular relational paths in its being 'downloaded' into the routine space of the hospital.

It was quite often that freakish pictures from the Web found their way into portering life, and the effecting of the exceptional-within-the-normal usually took place by way of an insulting, localizing graffito being scribbled on the picture which was then pinned to a wall. Roger confided in me that sooner or later he expected to be the subject of one of these visual practical jokes and how when it occurred he would merely laugh. 'Wouldn't you?', he asks me, seeing I am taken aback? For, 'it would mean fame!'. And it so happened that I was in the buckie the afternoon that Roy (like Bob, on his way home) showed off photo-copies of his latest Web finds before replacing them in his bag: a full-breasted figure with knickers lowered also to reveal a penis, which Roy has labelled, 'Trigger's Bride' ['Trigger' being the nickname of a particular porter]; a wizened hag, with the label 'Peter Hendry's first date'; a cartoon of an oversized dog trying to manoeuvre a toy car, with the label 'New Trolley, one careful owner: Contact Roger Weir in ENT Theatre'; and a picture of a naked woman excreting into a man's mouth (as yet untitled). Crowding round Roy in the buckie, porters are both enthralled and disgusted. Roy pins one of the pictures to the buckie noticeboard (that of Trigger), promises copies of pictures to those who request them, and leaves. When he has gone, his audience wonders, with amazement and admiration, where Roy regularly finds 'these things' – and Desmond teasingly asks if that was me with my mouth full of faeces.

This 'Roy' is of course the same Roy of black-market sales mentioned earlier, using his facility with the Internet to different effect. But it is significant, I feel, that he shows a certain edginess when in the buckie – more the catchment area of Albert's black-marketing – even though he must come there daily to clock in and out. He spends most of his time in the E[ar] N[ose and] T[hroat] Operating Theatre and it is there that his strongest relations with other porters are based. He posts only one picture in the buckie, then, and saves the others for areas of the hospital that pertain more to the relationships that they caricature (such as Roger's difficulties manoeuvring hospital trolleys). Like Bob, moreover, Roy is most relaxed when the pictures are safely back in his bag and ready to leave the hospital site; there is still something about handling and posting these excep-tional pictures – even for such a practised hand as Roy – that sits uneasily with one's normal public persona. This is also perhaps why the faecal picture was unnamed: because even domesticating the exceptional has its limits; purporting freakish tastes, even androgyny, is one thing, but excretion is a taboo too far.[2]

Finally, it should be said that the sexually exceptional is not the only kind of extreme uncouthness or uncivility to which the Web affords access. Roy and pals were responsible, I am told, for the accomplished practical joke of downloading a fake but official-looking letter from the Web, complete with imposing letter-head, instructing the addressee that they had been 'assigned five Asians to look after for six months: feed them only rice and dog biscuits; you will be paid £10 per week towards expenses'. This letter (a comment both on the Pakistani pres-ence in Easterneuk, and on the number of refugees seeking asylum in Britain) was then sent by internal mail to various portering managers and submanagers whose reactions Roy et al. then did their best to discover (if not espy).

Besides the titillation of the exceptional, uncivil and uncouth which the tech-nology of the Web gives onto, clearly there are elements here of subversion. One overturns norms of politeness, of sexual possibility, and also of hierarchy. The Web allows porters to enjoy the liminal reaches of an upside-down world where men return their heads to birth canals and have breasts, where mouths eat excreta, and where one threatens one's bosses with the strictures of officialdom. One comments subversively on relations – with work colleagues, with ethnic neighbours – that one would, in the normal way of things, simply put up with.

The Thieving of Computing

One of the tasks to which the hospital might assign a porter is Security, a combi-nation of nightwatchman, receptionist and bouncer, and Bob, an amateur weight-lifter, intermittently found himself in this role. After work, Bob and I had weight-trained together, and become friendly (cf. Rapport 2001). One day at work, asking after Bob whom I had not seen for a few weeks, Luke jokingly asks me in return if Bob had not tried to sell me a computer last time we had weight-trained together? For, 'haven't you heard?', Luke continues:

> Bob tried to steal a computer from upstairs, in the admin. block – the most important
> part of the whole thing! But he was caught on camera; wearing gloves, the works. It
> seems the day before there had been no cameras there, they'd just been put in, so Bob
> didn't know.

I am amazed – Bob is my pal – and Luke eagerly fills in more of the details for me: how the police came and arrested him at the hospital; how he made a court appearance some days later; how Ron read in the local paper that the case had been deferred; how it was then in the paper again, with Bob admitting his guilt; how, seemingly, he had been 'in trouble' before and they must have given him a second chance when he came to Constance (or else did not vet him very well); how he has now lost his job and will not get work here again. 'But him on secu-rity!', Luke concludes, 'That's so stupid! It's obvious who the culprit would be.'

There is a relative reluctance among other porters to discuss the case: embarrassment that a porter has been caught out like this, but also reticence inasmuch as this is a fate not difficult to imagine for themselves. Rather than moral censure, then, the common judgement on Bob's behaviour is that he is 'a fool': careless, and stupid considering what he has thrown away; 'I heard he could have bench-pressed for Scotland, he was so good [at weight-lifting]', as Robbie concludes with a shake of the head. Or again, it is instructive how Wilbur sees fit to reconstruct the case:

> I think it must have been the Thursday he stole it cos it was that day my wife asked me if a computer had gone missing; she works at Emilie Hospital and a friend there had told her the news ... It seems Bob had been doing it for a while; little things. But he was stupid going for such a big thing. You might take a ballpoint pen you see lying round, or a battery, but not a big thing: you'd never get away with it ... Mind you, I suppose he nearly did! It was only that they'd put in cameras that day cos the block was going to be closed down over the holidays for two weeks. And Bob didn't know ... And apparently they've got his fingerprints down at the police station from the time before, so this time he was wearing gloves, the lot. And its stupid, cos they're bound to think of security! ... Now, it seems he did other things too: like take the holiday fund for their night out from the girls in [Ward] 27. Cos it was in a locked room and they couldn't understand how someone could've done it. But then they found a master-key on Bob when they got him; so they're trying to pin that one on him too [sounding unconvinced].

Wilbur places the case in a precise time-frame and memorizes it 'genealogically': in terms of an existing gossip network that links him in Constance with his wife in Emilie Hospital and with their respective friends. Moreover, Bob remains one of us, whom 'they' are trying further to dishonour in terms of their own history of interests (solving difficult cases). Bob's actions were stupid inasmuch as they were excessive: going beyond the bounds of proportionate thieving and the credibility of possible excuses.

The expectation among the porters is that Bob will avoid jail and be fined and ordered to work some hours' community service (probably in an old-age home since he already had experience of working in a hospital); after all, he has two teenage children to look after. In the event, however, the local newspaper reports that he has been sentenced to four months' jail. It must have been his previous convictions, porters conclude; also that the Sheriff who tried him, McArthur, was, in Sid's words, 'a loony'.

Sitting in the locker room some weeks later, I find Robbie experiencing the Schadenfreude that: 'Nigel's mate Bob' has been 'sent away!' – even if his four-month sentence would likely be commuted to 40 days. Nevertheless, Robbie still cannot believe that Bob stole the nurses' money: stealing a computer is something very different; while Bob 'seemed an okay guy', once helping a busy Robbie complete a long list of jobs at Occupational Therapy even when Bob had his own Security duties to fulfil.

In short, in the interpretation of Bob's thieving of computing *materiel*, personal relations predominate. Bob is one of the porters' own, whose behaviour they can sympathize with and will not condemn; and even if not a particular pal, there are still instances to recall where the mundane drudgeries and indignities of the portering lot were gratefully shared.

Summary

What is there that substantively links the five computing scenarios ('genealogy', 'marketing', 'black-marketing', 'the uncivil and uncouth', and 'thieving') that I have described? Perhaps it is this: that in each case we see new technologies being brought within the ambit of established relations and practices among the porters; the new technologies become further ways in which the distribution of meaning and practice beyond the 'microcultural domain', the subculture, of portering is restricted (cf. Wulff 1988: 22–4). Computing is introduced into portering worlds of kinship and friendship, marketing and black-marketing, uncivility and thieving which preceded its invention and distribution. The 'virtual', in Miller and Slater's terms, remains part of the real of the ongoing and 'everyday' (2000: 6–8). And yet it has had a noticeable, even profound effect: *computing has added a scalar dimension to these existing worlds, significantly extending them.* One has greater, even excessive opportunity for theft; greater; even excessive opportunity for sexual voyeurism and insult; greater, even excessive opportunity for marketing and black-marketing, for extending oneself and one's relationships and imagining other lives (cf. Appadurai 1996). The lesson contained in the above conversations is on occasion the admonitory one, moreover, that the excess of computing opportunities can blinker the user to the normal measures of moderation by which he would abide: he downloads without limit, buys without safeguards, steals beyond sense.

In titling this chapter 'The Computer as a Focus of Inattention' I have also emphasized the way in which the established and excessive relations which computing technologies give onto are, for the porters, set over and against the institutionalism of the hospital and its daily round. An attentiveness to computing is an inattentiveness to the duties of portering; the excessiveness of computing correlates perhaps with the strict institutionalism of the hospital thereby overcome. This is seen most starkly in the scenario of thieving but also characterizes the others where one's genealogical placements, one's buying and selling, and one's voyeurism and subversion undermine the hierarchies of the hospital, its temporal and spatial regimes, the seriousness of its purpose, and the efficiency of its workings. Computing is part of a number of extra-hospital worlds which the allure, the sexiness, the importance and the power of new technologies bring closer, whose very logistics make it hard for the hospital regimen to keep in abeyance, and whose newness makes its potentially subversive deployment difficult to forestall. Inasmuch as the hospital employs information and communication technologies in the work practices of so many of its functionaries, removing the possibility of porters using them as foci of their inattention is made all the harder – and the 'transcendence' thereby achieved all the sweeter (Rapport 1997); the possibilities of the technology, it might be said, exceed the hospital's controlling regimen.[3] (Even the 'total institution' (Goffman 1961), even the 'disciplinary detail' of the panopticon (Foucault 1977), must admit those spaces where, in Levi's words (1996: 31), '[s]ome form of reaction, a corrective of the total tyranny' continues to prevail.)

As Garsten and Wulff suggest in their Introduction to this volume, a major impact of new technologies on the work practices and identities of the porters in Constance Hospital has been a complexifying of any clear distinction between 'work' and 'recreation'. Through their computing, porters are able to increase the ways and extents to which their recreational lives impinge on and colour their time working in the hospital. (Alternatively, the blinkered excesses of computing may be said to involve individuals in new work-like regimens, albeit ones of their own choosing.) Talk of sex, drink, TV and football might previously have been available to the porters to effect such a transcendence, but the importance of computing, its authority, accessibility, ubiquity and mystique – not least to the hospital authorities themselves – makes this technological route to transcendence all the more conclusive and satisfying.

Conclusion: Appropriation and Personalization

'Consumption as the new production' has become an effective slogan in the anthropological armoury of empowerment. Appropriating impersonal objects is a powerful contemporary means of producing modern personal identities, Miller has argued (1994); one thereby overcomes the sense of alienation born out of being separated from one's creativity and its products (1987). Using a computer in one's house in London, for instance, making it part of the furniture of one's selfhood as well as one's home furnishings, can be a means of overcoming anomy in a variety of social contexts, both within and beyond the house (Hirsch 1998). And while one must not pretend that anyone 'lives by consumption alone', as Strathern counsels (1992: xiii), it is pertinent to recognize the individual agency involved in being if not author of what is consumed then 'author of how things will be consumed'. Here is the consumer as 'processor': 'active in the self-referential authorship of [his or her] own processes of consumption' (ibid.).

In a prescient work Turkle (1984) termed computers a 'second self', in recognition of the way she found the new technologies entering into human theorization of 'the self' as such. While taking on many shapes – as objects to think with, as a descriptive language per se – computers and computing seemed deployed especially in the projection of parts of the self: mirrors of the mind, intelligence, consciousness, determinism and free will (1984: 15–24). (It is surely no accident that Strathern employed the word 'processor' to describe the agency that accrues to individuals through their consumption of computing technologies.) This chapter has examined the ways in which porters have, if you will, processed their experiences through computing technologies. I would not say, with Turkle, that these latter provide a language for something not expressed before – that the technology elicits a certain form of subjectivity and self-expression – for I would maintain that the relationship between symbolic forms and the meanings they harbour is indeterminate (Rapport and Overing 2000: 136–41). But I would allow that the newness of the technologies makes them into a symbolic form whose meaningful potential is barely tapped (non-routinized, non-clichéd) and thereby all the more attractive (Rapport 2000). It is also the case that individual porters invest in computing something personal which is highly significant to themselves, namely: *a sense of self which lifts them above and beyond the hospital site, its confines and routines, to where they become active in contexts (entrepreneurial, translocal, communitarian, wanton) only partially connected to their workaday lives.* The porters' various 'personalizations' of computing technologies afford them individual transcendence, however fleeting.

Finally, then, there is much in this ethnography which might lend itself to an analysis of those 'weapons of the weak' (Scott 1985) whereby low-key and limited but nonetheless endemic conflict is prosecuted by lowly actors involved in hierarchical institutions; also to a critique of those who would see actors immersed in seemingly hegemonic, self-reproducing social systems as merely 'bodies totally imprinted by history' (Foucault 1977). Echoing Scott (1990: 72–7), the porters may be said to practise all sorts of subtle ways of reflecting upon, discussing, confronting, resisting and undermining the inequalities predominant in their workplace (as well as instilling their own), and to inscribe 'hidden transcripts' (Scott 1990: 215), opaque sets of understandings unintelligible to the outsider, which validate the 'underlife' of the portering microcultural domain and its 'alternative moral career' (Marsh, Rosser and Harre 1978: 7,19).

In closing, however, and talk of porters' microcultural perspective within the wider organizational culture of the hospital notwithstanding, I would not want a parting impression to be that the porters among whom I primarily worked at Constance represented a necessarily cohesive group with a singular world-view. It is more true to say that no overarching or organizing ideological consensus existed among them regarding the institutionalism of the hospital, and their aspirations relative to its hierarchy were diverse. Nor should it be concluded that the above acts of transcendence are particular to the porters alone. When a doctor programmes in as a screensaver on his ward computer the message: 'UROLOGY NURSES ARE BABES: Now, where's my white stick?', when a nurse recounts to a doctor that a patient, a university professor, told her how he had been 'surfing the Net' for data on his condition and so she thought she had better take a look too (to check she knew what he now knew), and when a male nurse – fresh from working on oil rigs in the North Sea and now anxious to get a job on land – tells me he is going to 'get on the Internet to check out Constance and what it's got' ... here too are individual appropriations of computing technology toward the end of personalizing the hospital regime (resisting its impersonalism) and making it homelier to the self: recreating the world of the hospital – subverting the attention it would levy – by way of personal connections with worlds beyond.

Acknowledgements

The research on which this chapter was based was funded by the Leverhulme Trust (grant no. XCHL48), under the aegis of their 'Nations and Regions' programme, and part of the 'Constitutional Change and Identity' project convened by Professor David McCrone of Edinburgh University. I am very grateful to Helena Wulff for encouraging me to publish expeditiously on this new fieldwork, and to members of seminar audiences in St Andrews and Oxford where this material was also presented.

Notes

1. My fieldwork practice was, as ever, not to tape-record informants but still to aim at a precise memorialization of interaction by writing down as much of exchanges between porters as I could remember, as soon after the event as possible.
2. It is not insignificant, perhaps, that Roy, the source of much sexually exceptional or freakish Internet material on the body, works in an operating theatre and is there witness to a radical transformation of the body: identity to mechanism, integrity to section. To then focus upon body parts recreationally, as source of fascination and titillation, may be to transform the freakishness and exceptionalism of the work situation into something more akin to normalcy. (I am indebted to the volume editors for this observation.)
3. I am reminded of Simmel's discussion of modernity, epitomized by the urban, as an era and an attitude of mind characterized by excess; an excess of stimulation may lead to a blasé attitude to experience but also instantiates a freedom from limitations and constraints (1971: 329ff.).

References

Appadurai, A. (1996), *Modernity at Large: Cultural Dimensions of Globalization*, Minneapolis: University of Minnesota Press.

Foucault, M. (1977), *Discipline and Punish*, New York: Pantheon.

Goffman, E. (1961), *Asylums*, Harmondsworth: Penguin.

Hirsch, E. (1998), 'Domestic Appropriations: Multiple Contexts and Relational Limits in the Home-Making of Greater Londoners', in N. Rapport and A. Dawson (eds), *Migrants of Identity: Perceptions of Home in a World of Movement*, Oxford: Berg.

Levi, P. (1996), *The Drowned and The Saved*, London: Abacus.

Marsh, P., Rosser, E. and Harre, R. (1978), *The Rules of Disorder*, London: Routledge & Kegan Paul.

Miller, D. (1987), *Material Culture and Mass Consumption*, Oxford: Blackwell.

—— (1994), *Modernity: An Ethnographic Approach*, Oxford: Berg.

Miller, D. and Slater, D. (2000), *The Internet: An Ethnographic Approach*, Oxford: Berg.

Rapport, N.J. (1997), *Transcendent Individual: Towards a Liberal and Literary Anthropology*, London: Routledge.

—— (2000), '"Criminals by Instinct": On the "Tragedy" of Social Structure and the "Violence" of Individual Creativity', in G. Aijmer and J. Abbink (eds), *Meanings of Violence*, Oxford: Berg.

—— (2001), 'Bob, Hospital Bodybuilder: The Integrity of the Body, the Transitiveness of "Work" and "Leisure"', Paper presented at the American Anthropological Association meetings, Washington.

Rapport, N.J. and Overing, J. (2000), 'Form and Content', in *Social and Cultural Anthropology: The Key Concepts*, London: Routledge.

Scott, J. (1985), *Weapons of the Weak*, New Haven: Yale University Press.

—— (1990), Domination and the Arts of Resistance, New Haven: Yale University Press. Simmel, G. (1971), *On Individuality and Social Forms* (ed. D. Levine), Chicago: University of Chicago Press.

Strathern, M. (1992), 'Foreword: The mirror of technology', in R. Silverstone and E. Hirsch (eds), *Consuming Technologies*, London: Routledge.

Turkle, S. (1984), *The Second Self: Computers and the Human Spirit*, New York: Simon and Schuster.

Wulff, H. (1988), *Twenty Girls: Growing Up, Ethnicity and Excitement in a South London Microculture* (Stockholm Studies in Social Anthropology no. 21), Stockholm: Almquist & Wiksell.

–3–

Digital Ditches: Working in the Virtual Grass Roots

Sarah Green

It was yet another one of those uncomfortable management committee meetings at the Manchester Women's Electronic Village Hall (WEVH) during early 2001, and in uncomfortable surroundings. There used to be a proper meeting room, but recently there had been so much pressure on space and money that the meeting room had been turned into an office. We were now perched on chairs in among banks of computers that were part of a 'drop-in centre' which had recently also become one of the 'UK Online Centres' and 'Learndirect' course centres. These were two of the latest initiatives by the British Government to draw in those who did not have access to computing facilities or sufficient training or knowledge about using computers. The Government is extremely keen that everyone should have access to and be able to use these technologies, something Penny Harvey and I came to call 'the imperative to connect' during our research on the introduction of high bandwidth computing capacity to the public sector in Manchester (Green and Harvey forthcoming). The Learndirect scheme aims to use computing facilities to pursue the government's objective of encouraging people to engage in 'lifelong learning' by taking courses via the Internet.[1] There had been many earlier British Government plans, including the policy that by 2005 all schoolchildren in Britain should have access to and training in computing, and most especially the online aspects of it. This ambition was expanded and had now become the UK Online scheme, in which not only schoolchildren but *everyone* should have access to the Internet by 2005.[2] There had also been the National Grid for Learning, which was to provide, 'educationally valuable content on the Internet, and a programme for developing the means to access that content in schools, libraries, colleges, universities, workplaces, homes and elsewhere ...'.[3] That has developed into Learndirect. There had further been a plan to collect second-hand computers from commercial companies and redistribute them to those who could not afford to buy their own computers. Many people working in the voluntary sector in this field, in Manchester at least, predicted that the main problem with that scheme would be lack of provision of ongoing maintenance, training and trouble-shooting for these machines.

In fact, a general lack of sustained support for the mundane practicalities of introducing computing technologies to the 'socially excluded' was seen, by many voluntary organizations in Manchester, as a key difficulty for a whole range of public-sector plans, strategies, programmes and otherly-named projects in the information and communications technologies (ICT) sector. The WEVH, a voluntary, non-profit organization aimed mostly at providing ICT training to women in Manchester, was experiencing the sharp end of that lack in 2000 and 2001, as were hundreds of other voluntary sector organizations in the country. On the strength of the considerable commitment given to the promotion of 'universal access' to ICTs during the mid- to late 1990s, both by the British government and the European Union, the WEVH had grown into an organization with several full-time permanent staff (administrators, technicians and trainers), in addition to a considerable team of IT and ICT trainers who were paid only for the courses they taught (sessional trainers); it was simultaneously running a series of short-term specialist projects funded from a range of different sources, along with regular IT and ICT training courses offered by local further-education colleges that had been contracted out to the WEVH. The organization had become less able to cut ongoing running costs in times of economic difficulties than it had done in the past.

This chapter explores the WEVH story as an example of what happened in the voluntary sector during that heady and somewhat turbulent period. It argues that the rhetoric used to promote the use of ICTs – rhetoric which informed the way in which voluntary organizations were given funding – effectively separated the world in which people currently lived (the 'mundane practicalities' referred to above) from the 'future', from a world lived through or with these new information and communications technologies. This was a temporal as well as a spatial separation: the 'pre-ICTs' world was cast as one that was rapidly fading, replaced by a 'post-ICTs' world, in which lived existence would be mediated by computers. Those who did not gain access to ICTs would be left behind, drifting in a past that literally had no future. The effect of this rhetoric in terms of voluntary organizations was twofold. First, it made the way people lived before the introduction of ICTs appear relatively insignificant: everything was axiomatically going to change, so conditions for people before the change were not that important. In effect, this meant that the social contexts into which ICTs were introduced were discounted in the programmes that promoted them. Secondly, this rhetoric assumed that once access to ICTs were provided, the 'revolution' would inevitably occur; people who had access to ICTs would automatically become part of the 'information revolution'.

For people working in the voluntary organizations funded to provide such 'access', this generated a disjunction between the conditions in which they worked and the conditions of the funding they received. Such organizations worked mostly with low-income populations for whom access to ICTs did not obviously resolve any of their immediate problems – such as bad housing, lack of access to secure jobs, lack of sufficient childcare and so on. The content and design of the Internet in the late 1990s was aimed mostly at people who already had money and resources, who were accustomed to processes of learning how to use them and who could afford to continually keep up with changing technologies. For example, public listings of job vacancies on the Internet in the Manchester area in the late 1990s were mostly for white-collar posts that had a minimum starting salary of £20,000 per annum (considered a decent salary, and one that few unskilled or semi-skilled workers could ever hope to achieve). Another example: using the Internet for purchasing goods or joining groups that required payment of a subscription fee also assumed that people owned a credit card, something that few people on very low incomes possessed. And a final example: what was the point of learning how to use e-mail if nobody you knew actually owned a computer, let alone an e-mail account? The effort involved in having to travel to a public access point, during the few hours when it was open, in order to read and answer e-mails to discuss matters that could be discussed much more easily by dropping by and seeing someone locally, seemed somewhat pointless to many people in this position. In short, access to ICTs in and of itself was not going to make such people members of the 'information revolution'.

In the case of the WEVH, one result of this lack of fit between what these computing technologies offered and the lives of many of the people they were trying to reach was to eventually limit the range of people who could make use of the service, or who could see a point in doing so. By the late 1990s, the majority of women who attended courses already had some experience of computing, or were involved in jobs that made them feel a greater knowledge of it would be useful to them, or who felt, after a career break (e.g. to have children), that they might benefit from a course in getting back into work. In other words, the service reached out to those who were looking for such a service because their particular circumstances had already indicated that they might benefit. It had not always been thus; as will be discussed later, the WEVH initially managed to reach a much wider audience of women. Changes implemented as a result of the constraints imposed by funding led to the narrowing of people who perceived the service as relevant to them.

The second difficulty for voluntary organizations given the task of making ICTs accessible to the 'socially excluded' was a conceptual one. The WEVH story highlights the way the rather fantastical narratives being expressed during the 1990s about the potential for ICTs to alter everything, to bring forth some entirely new world, became embroiled in public policies. Those policies simultaneously aimed to encourage everyone to join the 'information revolution' and, which was not the same thing, to change the relationship between the 'socially excluded' and this 'new globe'. In brief, that latter relationship was to be transformed from an ideal of collective social responsibility into an individualized and broadly market-oriented relationship: the 'socially excluded' were *also* to become independent, flexible, multiply-skilled, lifelong learners along with everyone else, that being the means for them to achieve social inclusion (and ideally cease to be dependent upon state benefits).

In contrast, most voluntary organizations, until recent years, used the concept of 'social responsibility': that there is a responsibility for any collectivity to care for the collectivity as a whole; if people are in need, then they ought to be helped, whatever the outcome is in terms of public resources. This conceptual contrast will be discussed in more detail later; here, I want to note that the contrast was often experienced as a conflict in many voluntary organizations, because the structure of public funding and the regulations attached to them meant that they were increasingly pressured into changing their underlying approach toward voluntary activity. In particular, they were encouraged to run their organizations like businesses, were judged by pre-defined *measurable* 'outcomes' that audited the 'efficiency' of the services provided (e.g. how many people successfully completed courses and then went on to use those skills to gain employment), and were made to compete for funding that was increasingly linked to pre-existing large projects, rather than allowing voluntary organizations to define their own projects based upon the perceived needs of their particular area. As funding became increasingly scarce and competitive at the end of the 1990s, many voluntary organizations found themselves ill-equipped to cope with the combination of both this change in philosophy and the sudden loss of income. In the case of the WEVH, the organization had, unlike many other groups in the city, restructured itself to suit the new funding conditions; but it now had large quantities of computing equipment and expertise that needed continual maintenance and updating; a complex network of insecure and small-scale funding projects that never quite fitted with the original aims of the organization; formal employment regulations that were designed for large businesses, and with which they struggled to cope when cash flow became particularly difficult.

The WEVH is thus one example of what happened when voluntary organizations became involved, through their funding, in a complex admixture of euphoria about new media, changing public policies in Britain about social welfare, and European Union-initiated policies about combating social exclusion as well as the notoriously complex and cumbersome bureaucracy and auditing procedures imposed by the EU. While media headlines have endlessly discussed the dramatic boom-to-bust trajectory of the commercial new media technologies sector through the 1990s, a similar trajectory in the voluntary sector has hardly been noted at all. This chapter aims to trace how the experience not only left many voluntary organizations in an extremely vulnerable position by the time the funding 'boom' had ended, but is also one example of how the rhetoric surrounding the introduction and promotion of these technologies, rather than the technologies themselves, constituted the 'impact' they would have.

The WEVH Experience

The WEVH was founded in 1992, a year before the launching of the Internet as we know it today, as a result of a project called The Manchester Host, developed jointly by Manchester City Council, a research unit at Manchester Metropolitan University (the Centre for Employment Research (CER)) and a small workers' cooperative computing services company, later called Poptel. Funding initially came from the city council, British Telecom and the European Union.

The WEVH was one of three 'electronic village halls' (the other two were Chorlton EVH and Bangladesh House EVH) set up around Manchester in order to give minority and disadvantaged groups access to computing facilities. The WEVH was the only one of the three which had not been based on a pre-existing community voluntary organization, though that was by accident rather than design: initially, the WEVH was to be run by the Pankhurst Centre, a feminist organization in the centre of Manchester, but relations between the funders and the Centre deteriorated, and the Pankhurst Centre had pulled out.

Having lost the Pankhurst Centre as a venue for the WEVH, the organization was first located in a residential district at the edge of the city centre, in an area called Whalley Range. However, soon afterward, the management committee decided to move the organization to a much more central location, just to the north of the main shopping district. The reason, according to the WEVH's first director, Clem Herman, was that they wanted to get away from the idea that the WEVH served a particular community within Manchester, and therefore wanted to find a location that was more central and less specifically identified with a particular residential area.

The new location was certainly lacking in any sense of a residential community: it was in a run-down district composed mostly of Victorian and early twentieth-century warehouses and closed down factories, interconnected by a network of small and fairly badly lit streets. Less than ten minutes' walk away, the 'urban regenerated' city-centre shopping district began, full of the bustle of a growing town, with fairly pricey high-street shops, department stores, cafés, bars, restaurants and night clubs. However, the building used by the WEVH was tucked away from all of that, in one of the old warehouse side streets, and it felt like an entirely different world. One of the issues that had concerned the WEVH workers and volunteers from the earliest years was that the location neither was visible nor felt particularly safe for women to visit. Plans were continually being made to develop a dedicated 'women's technology centre' somewhere much more central, and a number of applications for grants were submitted (and often granted) to pay for such a venture. But such plans were slow to be brought to reality, and for now, the warehouse district was cheap.

Initially, the WEVH ran a range of services, including providing access to computers, working with women's groups around the city to discuss the relationship between women and new technologies and providing some training on using computing technology. The aim then was focused on 'empowering' women and keeping 'close to the grass roots', working alongside other women's groups to serve the needs of the women involved in them. In particular, there was no direct link made at the time between providing access to these technologies and enabling women to compete more effectively in the job market. That might have been the aim of some of the women who used the WEVH services; but it was not the *raison d'être* of the WEVH. Rather, the aim was to make it possible for women to use these technologies for whatever they wanted to use them for, including to simply satisfy their curiosity about them.

Moreover, the promised capacity of these technologies to allow greater communication between groups, through on-line bulletin boards (as they then were) and nascent e-mail systems, was also seen as something that could empower women in Manchester: it would make it possible for scattered groups and individuals to keep in touch, share information and perhaps organize events or meetings together. The potential links with other women's groups across Europe, made possible through the European part of the funding for these projects, was also seen as having potentially 'empowering' characteristics. Clem Herman, the first director of the WEVH, spent a great deal of her time going out on visits to other European women's groups and saw this potential for ICTs to allow greater communication and organization between women as one of its more exciting aspects.

However, things were to change radically over the years. After the initial 'seed money' to develop the project had run out, the WEVH began to search around for further funding. The immediate funding gap was filled by setting up contracts with Manchester City College and Manchester Adult Education Services to provide IT training skills for women. As Clem Herman recalled, 'We had to reinvent ourselves as a women's training organization'.

That was the beginnings of the shift toward a less directly 'socially motivated' and more 'economically motivated' slant to the work of the WEVH. In the following three to four years, 1995–9, there was a rash of public funding that began to become available, both from the British government and the European Union, for anything that had to do with information and communications technologies. The WEVH, having been in existence for three years already, and having developed a wide network of relations with other groups both within Manchester and around Europe, was very well placed to apply for such funding. As a result, the WEVH expanded rapidly, to such an extent that new training rooms were secured on two floors of a new building near the original offices. However, this coincided with a shift in emphasis from the original concept of the WEVH, as the organization had to accommodate to the conditions set by the grant-funding bodies, which at the time were in the grip of the 'information revolution fever'. That approach was strongly informed by the belief that ICTs would help to solve economic problems – and, in particular, the need for Europe's workforce to become 'lifelong' and 'flexible' learners.[4] The WEVH was increasingly becoming an organization that provided training for individual women so that they could take advantage of ICTs, especially in terms of 'enterprise', rather than one representing a 'social community' of women.

By 1996, the WEVH was receiving funding from nine different sources, and the sheer level of paperwork to run the various projects, produce reports and provide the auditing accounts was becoming immense. In addition, there was an increasing need to keep looking for more funding, and the process of completing applications for grants and sponsorship was hugely time-consuming. The Director ceased to provide any training herself in order to try to keep up with all this paperwork, as well as to attend numerous meetings in other European countries to meet partners on European projects; an increasing number of members of staff began to work mostly on specialist projects, thus fragmenting the sense of group working within the office.

It was toward the end of this 'boom' period that I came into contact with the WEVH as part of a wider research project looking into the introduction of high bandwidth ICTs to Manchester (see Acknowledgements, p. 61). I had already visited a couple of other voluntary organizations, such as the Manchester Community Information Network (MCIN) and Hulme Community Computing. As a result, I had experienced some sense of the difference between the 'haves' and the 'have nots' within the ICT sector in Manchester. Both MCIN and Hulme Community Computing were located in run-down areas of the city with reputations for high unemployment and high crime rates. Both organizations were under-funded and neither had enough staff or resources to develop their projects as they might wish. The people working in them had explained the difficulties of their situations, both in terms of the problems they had in 'fitting' their work into the rules set out by the funding available, and in terms of a lack of 'fit' between the needs of the people they were supposed to be serving and what was being provided by ICTs. Margo (a pseudonym), who was then the director of the MCIN project, pointed to a file of printed e-mails that she had collected from public information 'kiosks' (touch-screen computer units placed in public areas such as supermarkets and libraries by MCIN) as an example. One such e-mail read,

'Here's some information you can give me: how the f*** am I supposed to survive on £23 a week?'

'People around here have a problem seeing how these technologies are really going to change anything for them,' Margo sighed, 'and I can see their point sometimes.'

I was expecting something of the same story from the WEVH. Even though I had heard that the WEVH was one of the most successful ICT voluntary projects in Manchester, I imagined that it had experienced similar things as others around the city: a sense that neither the technologies, nor the funding, were really meant for them; that they were included in larger funded projects because the larger projects were required to show a concern about 'social exclusion' as a condition of receiving grants, and not because the larger organizations had any genuine commitment to 'social exclusion' (which usually led to chronic under-funding of the voluntary organizations); and that the population they were supposed to serve were singularly indifferent to the services offered by ICTs, and for good reason.

However, I was surprised to find that in 1998, most staff at the WEVH expressed no such doom and gloom. The offices, although once again located in a less than salubrious part of the city, were bright and airy inside, and there was a buzz of activity in every room. There were posters on all the walls advertising this or that ICT training programme or project; computers filled most rooms, along with files, books, papers and all the usual office clutter. It was cramped, but it was clearly a very active environment, and the women working there or participating in courses did not seem in the least bit demoralized, as I had found elsewhere. This was during the height of the boom years for funding for ICTs, and the WEVH had reached the peak of its expansion before the 'bust' years for public funding that were to come in 2000 and 2001. The key difference between the WEVH and the other voluntary projects I had been visiting was that it had 'transformed itself', as Clem Herman had put it, into a training organization that suited the requirements of funding much more effectively than many other projects.

As I would later discover, this had not gone down well with some of the earlier women involved in setting up the WEVH. For example, one member of staff, whose job had originally been to work with women on helping them to use the technologies for whatever they wanted, as well as to maintain links with women's groups around the city, had increasingly found that her work was 'reduced' to training activities. The links with women's groups had begun to dissipate, and the changing direction of the WEVH had meant that the focus was on delivery of training rather than on all the other elements that had been envisaged at the beginning of the WEVH. Eventually, that particular trainer left the organization. However, despite these underlying conflicts, during 1998, it seemed as though the shift in emphasis had paid off overall: the WEVH was thriving where other organizations were struggling and demoralized.

A sense of what this transformation meant in practice can be seen in the comments of another woman who worked at the WEVH as a senior trainer. She had previously worked as the co-ordinator of the Chorlton EVH project, and recalled her experiences there in a conversation with me in 1998. It is worth quoting her at some length:

> There was a lot of good work done in the early years at Chorlton EVH, 1993, 1994. Unlike the WEVH, it was a geographically based community project, and they were very committed to social welfare issues. For example, they ran courses for people with disabilities from the money from the EVH grant. Then they got further education funding, but the requirements of the grant were very constraining, and against the philosophy of the Chorlton EVH. The funding was too difficult to administer and it wasn't worth the effort put into it; it was good for providing a few core courses, but there was no money for personal support of the people participating. Life was very hand to mouth ...

> Chorlton was run as a cooperative. At the WEVH, it's consultative, a management committee, which I prefer; it makes it easier to move on with the new world we're in. Chorlton Workshop started as a community group in the early 1980s via Manpower Services. That set in train the 1970s-style 'disadvantaged group philosophy'. It just doesn't fit with the current funding regime. In contrast, the WEVH began as a new organization, so it didn't have that much of that 1970s philosophy about it; it was more flexible and able to change ...

> Basically, working with disadvantage is not what it's about anymore; it's about running voluntary organizations as businesses – or to help people get into business themselves ... The collective ethos of Chorlton did give it problems; it's very worthy, you can't knock it; but it's hard to get money for that sort of thing today. The difference with the WEVH is that it's willing to develop new things and new approaches in order to fit with new funding and technical conditions. That's why it survives. Chorlton tried to do their best within their anachronistic philosophy; but it drove them mad, really.

What had happened, in effect, was that the WEVH had not only transformed itself into a training organization; it had also fundamentally shifted its underlying philosophy toward voluntary work, as well as its original aims in bringing women and new technologies together.

The costs of this conceptual flexibility started to become evident as the funding began to dry up toward the end of 1999. A series of tensions between staff and the directors of the WEVH, as a result of the changing direction of the organization, the formalisation of working practices and the fragmentation of the work done by members of staff through being involved in a series of unconnected projects, began to surface more visibly as the strains of lack of funding began to take hold, particularly in the the higher workload it involved for many. Some of the older members of staff began to leave or to express deep dissatisfaction with their working conditions, while the mood in the office became increasingly tense. The WEVH managed to survive the crisis of the funding 'bust', but by the end, it had become a different organization, delivering ICTs to the 'socially excluded' in an entirely different way from that originally envisaged.

The Rhetoric Explored: Constituting ICTs as a Revolution

Given my suggestion that what happened within the ICT voluntary sector in Manchester had much more to do with shifting policies about social welfare combined with a particular set of assertions about what ICTs could or would achieve, it is worth attempting to unpack the rhetoric that came with the public funding 'boom' of the mid- to late 1990s. The drives to get everyone on-line in the mid- to late 1990s were backed up by what today may seem incredible amounts of financial resources as well as extremely strong public pronouncements about the urgency of this endeavour. Particularly relevant here was a stated concern about the potential danger of 'social exclusion' from the new 'information society' and 'information economy' as the reason for providing access to ICTs for those who could not, or would not, do it themselves. The British Government has been replete with such statements in recent years,[5] but so have international organizations. For example, the United Nations' statement on 'Universal Access to Basic Communication and Information Services'[6] starts by saying that, 'the world is in the midst of a communication and information revolution' and that the greatest danger for the poorer and less developed countries in this is being given little if any opportunity to connect. As the UN statement puts it:

> We are profoundly concerned at the deepening mal-distribution of access, resources and opportunities in the information and communication field … a new type of poverty – information poverty – looms. (ibid.)

The UN was explicit about what they thought was happening. ICTs are, the report says, 'at the heart of the intensifying globalization trends – and drive the emergence of a tele-economy with new global and societal organizational models … In many instances, physical location is becoming irrelevant …' All of this leads the UN to 'embrace the objective of establishing universal access to basic communication and information services for all.' (ibid.)

Similarly, in 1994 the European Union published a lengthy report, the Bangemann Report (Bangemann 1994). This also laid the basis of the argument that the need to prepare for the 'revolution' was urgent, and that the need for 'universal access' was particularly urgent. This report was at the root of a prolif-eration of programmes, research and projects funded by the European Union to promote this aim. The European Union particularly emphasized, and continues to emphasize, the issue of 'social exclusion' as a matter of general inequality in terms of 'quality of life',[7] whereas the British Government tends to emphasize 'social exclusion' as a matter of lack of access to the economic potential of the Internet. However, the outcome for voluntary organizations was the same: from the mid-1990s, there was an enormous publicity campaign and visibility of this issue, and considerable amounts of funding available to help people 'get on-line'. At the same time, the commercial sector was in the middle of the 'dot com boom', during which incredible amounts of money could be made in very short periods of time through an apparently infinite willingness for wealthy sponsors to invest in 'dot com' companies.

A key element in this euphoric debate about ICTs was the idea that people's current experiences were soon going to be 'the past': the world would never be the same again. It is worth taking a moment to remember the outline of this debate; apart from the fact that it is still continuing, if in a more muted and less fantastical way than it was during the 1990s, it draws out the discursive form in which ICTs were constituted in public discussions; the way in which they were represented, imagined and brought into relation with other things. The following outline draws out the main common elements that characterized each side of the debate, and as such, it is not intended to represent the views of particular people or organizations. The aim is to get at the underlying implications of the differing perspectives.

I will begin with outlining the positive perspective. In that narrative, these technologies, and particularly the Internet (mobile telephony and digital interac-tive television would be added later) were generating a new and wonderful revo-lution in both space and time.[8] They were creating conditions that would allow more autonomy, more self-expression, more flexibility, more access to the things to which only the privileged had access before. For some, the most important aspect of this was economic: it would provide genuinely new economic opportu-nities, allowing a previously inconceivable expansion of the global economy that would eventually benefit everyone. For others, what was more important was that ICTs might provide a new kind of social, cultural and intellectual space for people to inhabit and in which to interact. It would be a space free of the ties that bind, as it were: free of those relations and conditions that constrain or restrict us to what our material, physical and social position in the world allows us to be or do.[9]

This side of the debate usually provided a deeply individualistic vision, one that was steeped in the political and philosophical tenets of classic western liberal epistemology, albeit in its current flexible, diverse, consumption-oriented form.[10] The image of the user (it was always *a* 'user') of ICTs in this vision was an individual, a single person, who would be limited only by his or her imagination in what, who or where he or she could do or be. New social groups and communities would be generated within cyberspace, out of the interactions of these free-floating individuals.

In the earlier periods within this vision, the image of people actually getting on-line was also often presented as an image of an individual, sitting alone in front of the computer screen, engaging with the information on the screen rather than anything that was going on around him or her. In social and cultural terms this image is nonsense, of course. First, it assumes that 'new' sociality will be generated with no reference to the sociality in which people are currently engaged, something that Stone, among others, questioned many years ago (Stone 1992); secondly, it assumes that technology generates its own realities, as if the technologies themselves exist autonomously of the context in which they were developed, something that many have demonstrated is part of the (Euro-American) social construction of the concept of technology itself (e.g. Bijker et al. 1987; Dovey 1996; Downey and Dumit 1997; Escobar 1994; Haraway 1985; Law 1991); and thirdly, more recent ethnographic studies, such as those of Miller and Slater on Trinidadian use of the Internet (Miller and Slater 2000) and Downey's work on computer engineers (Downey 1998), have demonstrated that people actively and often seamlessly combine those social interactions which are mediated by computers and those which are not.

In short, the idea that 'cyberspace' is an autonomous social space in which individuals engage independently of their existing social relations has not been borne out in practice. Nevertheless, this kind of culturally-marked image did inform the way new information and communications technologies were represented and promoted. In that sense, that image formed part of the social construction of these technologies, and it contributed significantly to the way it was possible to treat computer-mediated interaction *as if* it was independent of other forms of interaction in which people were engaged. I will return to this point.

The alternative view being expressed in the 1990s was that these technologies were indeed revolutionary, but ran the risk of simply exacerbating existing inequalities, because they were part of late- or post-industrial global capitalism, patriarchal or otherwise. Associated with that view, but rather less extreme, was the sense that these technologies would create new forms of social exclusion, the 'information poor', living in the shadow of the 'information rich', and new kinds of sweatshop labourers, in both the northern and the southern hemispheres of the globe.[11] Unsurprisingly, these newly excluded people would be much the same people as they had been before: those with little money, those with few white-collar skills, those who were unfortunate enough to be born in countries with crippling debt, those who in the past had little status or influence, including women, and who would continue to have little status or influence today.

Some holding this perspective suggested that therefore, these technologies ought to be avoided at all costs.[12] Others, however, sent out a call for action; these technologies must be made to work for campaigns against the forces of economic and political globalization.[13] Somewhat similar to implications of Donna Haraway's approach towards cyborg technologies in the 1980s (Haraway 1985), this perspective argued that new media technologies should be embraced rather than rejected by those against the forces of 'Western' (largely American, in the case of the Internet) global hegemony.

Rather differently from the first perspective, which argued that these new technologies would provide a space for the mind to soar over its constraints and finally achieve the Cartesian fantasy of the triumph of the mind over the body, this second perspective kept its feet firmly located in the world of political economy. These technologies, so the argument went, would do nothing to change the social, economic and political inequalities of that world simply by being what they are – in fact, rather the opposite. The only hope was to seize these technologies, to use them to enhance and improve the kinds of protests against oppression that had been going on anyway; to use these technologies for purposes for which they were not designed, in order to undermine those purposes.

This perspective, which was reflected in the attitudes of the consortium in Manchester that funded the electronic village halls, was also in its way visionary, and also quite strongly culturally marked. Rather than the triumph of individualism for the individual's sake, you would campaign for the triumph of the group, of the little people, against the powers that be; if in the past the weakness of the masses was that they could not organize their large numbers into a co-ordinated force, then these technologies gave them the means to do it now. The constraints to freedom that were imagined in this perspective were not bodily, intellectual or geographical constraints, but the constraints of global economic and political forces.[14]

In fact, and as implied in telling the WEVH story above, the political imperative to provide 'universal' access to ICTs utilized parts of both sides of this debate: both the positive view that there were genuinely new social and economic opportunities to be had through ICTs, *and* the more negative notion that certain groups and people would be excluded from the 'revolution' unless there were political intervention.

I would suggest that the debate as a whole was, in Judith Butler's terms, a citation (Butler 1993): its terms borrowed and quoted from very similar, and markedly Euro-American, forms of debate concerning the relationship between the individual, the social, the economic and the technical. In Butler's terms, the debate was performative; it constituted the realities it was describing, through iteration, through borrowing from culturally marked ideas that were well known and well understood. And the thing about performative utterances for Butler is that they mask the way they create the realities they talk about: it appears as if the utterances are made *because of* the way things are, not that the utterances *constitute* the way things are. In the ICTs debate, it appeared that the inherent characteristics of ICTs (their technical capacities to store, process and manipulate data; to connect information and people together; to allow communication across previously unimaginable distances and at incredible speeds, and to allow the crossing of previously apparently impervious boundaries) would generate the 'information revolution', and this would be either good or bad. Butler's approach would imply that it was the other way around: that the way people made ICTs into something meaningful – the way ICTs were linked, through citations of both form and content, to other things – would constitute that 'revolution' (even to the extent of seeing it *as* a 'revolution' in the first place). This implies that from the beginning, what ICTs 'are' and what effects they would have is constituted by the forms of debate about them.

Butler's analysis has its limitations, as many have noted in recent years (Adkins 2002; Adkins and Lury 1999; Hennessy 1993; Hennessy 1995; Fraser 1997; Lloyd 1999). The critics suggest that the fact that citation and performativity occur within particular economic, cultural, political and historical contexts matters a great deal, deeply affecting how performativity 'works', and especially how it 'works' better for some people rather than others. In this, the ability to be 'visible', to have yourself be 'recognized' (as opposed to 'misrecognized' as an effect of normative performativity), is crucial. For the critics, this is simply not possible for many people in practical terms, both because the dominant form of the debate (in this case, a pairing of opposed positions within a single discursive frame)[15] and their weak socio-economic position leaves them without 'something' to be recognized.[16] In short, it is not enough to be 'playing with representations and images' in order to challenge 'social exclusion'; material changes need to occur as well that give people the ability to live differently.

I suggest that this was at the heart of the lack of fit between the rhetoric about ICTs that informed the way in which they were promoted and funded, and the lives of many people who were 'socially excluded'. The form of the debate, both the positive and negative versions, placed ICTs at the centre of a 'new' social, economic and political world (or rather 'globe'); ICTs were both the cause and the crucial enabling factor that would reshape everything. For some, this had the positive potential of creating new opportunities and spaces; for others, it would reproduce previous inequalities, but in a new guise. Either way, ICTs were at the centre of it, and what would happen next would be unlike what had come before. Of course, the tendency to mask inequalities by using temporal assertions of difference – 'backwardness' or, in the case of technologies, 'Luddites' – is also a marked characteristic of much modernist rhetoric.[17] In this case, the constitution of a 'pre-ICTs era' created a separation between what people in the voluntary organizations were experiencing (the 'mundane' world of 'social exclusion') and the grinding logic of the policies that were behind the funding for providing wider access to ICTs. Yet voluntary organizations were having to deal mostly with what was now being constituted as the past (the 'pre-ICTs era'); the funding was supposed to assist them to draw this past into the future. Even the 'social exclusion' of the future would be different, involving a gap between the 'information poor' and the 'information rich' (Haywood 1995). The fact that the 'information poor' would in all likelihood be exactly the same people as were currently poor with or without ICTs seemed, if not entirely irrelevant, somehow beside the point.

That shift toward seeing the 'poor' in this context as the *information* 'poor' is important, for it allowed a sense that the problem for the 'socially excluded' was somehow the same as the problem of persuading people in general to use these technologies. Within the new world that ICTs were supposed to usher forth during the 1990s, it was predicted that there might initially be two key problems. First, enough people needed to be persuaded to 'become connected' to achieve the 'take-off' of these new technologies. This rapidly came to be known as the 'critical mass' problem: many early enthusiasts of ICTs assumed that these technologies were so important that the only barrier to their general and widespread use was to convince the unconverted to see the light. The people who needed persuading were 'the public', both those running businesses and all those millions of potential consumers. These people were assumed to be largely technically illiterate and, crucially, *that* was assumed to be the main problem in persuading them of the potential of these technologies: a 'practical' problem of appropriate knowledge and information, not a problem of whether, even with appropriate knowledge and information, people would want to use these technologies (the 'Luddite' issue mentioned above).[18] Secondly, there was the possible problem of the development of a mass of 'socially excluded' people who, for one reason or another, would not have access at all, and therefore would not be able to participate in the anticipated revolution – which, in the UK and some other parts of Europe, was usually termed the 'information society'.[19] They would become the 'information poor'.

These two concepts – 'critical mass' and 'information poor' – are obviously quite different, but a focus on the idea that access to and willing use of these technologies was the key problem meant that they were frequently blended together as if they were the same thing. The result was that 'social exclusion' was often treated, in practice, in the same way as the need to achieve a 'critical mass': get people on-line, using whatever means. Somehow, it seemed, the rest would take care of itself.

Through this kind of rhetoric, the technologies themselves were constituted as generating their own social, political and economic reality (the 'information society'), so long as enough people got on-line. This form of technical determinism is not new, of course; it has been repeatedly noted as a key aspect in modernist representations of technology.[20] And the implication was that the non-ICT world constitutes the past, a 'different country'.

In truth, many people both inside and outside of the voluntary sector during the 1990s wanted to believe in this disjunction between the past and the present. For the voluntary sector in Britain, there was not a great deal else to believe in at the time, having experienced years of a gradual erosion of state welfare services and an ever-increasing gap between rich and poor during the 1980s and early 1990s. That had put increasing pressure on the voluntary sector, to whom people in need were increasingly turning for help. By the mid-1990s, the sudden influx of relatively enormous quantities of public funding provided to pay for anything to do with information and communications technologies seemed like the one thing that could rescue voluntary organizations that were on the verge of collapsing under the strain. If, at the same time, providing access to ICTs for the 'socially excluded' could actually reduce their social exclusion, as the rhetoric strongly suggested, then this could be a genuine 'win-win' situation.

However, the way in which the rhetoric used to promote ICTs effectively masked the relationship between people's located lives and their experience of ICTs, through marking the first as 'the past' and the second as 'the future', left the voluntary sector involved in ICTs with the 'lack of fit' that I have described in the case of the WEVH. This was exacerbated, rather than helped, by the considerable changes for the voluntary sector in Britain following the election of the new Labour Government in May 1997. As part of the new government's 'Third Way' philosophy, a radical restructuring of the role of the voluntary sector for 'care in the community' was introduced. In this, 'compacts' were made between the government and the voluntary sector to provide services (Morison 2000). A number of researchers have argued that this change effectively imposed an economic or 'marketplace' model of social welfare, which emphasized individual choice and responsibility for services and welfare, rather than the social responsibility notions that had been implied in earlier ideas of citizenship (Turner 2001; Craig and Manthorpe 1999; Hudson 1998). In Manchester, the difference between MCIN, Hulme Community Computing and the WEVH was that the latter 'reinvented' itself in line with the new conditions, and it is one example of how the rhetoric, rather than the technologies themselves, was central to constituting the 'new world' involving ICTs. Issues arising out of peoples' lives that did not concern ICTs (now regarded as 'the past') and would not be solved by having access to them tended to be conceived as barriers, or sometimes as an afterthought, but rarely as the central issues that needed to be addressed.

In practical terms, the outcome of the new approach was an underlying lack of commitment to the long term that I mentioned earlier: few of the grants available lasted more than a couple of years; few provided funds for the basic running costs of organizations; most required new work, new projects, new ways to get people on-line, stretching resources rather than consolidating them; few provided funding for ongoing maintenance, trouble shooting, career development for staff, and so on.

So in conclusion, once the initial euphoria began to die down as the extent of the problems of the new media industries began to emerge, and as the voluntary sector 'boom to bust' period began to come to an end, the transformation in the ICT voluntary sector had been established. It was not achieved through the 'impact' of the technologies, but through the 'impact' of what these technologies were assumed to mean, assumptions which were backed up by public policies and the conditions of public funding for these projects. If there was a 'revolution', then it was constituted through empowered rhetoric, and through the creation of a split between people's located lives and an imagined future; but it was not through computers.

Acknowledgements

This chapter is based on ethnographic research supported by the Economic and Social Research Council's *Virtual Society?* programme, and was part of a research project within that programme entitled 'The Social Contexts of Virtual Manchester', carried out jointly by Penny Harvey (also an anthropologist), Jon Agar (a social historian of computer technology) and myself (Agar et al. 2002). The research included an exploration of publicly-funded projects aimed at encouraging greater use of, and access to, new information and communications technologies within the Manchester area. The underlying aim in the project was to analyse the relationship between concepts of 'virtuality' – the idea that new information technologies would allow forms of interaction that were not constrained by physical location – and the fact that all people, and computers, have to physically exist somewhere, and are also constituted by the historical and social contexts in which they exist. Aspects of the present discussion were presented to a number of seminars. Particularly important was the Surrey Sociology Research Methods Conference in Bournemouth in November 2001; a paper presented with Penny Harvey to the Manchester Social Anthropology Seminar series in October 2001; and an Equal Opportunities On-Line conference in Manchester in 2000. I have worked extremely closely with Penny Harvey on this project; the errors in this paper are my own; the shafts of light have been a joint endeavour.

Notes

1. http://www.learndirect.co.uk
2. http://www.letsallgeton.gov.uk
3. http://www.dfee.gov.uk/grid/challenge/open.htm
4. One of the many commentators on the 'flexible' version of capitalism in the current era is David Harvey (Harvey 1990), 'Flexibility' as a broader theme, particularly in the area of globalization and transnationalism, has received quite a bit of attention of late. Two notable examples are Ong's *Flexible Citizenship* (Ong 1999) and Emily Martin's *Flexible Bodies* (Martin 1994). See also Inglis and Rogan (1994) and Christensen-Dalsgaard et al. (1999).
5. The most recent version, the Communications White Paper, is available on-line (http://www.communicationswhitepaper.gov.uk). Particularly interesting is Chapter 3, 'Ensuring Universal Access' (http://www.communicationswhitepaper.gov.uk/by_chapter/ch3/index.htm). Another site of interest is the 'Let's All Get On' site, which outlines how the Government aims to assist people, particularly commercially and educationally, to 'get on-line' (http://www.letsallgeton.gov.uk/links.htm).
6. www.itu.int/acc/rtc/acc-rep.htm
7. See, just as examples, European Commission Directorate-General Information Society (2002); European Commission (2001); Houdart-Blazy (1996).
8. There are many sources to cite here, and I will just mention a few of them: Mitchell (1995); Springer (1996); Featherstone and Burrows (1995); Hayles (1999); Rheingold (1995); and Smith and Kollock (1999).
9. Some examples include Dovey (1996); Springer (1996); Featherstone and Burrows (1995); and Jordan (1999).
10. This is part of the idea that the 'bourgeois individual' has in recent years become one who 'celebrates diversity' and borrows continually from others in order to continually construct a constantly changing 'self' (Lury 2000; Lury 1998; Featherstone 1990).
11. For a fuller discussion, see Manuel Castells (1996), and also others who have contributed, including Haywood (1995); Norris (2001); Garnham (1990); Augé (1999); Boal and Brook (1995); Slouka (1996); and Anderson (1996).
12. One of the more extreme examples is Mark Slouka (1996); a rather less extreme argument can be seen in Noble's critique of 'distance learning' in universities (Noble 1998b; Noble 1998a).
13. The most notable recent publication to argue this position is Hardt and Negri's *Empire* (2000).

14. The way this debate mirrors right- and left-wing perspectives is obviously not accidental; but these days, it is difficult to place the two neatly into a right- or left-wing approach, and certainly not in Britain since the advent of New Labour.
15. A point made by Foucault (1986).
16. A particularly interesting example of this argument is Adkins and Lury's study of working-class women's position in the workplace (Adkins and Lury 1999).
17. Fabian (1983) describes this in terms of 'others' elsewhere, and Haylett (2001) in terms of the construction of the working class in Britain as 'backward'.
18. Whether people would want to use the technology or not was later glossed as a 'cultural' problem; for example, see the UK Cabinet Office's Performance and Innovation Unit report, 'e-commerce@itsbest', http://www.cabinet-office.gov.uk/innovation/1999/ecomm.shtml, in which it was suggested that two of the four main barriers to e-commerce succeeding were 'understanding' and 'trust'.
19. In fact the idea of an 'information society' long pre-dated the introduction of the Internet (Salvaggio 1989; Beniger 1986), but increasingly became a 'self-evident fact' following its introduction (Webster 1995).
20. See, for example, Bijker et al. (1987); Dovey (1996); Downey (1998); Downey and Dumit (1997); Haraway (1985); Ingold (1987); Latour (1993); Law (1991); MacKenzie and Wajcman(1985); Rapp (1997); Woolgar (1988).

References

Adkins, L. (2002), 'Sexuality and Economy: Historicisation vs Deconstruction', *Australian Feminist Studies*, 17(37): 31–41.

Adkins, L. and Lury, C. (1999), 'The Labour of Identity: Performing Identities, Performing Economies', *Economy and Society*, 28(4): 598–614.

Agar, J., Green, S. and Harvey, P. (2002), 'From Cotton to Computers: How Manchester made its Place in Technical Revolutions', in S. Woolgar (ed.) *Virtual Society? Get Real!*, Oxford: Oxford University Press.

Anderson, J. (1996), 'On the Social Order of Cyberspace – Knowledge Workers and New Creoles', *Social Science Computer Review*, 14(1): 7–9.

Augé, M. (1999), *The War of Dreams: Studies in Ethno Fiction*, trans. L. Heron, London: Pluto Press.

Bangemann, M. (1994), *Europe and the Global Information Society: Recommendations to the European Council*, Brussels: European Council.

Beniger, J.R. (1986), *The Control Revolution: Technological and Economic*

Origins of the Information Society, Cambridge, MA and London: Harvard University Press.

Bijker, W.E., Hughes, T.P. and Pinch, T.J. (eds) (1987), *The Social Construction of Technological Systems: New Directions in the Sociology and History of Technology*, Cambridge, MA and London: MIT Press.

Boal, I.A. and Brook, J. (eds) (1995), *Resisting the Virtual Life: the Culture and Politics of Information*, San Francisco and Monroe, OR: City Lights: Subterranean Co. (distributor).

Butler, J. (1993), *Bodies that Matter: On the Discursive Limits of 'Sex'*, London: Routledge.

Castells, M. (1996), *The Rise of the Network Society*, Oxford: Blackwell.

Christensen-Dalsgaard, B., Donnelly, W. and Griffith, M. (eds) (1999), *Flexible Working: New Network Technologies*, Amsterdam and Oxford: IOS Press.

Craig, G. and Manthorpe, J. (1999), 'Unequal partners? Local Government Reorganization and the Voluntary Sector', *Social Policy and Administration*, 33(1): 55–72.

Dovey, J. (1996), *Fractal Dreams: New Media in Social Context*, London: Lawrence & Wishart.

Downey, G.L. (1998), *The Machine in Me: an Anthropologist Sits among Computer Engineers*, New York and London: Routledge.

Downey, G.L. and Dumit, J. (eds) (1997), *Cyborgs and Citadels: Anthropological Interventions in Emerging Sciences and Technologies*, Santa Fe, NM: School of American Research Press.

Escobar, A. (1994), 'Welcome to Cyberia – Notes on the Anthropology of Cyberculture', *Current Anthropology*, 35(3): 211–321.

European Commission (2001), *eEurope: an Information Society for All*, Luxembourg: Office for Official Publications of the European Communities.

European Commission Directorate-General Information Society (2002), *Systems and Services for the Citizen – Synopses of Research Projects: Applications Relating to Persons with Special Needs including the Disabled and the Elderly*, Luxembourg: Office for Official Publications of the European Communities.

Fabian, J. (1983), *Time and the Other: How Anthropology Makes its Object*, New York and Chichester: Columbia University Press.

Featherstone, M. (1990), *Consumer Culture and Postmodernism* (Theory, Culture & Society), London: Sage.

Featherstone, M. and Burrows, R. (1995), *Cyberspace/Cyberbodies/Cyberpunk: Cultures of Technological Embodiment* (Theory, Culture & Society), London: Sage.

Foucault, M. (1986), *Power/Knowledge: Selected Interviews and Other Writings 1972–1977 by Michel Foucault*, Brighton: Harvester.

Fraser, N. (1997), *Justice Interruptus: Critical Reflections on the 'Postsocialist' Condition*, New York: Routledge.

Garnham, N. (1990), *Capitalism and Communication: Global Culture and the Economics of Information* (The Media, Culture and Society Series), London: Sage.

Green, S. and Harvey, P. (forthcoming), 'Scaling Place and Networks: an Ethnography of ICT "Innovation" in Manchester'.

Haraway, D. (1985), 'A Manifesto For Cyborgs – Science, Technology, and Socialist Feminism in the 1980s', *Socialist Review*, 80: 65–107.

Hardt, M. and Negri, A. (2000), *Empire*, Cambridge, MA and London: Harvard University Press.

Harvey, D. (1990), *The Condition of Postmodernity: an Enquiry into the Origins of Cultural Change*, Oxford: Blackwell.

Hayles, N.K. (1999), *How We Became Posthuman: Virtual Bodies in Cybernetics, Literature, and Informatics*, Chicago and London: University of Chicago Press.

Haylett, C. (2001), 'Illegitimate Subjects?: Abject Whites, Neoliberal Modernisation, and Middle-class Multiculturalism', *Environment and Planning D: Society & Space*, 19(3): 351–70.

Haywood, T. (1995), *Info-rich–Info-poor: Access and Exchange in the Global Information Society*, London: Bowker-Saur.

Hennessy, R. (1993), 'Queer Theory – a Review of the "Differences" Special Issue and Wittig's "The Straight Mind"', *Signs*, 18(4): 964–73.

—— (1995), 'Queer Visibility in Commodity Culture', in L.J. Nicholson and S. Seidman, (eds), *Social Postmodernism: Beyond Identity Politics*, Cambridge: Cambridge University Press.

Houdart-Blazy, V. (1996), *The Information Society: a Challenge for Women* (Women of Europe dossier no. 44), Brussels: Information for Women Directorate-General X Information Communication Culture and Audiovisual Media European Commission [1996].

Hudson, P. (1998), 'The Voluntary Sector, the State, and Citizenship in the United Kingdom', *Social Service Review*, 72(4): 452–65.

Inglis, J. and Rogan, L. (1994), *Flexible Families: New Directions for Australian Communities*, Leichhardt, NSW: Pluto.

Ingold, T. (1987), 'Tools, Minds and Machines: an Excursion in the Philosophy of Technology', in L. Holy (ed.), *Comparative Anthropology*, Oxford: Basil Blackwell.

Jordan, T. (1999), *Cyberpower: the Culture and Politics of Cyberspace and the Internet*, New York: Routledge.

Latour, B. (1993), *We Have Never Been Modern*, New York and London: Harvester.

Law, J. (ed.) (1991), *A Sociology of Monsters: Essays on Power, Technology, and Domination* (Sociological review monograph; 38), London and New York: Routledge.

Lloyd, M. (1999), 'Performativity, Parody, Politics', *Theory Culture & Society*, 16(2): 195–213.

Lury, C. (1998), *Prosthetic Culture: Photography, Memory and Identity*, London: Routledge.

—— (2000), 'The United Colors of Diversity: Essential and Inessential Culture', in S. Franklin, C. Lury, and J. Stacey (eds), *Global Nature, Global Culture*, London: Sage: 146–87.

MacKenzie, D.A. and Wajcman, J. (eds) (1985), *The Social Shaping of Technology: How the Refrigerator Got its Hum*, Milton Keynes: Open University Press.

Martin, E. (1994), *Flexible Bodies: Tracking Immunity in American Culture from the Days of Polio to the Age of AIDS*, Boston: Beacon.

Miller, D. and Slater, D. (2000), *The Internet: an Ethnographic Approach*, Oxford: Berg.

Mitchell, W.J. (1995), *City of Bits: Space, Place, and the Infobahn*, Cambridge, MA and London: MIT Press.

Morison, J. (2000), 'The Government-Voluntary Sector Compacts: Governance, Governmentality, and Civil Society', *Journal of Law and Society*, 27(1): 98–132.

Noble, D.F. (1998a), 'Digital Diploma Mills, Part II: The Coming Battle over Online Instruction', *Sociological Perspectives*, 41(4): 815–25.

—— (1998b), 'Digital Diploma Mills: The Automation of Higher Education', *Monthly Review – an Independent Socialist Magazine*, 49(9): 38–52.

Norris, P. (2001), *Digital Divide: Civic Engagement, Information Poverty, and the Internet Worldwide* (Communication, Society and Politics), Cambridge: Cambridge University Press.

Ong, A. (1999), *Flexible Citizenship: the Cultural Logics of Transnationality*, Durham, NC and London: Duke University Press.

Rapp, R. (1997), 'Real-Time Fetus: The Role of the Sonogram in the Age of Monitored Reproduction', in G.L. Downey and J. Dumit (eds), *Cyborgs and Citadels: Anthropological Interventions in Emerging Sciences and Technologies*. Santa Fe, NM: School of American Research Press: 31–48.

Rheingold, H. (1995), *The Virtual Community: Finding Connection in a Computerized World*, London: Secker & Warburg.

Salvaggio, J.L. (ed.) (1989), *The Information Society: Economic, Social, and Structural Issues* (Communication), Hillsdale, NJ: Lawrence Erlbaum Associates.

Slouka, M.Z. (1996), *War of the Worlds: Cyberspace and the High-tech Assault on Reality*, London: Abacus.

Smith, M. and Kollock, P. (eds) (1999), *Communities in Cyberspace*, London and New York: Routledge.

Springer, C. (1996), *Electronic Eros: Bodies and Desire in the Postindustrial Age*, London: Athlone Press; Austin: University of Texas Press.

Stone, A.R. (1992), 'Virtual Systems', in J. Crary and S. Kwinter (eds), *Incorporations*, New York: Zone Books.

Turner, B.S. (2001), 'The Erosion of Citizenship', *British Journal of Sociology*, 52(2): 189–209.

Webster, F. (1995), *Theories of the Information Society* (The International Library of Sociology), London and New York: Routledge.

Woolgar, S. (1988), *Science: the Very Idea (Key Ideas)*, Chichester and London; New York: Ellis Horwood; Tavistock Publications.

–4–

Real-time, Real-place Market: Transnational Connections and Disconnections in Financial Markets

Anna Hasselström

The financial market of today is often pictured, by scholars as well as in popular media, as a global, electronic, out-of-control money-seeking monster (Castells 1996, Lash and Urry 1994, Strange 1988, 1998, Whimster and Budd 1992). Traders and brokers in New York, London, Stockholm, Tokyo, Johannesburg, Sao Paolo and other big cities are connected by huge real-time, on-line cyber networks. It is described as an electronic army of traders that can suddenly, without warning, be turned into a stampeding electronic herd (Friedman 1999) of a gigantic size, causing companies to go bust, central banks to quiver, national currencies to devalue, people to lose their jobs and money to mysteriously disappear into thin air.

So, has the world entered into a qualitatively new era organized around global financial markets? Do we now live in an information or perhaps a knowledge society driven by the anonymous actor we have learned to call 'global capital' and its much valued companion and sidekick 'information technology'? A society with no need for shared time and shared space (Castells 1998)?

I believe such accounts of global financial markets tell only half the story. Although contemporary financial markets are very much structured by various kinds of information technologies making real-time, on-screen trading possible, I hope to show that the work environment and practices of financial traders, brokers and analysts also are set in specific physical, temporal and social contexts (which make the often abstract 'Market' more tangible). I will further look at how these contexts contribute to images of 'the Market' as, on the one hand, global and interconnected, and on the other, disconnected from the world outside the financial arena.[1] But before developing this argument further let us visit 'the Market'.

Spring 1998, New York, Wall Street, 7.45 a.m.: Waiting for the Action

At 7.45 a.m. I enter the doors into one of the larger brokerage houses in New York. Today is a special day: the latest American employment figures are to be released at 8.30 a.m. and brokers and traders all over the world will be waiting by their screens keeping a close eye on the *Reuters* news-ticker.[2] As a visitor I am first shown to the waiting area which is furnished with two small sofas and a coffee table, and is located between the reception desk and the bond-trading floor. Separating the two areas is a glass wall that allows the visitor full view of the trading floor – 'the Market' is, so to speak, on full display.

Looking out across the trading floor I see a large open-spaced area with no office cubicles or other kinds of walls. There are no curtains and the wall-to-wall carpet is in a dull, dark-blue colour and looks dirty and messy. The floor seems over-crowded with people, computers and telephones. The brokers, numbering roughly around 100–120, are mainly white men between 20 and 40 years old. They sit at or stand by their desks that are placed in long rows covering the trading floor. Each workstation is equipped with several computer screens, telephones and microphones.

Peter, the broker who invited me to sit in, sees that I've arrived and rushes toward me. He explains that he won't have time to look after me, and introduces me to another young man, Mike, who takes me on to the floor.

The floor is fairly calm: some brokers are standing around in small groups, talking and laughing, whereas others are on the phone by their desks. All of a sudden there is a commotion among a small group of brokers sitting at the left-hand corner of the room. They get on their feet, with phones pressed to their ears, and start shouting quotes to each other, while occasionally bending down to look at the screens. Buy quotes, sell quotes and orders fly through the air, either via loud shouts or hand signals. The brokers not involved in the commotion seem totally disinterested in what is going on. The screaming and hand signalling goes on for a couple of minutes only to die down again. The brokers put down the phones and sit back down.

According to Mike most clients (in this case mainly traders working for big companies and banks) want to stay on the phone line while the broker executes the transaction order to hear if the broker 'fucks up', i.e. buys or sells at the wrong price, or if something else is going on. If the broker 'fucks up' he usually gets an instant outburst of abuse from the client.

A couple of minutes after the first commotion the same thing happens again, this time in another corner of the room. These waves of activities continue, sometimes including more than one desk, until about 8.29 a.m. when the noise on the floor slowly dies down and most brokers turn toward the big *Reuters* screen placed in the left-hand corner of the room. It is one minute before the figures are to be made public. Most heads are by now turned to the screen. Finally the figures flash up on the *Reuters* news ticker: the numbers are slightly up.

I was unsure what to expect after the figures were released but I did think *something* would happen. Instead, the brokers quietly turn away from the *Reuters* ticker and back to their own screens. The scattered waves of commotion start again. However, at around 8.45 a.m. the intensity increases somewhat and about a minute later, all hell breaks loose. Almost all brokers on the trading floor stand up and take turns shouting, yelling, cursing and signalling. The intensity and frenzy completely engulf the trading floor.

Shortly after 9 a.m. the noise and commotion slow down, and brokers go back to chatting and laughing with each other. Mike explains that it takes about fifteen minutes for the clients to interpret the figures, i.e. to work out what this might mean for their positions and how others will act upon the information, hence the interval between the release of the figures and trading.

Just before I'm about to leave the floor I hear a broker say twenty-five – the rest of the sentence disappears into the general noise of the trading floor. Mike turns to me and says: 'Now when he said twenty-five, that means that bonds worth twenty-five million dollars just changed owner.' Twenty-five million dollars! I give Mike the reaction I assumed he was after: 'Wow! Twenty-five million dollars! Crazy ...' I say and shake my head. Mike smiles and looks pleased.[3]

Autumn 1998, London, the City, 7.15 a.m.: Collecting 'Added Value' and Becoming 'in-the-Know'

Steve's late! He puts down his takeaway coffee on his desk and starts shuffling papers around trying to find a note pad. There it is! He then runs across the trading floor of the large American investment bank he is employed by, and sneaks into the auditorium where the other equity traders and sales traders are seated. The morning meeting is already on the way, and one of the in-house economists is busy talking about a management changeover in a European company that may affect the share price.

It is a smallish auditorium seating roughly 80 people. A table with microphones is placed on the centre of the stage. The traders and sales traders listen, take notes and ask the odd question.

The economist finishes his briefing and Frankfurt is put through via the speaker system and a sales trader from the German office gives her on-the-spot view. She talks for a few minutes but according to Steve she doesn't 'add any value' – i.e. she doesn't really say anything new that Steve himself could not 'read off the screen', as he puts it. Here 'the screen' refers mainly to the financial news offered on-line by the large news agencies such as *Reuters* and

Bloomberg. After that other economists and traders take turns in talking about the coming day's events.

London, the City, 7.30 a.m.
On his way out of the auditorium Steve picks up a bunch of photocopied papers lying by the exit. The papers contain abbreviated versions of what has just been said. He returns to his desk and starts calling clients. The idea is to 'add value': to give the client information on what is going on in the market. Steve simply reads off his own short notes but sounds as though he knows a lot more than actually he does.

Later that morning when checking his e-mail, Steve suddenly discovers a message from the in-house Latin-American analyst. It had arrived earlier that day and he had somehow missed it. The e-mail was about a political decision in Brazil affecting IMF (International Monetary Fund) funding. This could be a possible problem for Steve's clients. After reading the e-mail, Steve rushes over to the analyst who had written it and asks for more information about what this might mean. He then calls two of his clients and tells them about this possible 'hot spot'. Both clients listen quietly when Steve explains what has happened in Brazil. When he finishes they ask him what this could mean, what the consequences might be and why it has happened. Steve, with his new-found knowledge on the topic, answers in a very authoritative and convincing manner, sounding very much 'in the know' of things. After hanging up, Steve walks around to the some of the other sales traders and traders and tells them about the Brazil news.

London, the City, 12.30 p.m.
There is a lunch and investor/client meeting upstairs. Steve's bank has invited five Nordic companies together with possible investors for a day's meeting. The company representatives take turns in promoting their companies in order to attract investors. With fancy PowerPoint presentations and lots of neatly printed hand-outs they try to convince the present traders and sales traders that their particular company offers a lucrative future investment. After leaving the meeting early, Steve complains: 'What a waste of time! It didn't add any value at all!' That is, the company representatives did not reveal any kind of information that Steve could pass on to his clients for them to 'trade on'. It was all old news.

For Steve, the aim of the meeting is to collect 'added value' to pass on to his clients. At the morning meeting Steve's boss told Steve and his colleagues to call their clients directly after each company presentation to let them know what had been said. Steve did not do this since he regarded the presentations a waste of time and since he did not want to annoy his clients with useless information and thereby waste their precious and valuable time.

The afternoon turns out to be fairly quiet. Steve makes a few client calls before going out for a quick drink with me, the visiting anthropologist. It's his only free evening this week. Christmas is closing in and there is a lot of client entertaining to do.

Autumn 1998, London, the City, 9 p.m.: Working while Drinking

It's Thursday and the bar is crowed with men in suits and dressed-up women. I'm there with some Swedish traders who have flown in from Stockholm to visit and take out a couple of English traders from a larger bank in London. We are standing by the bar, drinking and talking. A large part of the conversation centres on how drunk one of the English traders had been the night before. After I've been talking some time with the senior Swedish trader, Per, about his job and about my dissertation, he half-jokingly offers me a job. I ask him what I would be doing, whereby he answers: 'What you're doing now. Client-trader relations …'

I decline the offer and instead ask him about the entertaining[4] part of his job. According to Per it is really important to get drunk together with the people you do business with. He gestures towards the group of English traders that are standing around drinking with his own junior Swedish traders and says: 'This is actually work. You're not going to cheat someone you've been drunk with. A half-hour meeting in the office doesn't give anything. This is what is important!'

So, the 'disembodied phantasmagoria' of 'free-floating capital' moving with 'lightning-like movements' (Jameson 1998:142–3) has not as yet managed to out-run people, places and times.

The Global Economy: Information Technology and the Mundane Banalities of Everyday Life

The so-called global economy is often described in terms of buzzwords such as hypermobility, time-space compression, deterritorialization, privatization, liberalization and deregulation. These concepts are then combined with powerful metaphors such as turbo capitalism, virtual money, quicksilver money, mad money, etc. Manuel Castells is one of many commentators offering an analysis of the contemporary global economic order, and in his extensive trilogy *The Information Age: Economy, Society and Culture* (1996, 1997, 1998), he sees a new kind of information-technology paradigm developing where important functions of society have become organized around networks. Castells speaks of a kind of networking logic that in itself is more deterministic in relation to social activity than the actual social interests operating through the networks: 'the power of flows takes precedence over the flows of power' (1996: 469).

The most powerful networks today, according to Castells, are the global networks of capital, around which the new kind of economy is organized. Through the use of information technology, these financial networks have access to other kinds of technological know-how which in turn is the basis for production and competitiveness. The network society is characterized by timeless space (electronic flows of finance independent of human logic) that takes precedence over industrial clock-time. In this kind of society, capital is always on the move and never pinned down to place but only passing through different localities connected by information technology. So what we have is a 'culture of real virtuality' where technology 'compresses time …, de-sequencing society and de-historicizing history' (1998: 349). It is a culture where 'capital is allowed to escape from time' (ibid.). Space of flows and timeless space take over from place and clock-time and produce new cultures no longer depending on shared space and shared time.

Although his ideas on the network logic have some relevance, the global financial market I encountered during field work does not fit the Castellian picture all that well.[5] The main problem is that Castells' text, which I read as an attempt to analyse and critique a specific world order based on global financial networks, ends up actually *contributing* to the reification and mystification of 'global capital' – probably as a consequence of his emphasis on the power of flows over flows of power. In the hands of Castells, global financial flows become an uncontrollable, natural force following its own logic. But financial markets are not the natural outcome of a capitalist economy (Coronil 2000, Young and Theys 1999). Financial markets are culturally and politically constructed. They are the result of decisions and non-decisions made throughout history concerning national and international policies on trade and security, such as for example direct interventions to make transnational capital flows easier as a way to finance national budgets and trade deficits, and to compete internationally (Martin and Schumann 1996, Pauly 1997, Strange 1988, 1998, Trouillot 2001). And even if the hard discs somehow have been declared to be extraterritorial areas (Martin and Schumann 1996), financial markets '… cannot play a dominant role in the way in which a political economy functions unless allowed to do so by whoever wields power and possesses authority' (Strange 1988: 23).

Although Castells recognizes that electronic space is not simply a neutral, technological phenomenon but offers sites for concentration, power and contestation, as well as sites for decentralization and openness, he treats electronic networks as self-contained systems of dominant power over the surrounding society due to his emphasis on electronic networks as the true sources of power in its own right. But Castells's dematerializing account of the global economy (as denationalized, hypermobile, deterritorialized and timeless) only tells us part of the story, leaving out the fact that electronic flows of money have to be accommodated by actual flesh-and-blood men and women, living in actual cities, riding the actual tube to work, trading in actual trading rooms using actual computers hooked up with actual fibre-optics dug down in actual soil that still belongs to an actual political actor – i.e. the nation state (Sassen 1999, 2000). And since the state still plays a vital political role it is a mistake to assume the state is simply losing control over the economy due to financial deregulation. Instead novel institutional forms are created and old ones are altered, which means that deregulation is often better described as reregulation (ibid.).

So instead of mainly focusing on the 'cyber-hyper' aspects of financial markets – an approach that represents and reifies 'the global economy' and 'the Market' in a particular manner and leaves out the production and regulation of global capital – a more fruitful approach is to look at how financial flows weave in and out of digital and physical space thereby being both fixed and mobile (Sassen 1999, 2000). The nodes and switches of the network logic described by Castells do hit the ground now and again, thereby offering us an opportunity to empirically study how they are constructed and organized.

With such a focus we can then ask how this relates to images of 'the global economy' and of 'the Market', i.e. we can ask what 'projects of globalization' (Tsing 2000) *do* in the world, and thereby avoid reproducing instead of making explicit the construction of economic globalization. A starting point for doing this is to view capitalism and globalization as processes that can be both diverse and porous and that accommodate varied agendas and practices (Maurer 2000, Tsing 2000).

Having said that, financial markets *are* partly characterized by hypermobility and deterritorialization: large electronic and digital networks do connect people, banks and cities from all over the globe, and allow for the instant transferring of large volumes of money, information and rumours. Traders, brokers and analysts do have the world's different trading floors as their everyday work environment via 'real-time' video and audio links in a 'face-to-screen' manner (Knorr Cetina and Bruegger 2000). But financial markets are also very much located in actual cities and buildings and on trading floors. And every day, traders and brokers make use of physical, temporal and social resources and infrastructures in order to move electronic money around. Or in other words, digital space is very much embedded in physical space and vice versa.

Place, Time and Social Interaction in Financial Markets

What follows is a brief description of some of the physical, temporal and social aspects that make up the financial arena.

Physical and Material Setting

The New York Stock Exchange and other exchanges inhabited by screaming, gesturing men in colourful suit-jackets are powerful symbolic representations of financial markets. Those exchange floors that are on financial news on television for only a few seconds are *not* the focus of my research. When I talk about trading floors I refer to trading floors *within* investment banks, large companies and brokerage houses. A vast amount of financial trading takes place from and between these floors scattered across the world. The ones I have visited during fieldwork (whether in Stockholm, London or New York, whether brokerage houses, investment banks or institutional investors, or whether Japanese, Swedish, English, German, Swiss or American) have all been very alike in certain ways.

For example, the design and layout of the floors are similar: the first person a visitor is likely to encounter is the receptionist. The reception desks are usually fairly neat with a small waiting area, a couple of sofas, some plants, and a few financial newspapers such as the *Financial Times* and *Wall Street Journal* on display. It is here you sign in and get your entry pass. Once inside you are likely to come across a glass wall separating the trading floor from the rest of the office thereby giving visitors and the rest of the staff a full view of 'the Market'. No matter the size, trading floors can usually only be entered with a magnetic pass or by code.

On the actual trading floor an army of young to youngish men in designer shirts and ties, coats hanging off the back of the chairs, sit at desks placed in an open-spaced area. The floor is covered by row after row of desks equipped with computer screens, telephones and speaker-systems connecting the floor with other floors all over the world. Working as a trader or broker means being surrounded by others all the time. There are people sitting behind you, in front of you and next to you rubbing elbows with you, which make it virtually impossible to have any private telephone or e-mail conversations.

The physical and technological settings of trading floors structure, control and discipline brokers, traders and analysts into certain ways of moving about, talking, joking, trading, etc. This takes place in a kind of transnational panoptical environment where the individual broker or trader constantly sees and hears others – both on his own floor as well as on other floors scattered across the larger cities of the world, connected via real-time audio and video links. Conversely, he too is being observed by others, but without ever knowing exactly who it is that watches and listens. This transnational panoptical dimension is, however, not totalizing (cf. Lyon 2001) since information technology itself offers ways around it in the guise of mute and off buttons.

Some paraphernalia are more common than others on the floors, such as a number of clocks on the wall showing different time zones, large electronic boards displaying different trading rates and indices, and video cameras filming the white boards where the latest buy and sell prices are written down (the cameras broadcast these figures live to the other offices in the often transnational brokerage house).

As for individual technical equipment some traders, usually the proprietary traders,[6] are on-line to their markets all the time, even at home, through small beeper-like gadgets on which they check their positions. On the floor, brokers and traders usually have two to four computer screens each, plus one or two telephone lines. Telephones are pre-programmed to certain large clients. Brokers and traders are also connected to each other via direct speaker systems. Some banks have live videolinks connecting for example the London trading floor with the Stockholm trading floor. One of the traders I worked with said that the videolink at his bank was an attempt 'to make us feel part of the global company'. He called it 'a waste of money', but later admitted that 'the place would be dead as a library without all the videolinks, microphones and speaker systems'.

Traders and brokers customize their own computer screens to suit their specific needs. Their screens are programmed to show for instance certain regional news, specific markets indices and trading rates, tables, graphs, etc.

Trading and communicating between traders, brokers and analysts usually take place, directly or indirectly (Calhoun 1991, 1992), either via telephone or via on-line and/or real-time trading, news and message services[7] provided by e.g. *Bloomberg* or *Reuters*. Apart from accessing news and statistics and to trade, many traders and brokers use message services to discuss trading-related rumours and news as well as non-trading-related things such as what bar to meet in later that day or to send jokes back and forth to each other. When I was on the trading floor, I also often used the *Bloomberg* message service and found it a great way to keep in touch with my contacts without actually having to talk to them in person – it was an efficient way to keep a relationship alive with minimum effort made.

The speed and volume of trading, made visible through figures mediated by computer screens, videolinks, phones, speaker systems, etc., 'talk' to the traders and brokers, and are part of the knowledge process referred to, by traders and brokers, as a 'feel for the market', 'market sentiment' and 'gut feeling'. On the financial arena 'the Market' as an aggregate of action across the globe is produced and distributed in the guise of different-coloured figures on screens, electronic boards, via audio links, etc., in a manner that glosses complex political and economical interconnections (Dilley 1992). Complicated processes outside the financial arena and trading floor are transformed into different financial instruments (cf. Norberg 2001) such as shares, options, convertibles, etc. that in turn are transformed into numbers and into 'financial facts', and hence become an 'important source of authority' (Downey and Dumit 1997: 6).

An interesting point is how information technologies to a certain extent have to be 'invisible' or 'transparent' in order for us to use them in a unproblematic manner, as well as having to be visible 'in the form of extended access to information' (Lave and Wenger 1991: 103). The invisibility aspect of information technologies allows us to focus on the visibility of the subject matter (ibid.).

Temporal Cycles and Financial Flows

The description of trading given in financial textbooks tends to leave the reader with an image of the financial market as a technological, automatic, smooth-running machine. It is a description that leaves out people and the mundane practices and social structures that in fact affect trading. Some of these practices and structures follow very distinct temporal patterns, and are of both an official and an unofficial character.

For example, there are the official announcements and releases of economic news and figures made by central banks, corporations and governments cabled out as good as 'real-time' via the large news agencies' on-line services. These can be pre-scheduled to take place at certain days and at certain times or un-scheduled when for example Alan Greenspan and his colleagues want to surprise 'the Market'. (See the description, in the beginning of this chapter, about the New York bond-trading floor.)

The less official temporal cycles refer to more mundane matters. For example, trading in the summer is usually slower than during the rest of the year since even investors, traders, brokers and analysts go on holiday. So is the time around Christmas and New Year. Another example is Fridays – during fieldwork I was repeatedly told that Fridays can be somewhat different compared to other days of the week. On the one hand, Fridays can be a lot calmer with less trading and lower liquidity but with greater volatility. This means that rumours started on Fridays can cause large price movements and open up for possible high profits (or losses). On the other hand, Fridays can also mean *more* deals for brokers since many traders do not want to go home for the weekend having risky positions to worry about, and hence get rid of these positions before leaving the trading floor for the week.

Trading also varies during the course of the day, with usually some trading in the morning, when traders and clients come into their offices and check their positions and when the trading systems opens[8] (the volume varies in the morning as well due to time differences between countries which means that some traders and brokers start earlier than others), then trading quiets down at lunch time (because they have to eat), only to pick up pace again in the afternoon.

Obviously this generalized picture varies according to the kind of market a trader or broker works in, and to what happens during the day: sudden news or the release of economic figures as mentioned above usually also affect the trading volume.

These temporal cycles mean that a lot of time on the trading floor is spent waiting by your screens: waiting for business from clients, waiting for the market to go in a particular way, waiting for the release of new figures, etc. I have sat next to brokers where the phone constantly rang and deals were made all the time, but I have also sat next to brokers who didn't get to broke one single deal during a day. During these slow days being a broker seems very dull and boring.

Information technology has speeded up many aspects of the work practices of financial markets. This acceleration is both contagious and addictive (Eriksen 2001). The acts of quoting, trading, broking and exchanging information strive to come as close to 'real-time' as possible. Traders, brokers and analysts expect and give response almost instantaneously through the use of various communication technologies. This high-speed interaction abstracts and simplifies (ibid.) the workings of broking and trading, and offers little time for reflection. It further introduces a dimension of insecurity among traders, brokers and analysts consisting of a fear of lagging behind, of knowing less than others. However, this does not mean that financial markets are time-less and place-less as Castells and other with him would have it. Financial flows are organized along and punctuated by different, socially and culturally construed, temporal dimensions (some are very fast-moving, others less so) (cf. Wulff 1994). These dimensions are very much clock-bound and shared.

Social Interaction and the Financial Arena

Brokers and traders oftened used the word 'aggressive' to describe the work environment in financial markets. When I asked Maria, a Swedish sales trader in London, to elaborate a little on what this meant she had great difficulty doing so. Eventually she said that 'aggressive as in when your boss shouts: you fucking idiot!' She also said that 'aggressive' includes the fact that everything is measured in figures and numbers: your work is constantly monitored and measured, and thereby you are always under evaluation. There is a constant pressure to perform – i.e. to make lots of money. She further mentioned distrust between colleagues as an aspect of this aggressive environment, and talked about work in terms of a status ladder cramped with traders trying to get higher and higher. Being on the ladder meant always worrying about the ones behind you, trying to get past. For example, Maria would not trust just anyone of her colleagues with handling her clients when on holiday. Not because she thinks some of her co-workers are less competent, but because she is afraid they might steal her clients away from her.

In short, financial markets are highly competitive and individualizing (cf. Abolafia 1996, Norberg 2001), and the work of brokers, traders and analysts is constantly 'audited'.

The brokers and traders themselves often nurture the popular image of brokers and traders as hot-shot, aggressive go-getters. There was a lot of swearing and shouting going on at the larger trading floors I visited in London and in New York – especially on busy days. At the English brokerage house where I spent most time, it was not uncommon to hear loud abuse along the lines of 'fucking cunt' or 'fucking idiot' flying through the air. Matt, a trader working for a large Japanese bank in London, gave another example: he was new at the desk and a trader from another desk approached him and wanted a price. Matt didn't really know what to do and replied: 'I'll get back to you in two minutes', whereby the trader responded: 'No, I want it now, you idiot!' Luckily, Matt explained, he had good desk colleagues that told the trader to 'fuck off'.

It is not only the relationship between colleagues that can be somewhat strained and unpleasant – the relationship between traders (clients) and brokers is also far from a frictionless one. The financial trading system is, in theory, based on opposing interests: both parties want to make as much money as possible out of the other party, which means that certain systematic tensions are built into the very structures of trading. When talking about the relationship between brokers and traders one broker said: 'We hate them and they hate us. They all think we're wankers. They treat us like shit and we still have to go out with them.'

The aggressive work environment is often referred to by traders and brokers themselves when explaining 'entertaining' which is seen, by many of them, as a way to create trust and to patch up relationships in a world characterized by uncertainty. But as I have argued elsewhere, the particular kind of social interaction (aiming at friendship-like relationships) that characterizes 'entertaining' results in another kind of uncertainty, having to do with the mixing of two sets of ideals: business vs friendship (Hasselström 2000; cf. Wulff 1998: 78–80 on how competitive situations create allies but not friends).

The Social Virtuality of Financial Markets

The work practices of financial markets weave in and out of digital and physical space and place. Throughout the rest of this text I will use the concept of social virtuality when referring to the specific physical, temporal and social contexts of financial markets as described above. The concept allows us to focus on virtual and social life as intertwined and connected to places (see introduction in this volume and Miller and Slater 2000; see also Carrier 1998, Thrift 1998). Take the following example:

At the London office of the large American investment bank the first traders arrive before 7 a.m. At around 8 a.m. most traders seem to be in place, and the level of activity rises. The convertibles desk (consisting of about eight traders) has their morning meeting over the phone even though they sit right next to each other. Each trader tells the others what they intend to do during the day. This takes about ten to fifteen minutes. On this occasion, one of the traders, Dick, talked some about Tokyo and what had happened there overnight, and Jake told the others what was happening to a certain company in Holland. Earlier that morning a broker in Holland had sent a *Bloomberg* message to Jake concerning a financial decision made by the company that probably would affect its shares. Jake called the broker before the morning meeting and asked for more information and an explanation of what was going on. The broker explained what he knew but for some of the questions Jake asked, he in turn had to ask his analyst while Jake waited on the line. The Dutch broker sounded very convincing and in-the-know, and Jake sounded just as convincing when he a few minutes later recapitulated the information to the rest of the desk on the morning meeting via the phone. He also emphasized that the information came from 'the broker we usually use in place'. This emphasis I took to be another way for Jake to say: 'I am not responsible for this information, I only pass it on. The information is, however, reliable since it comes from a broker we know and usually use'. (Jake and most of the others have met this broker on several occasions while being entertained.)

Most of the traders, brokers and analysts I worked with were in constant touch with each other: they talked on the phone, via speaker systems, via on-line message services, travelled routinely to see each other, and so on. Further, it was not uncommon to have done business together for years. Obviously the importance of these kinds of personal contact differs depending on what market we deal with, and what the traders, brokers and analysts themselves think about entertaining, but despite this, face-to-face meetings are very much part of global financial flows and financial markets. The super-efficient, anonymous 'textbook market' is through these practices personalized, contextualized and given a face; business and information come from someone you have probably dealt with before. Financial markets are not only about accessing already packaged information via digital media – this information is set in relation to where it came from; set in relation to someone you can contextualize, someone you have met, worked with before, and someone you might even call your friend (with whatever implications that might bring for how financial markets are organized).

Despite the very brief and general description given above of what I encountered at different trading floors during fieldwork, it should be apparent that information technology provides an important backdrop for the organization, production and distribution of financial flows as argued by Castells. But the seemingly hypermobile, placeless and timeless financial flows of information-technology-based financial markets are in fact deeply intertwined with certain shared place-bound, time-bound and social practices of trading. Financial markets are simultaneously territorialized and deterritorialized, in physical as well as in digital space. Time is not timeless and place is not dissolved into digital space.

Fragmented Globalization: the Including and Excluding 'Market'

What impact does the social virtuality of financial markets have on images of 'the Market' held both by financial professionals themselves and images of the market on a more popular level? Well, on the one hand 'the Market' becomes global and interconnected but on the other hand, it becomes *dis*connected from the world outside the financial arena. Let us start with what makes 'the Market' globally interconnected.

The Connected Market

Traders, brokers and analysts trade and communicate in 'real-time' with other traders and brokers sitting at trading desks all over the financial world. With a click on a button a trader in Stockholm can talk to a broker in New York. They make use of all kinds of information technology such as real-time audio and video links, on-line message services, speaker systems, open phone lines, pre-programmed dialling buttons connecting the broker or trader with other brokers or traders in an instant no matter where on the globe they sit. Traders, brokers and analysts also have access to real-time trading figures via computer screens or pocket-size beeper-like gadgets. All this is accompanied by the constant ticking away of real-time financial and political news broadcasting visible on the screens in front of them.

In short, trading and broking take place in similar surroundings in terms of physical and material layout of trading floors (placement of desks, clocks on the wall, electronic indices boards, the same financial newspapers, etc.); traders, brokers and analysts talk the same language (usually English when trading and communicating), use the same technological equipment and computer software, watch the same news, follow the same national and international political events, and even dress the same. The milieu is recognizable to financial professionals either visiting the floor in person or simply visualizing the floor while trading and communicating with others actually there. This sameness also make the trading floors recognizable to 'non-financial' people sitting at home watching the business news with footage from a floor in Frankfurt that looks more or less exactly the same as the one from New York shown on yesterday's news. Local particularities in terms of physical layout thereby give way to standardized images (Garsten 1994) of the financial market. Information technology turns 'the Market' into one interconnected place where global flows of money are moved at high volume and speed.

The official and unofficial temporal cycles of trading also add to the image of the market as one place. At the official release of certain economic figures, traders and brokers know that others will also hang by their screens, waiting. Feelings of excitement, anticipation and disappointment are shared not only with colleagues on a particular floor but also with traders and brokers sitting on other floors in other cities and countries (Knorr Cetina and Bruegger 2000). They are events to gather around, to anticipate, to relate to, to dread or to look forward to. These events are hence part of a global microstructure characterized by 'patterns of relatedness and coordination that are global in scope but microsocial in character, and which assemble and link together global domains' (Bruegger and Knorr Cetina 2002).

Further, the temporally structured trading with lower and higher volumes visible to traders and brokers when looking at their screens or at different indices also adds to the image of the market as one. News from across the globe is instantly translated into market activity visible on the screen in the guise of numbers. A certain 'global we-feeling' – a feeling of being part of something larger beyond the actual trading floor – is hence created among traders, brokers and analysts working in financial markets.

The image of 'the Market' as connected is further strengthened through the reoccurring causal explanations put forward by financial experts, linking different events with each other, such as an interest rate cut in the United States with my pension scheme in Sweden.

And when not sitting in this connected work environment (rubbing shoulders with others, hearing them getting excited when 'the Market' is going their way and angry when it isn't), traders, brokers and analysts are flying to other cities, countries and continents in order to entertain or to be entertained. Taking all this into account, how could the market be anything but global and connected?

The Disconnected Market

To start with, the information technology used in financial markets does not come cheap. You have to pay to get access to real-time news provided by e.g. *Bloomberg* or *Reuters*, pay to get access to trading systems, to on-line message services, to use beepers and so on. Apart from money you also need time – time to sift through and to take in all the information that technology provides you with. So, information technology offers access to real-time trading, real-time news, real-time communication, and research. But it is not enough to have lots of money and time in order to access these networks – you also need to be part of a particular organizational actor (e.g. an investment bank) that provides the legitimacy, besides the time and money, for you to use them.

The disconnection in relation to access to information technology is very much related to the disconnection in relation to what I have called the temporal cycles of official announcements. Even though these announcements are official, not everyone has access to them at the same time. Obviously, the absolutely best thing is to have access to these news and figures *before* they are released, but the second best thing is to have access to the kind of information technology that provides as good as real-time coverage of such events, i.e. to have access to the large private networks.

So, the so-called connected market is to a large extent dependent on private networks that provide these online, real-time services, and they charge a lot of money for access – the market is thereby global and exclusive at the same time (Knorr Cetina and Bruegger 2000, Comaroff and Comaroff 2000) and not everyone is invited to the party. Being part of these kinds of network is very important and in this sense Castells is on to something – the power of flows is truly strong – but information technology networks are not standing alone: they are, as have been demonstrated, better described as part of a kind of social virtuality.

Another very important factor contributing to the disconnection of 'the Market' from the world outside the financial arena is the use of figures and numbers in financial markets. Most traders, brokers and analysts interpret new releases of figures, news and rumours in terms of how it will affect their positions and the market, and not in terms of what it might mean for people outside the financial trading floor. The connection between figures on the screen and their translation for employment, savings, quality of life, etc. is lost on the way (cf. Norberg 2001). Part of the explanation is that many do not know the technical relation between the figures they trade on the screen and its working out in life outside the floor. Many of the traders and brokers I have worked with have a very poor understanding of the relations between instruments traded, underlying value and the figures on the computer screens (cf. Norberg 2001). Some of these brokers and traders have hardly any theoretical understanding of the instruments they broke or trade – they only trade on the actual figures on the screen, which seems to be enough in many cases. Also, some of the traders and brokers I have worked with have a very narrow interest in, and knowledge of, economic, political and financial news, and do not even pretend to be in the know, whereas others will always have something to say – usually in a very authoritative manner – when asked why certain things happened. These explanations may sound convincing but are usually only one explanation among many possible ones.

Another part of the explanation is that complex economic and political processes, interests and agendas are glossed by the presentation of the market in figures that either go up or down. Everything is translated into and measured in numbers – nation-states' monetary policies, the charisma of corporate leaders, the trader's own performance, etc. Complicated processes and chains of events are hence transformed into neat numbers.

The same process is evident in financial news reporting and research. In financial markets time is of the essence and the information available is massive. As a result, news, reports, research, etc. are presented at different levels of depth with the brief, general and abbreviated versions most accessible on the screen (short one-sentence news ticking away) or in the written texts (bold print, summaries, bullet points). The more in-depth versions are hidden behind the one-sentence news or further into the written material. Financial news and research are designed for speedy and easy access on behalf of the trader/investor/broker with very little time and so much money to spend (cf. Eriksen 2001).

As for the army of traders, brokers and analysts, they surely are a transnational crowd: they work abroad, they have colleagues from all over, they are entertained by counterparts flying in from Stockholm, New York, Frankfurt and they routinely travel themselves to other places. 'The Market' to a large extent consists of these people who are connected across the globe via information technology and personal visits. It is however a network of financial professionals that stretches *selectively* across the world – it stretches across the world of finance, of business and of money. True, they often live abroad, they often travel a lot, and they have the financial world at arm's length at their trading desks. But these global activities are, however, limited to certain areas and the 'home-away-from-home' (Hannerz 1996) for brokers, traders and analysts is a well-known place: they travel business class, from one business centre to another, from one fancy restaurant to another, from one business hotel to another, preferably by taxi and not by public transport. Apart from the ride in from the airport, they rarely see other parts of the city or country than the city centre with its nice hotels and bars.[9]

To conclude, by recognizing the physical, temporal and social settings of the global economy in general and financial markets in particular, in relation to various uses of information technology, we can contribute to a decoding and demystification of globalization processes. Global financial markets can thereby be understood as a transnational geography weaving in and out of digital and physical space and place, consisting of multiple linkages and networks simultaneously constituting and being constituted by electronic, material, temporal and social infrastructures, where time and space is both shared, placebound, compressed and dissolved.

Information technology organizes many aspects of the workings of financial markets, but so do the material, temporal and social settings that in many instances are directed at creating some kind of personalized physical proximity (real-time connections, shoulder-to-shoulder work places, entertaining etc.); 'the real-time, real-place Market' is thereby a far cry from the anonymous text-book example.

But as has been pointed out by many before, the use and knowledge of information technology results in both inclusion and exclusion (cf. Garsten 1994). Not anyone can access the information technology networks that connect traders and brokers across the world. Apart from the time and money you need to get hold of news, trading, research, communication, rumours, faster service, private networks, databases, Intranets etc., you also have to be a legitimate actor in this particular arena. 'The Market' is neither free nor accessible to everyone. But not even access in itself to these digital networks seems to be enough since many traders and brokers routinely interpret information from these in terms of where and whom it came from – information is placed in a personalized setting that guides, justifies and explains decisions and events.

The social virtuality of financial markets does connect transnational flows of money, people, ideas, information and knowledge, thereby contributing to the image of 'the Market' as globally interconnected. But if we decide to call this 'globalization' we should make sure to emphasize that we are dealing with a particular kind of selective and 'fragmented globality' (Trouillot 2001: 129) where not everyone can or is even invited to join in. So whereas information technology connects, it also disconnects, thereby being part of the fragmented process of globalization often referred to as 'the Market'.

Acknowledgement

I would like to thank the Bank of Sweden Tercentenary foundation for funding this project.

Notes

1. The text builds on research conducted on and off between 1997 and 1999 among financial brokers, traders and analysts working on different markets such as stock markets, interest rates markets, bond markets, etc. Fieldwork was conducted mainly in London and Stockholm, but also in New York. Conversations and semi-structured interviews were combined with observations on and off trading floors, together with the listening-in on phone conversations between clients and traders and brokers.

2. Low unemployment often causes concern in the financial markets. What seems as a paradox is explained in the following manner: low unemployment in the United States can be a sign of an overheated American economy, which might mean that the American Federal Reserve Board will raise the interest rate to counteract a possible inflation. Changes in interest-rate levels, whether up or down, usually result in some financial-market activity since traders and investors might want to alter their positions.

3. Talking in abstract symbols, such as in figures, is an important aspect of the increasing degree of abstraction and reductionism that characterizes financial markets as well as many other spheres of contemporary life (cf. Norberg 2001).

4. 'Entertaining' is a well-established activity in the business world. In the financial market context it refers to the different activities, besides trading, that traders and brokers do with their clients outside the work place, such as visits to strip clubs, going out for lunches, dinners, drinks, going to different sporting events, to the theatre, to the horse track and so on. And since banks, investment funds and other companies, that make use of financial markets, have clients and counterparts from all over the financial world, brokers, traders and analysts are routinely sent abroad, armed with the company credit card, to in person 'entertain' and 'be entertained'.

5. A central question Castells fails to address is why place is still very important in relation to the organization of financial markets despite access to information technology. He argues that access to information technology leads to the dominance of space over place but financial market transactions are still to a very large part centred in cities (organized in an hierarchical order with New York, London and Tokyo as important centres), and in particular areas of these cities such as Manhattan in New York and the City in London.

6. A proprietary trader trades 'his own account', i.e. the bank's money.

7. These message services function as large Intranets connecting banks, investors and brokerage houses.

8. Not all markets are open 24 hours a day.

9. I have only highlighted how some of the aspects of the social virtuality of financial markets contribute to images of 'the Market' as disconnected. There are many more, such as the particular language used when talking 'finance' which limits who can join in, paraphernalia such as the not very reader-friendly financial newspapers (e.g. the *Wall Street Journal*), the process of becoming an authorized actor of a trading floor, the entry passes and glass walls separating 'the Market' from the un-authorized, only to mention a few.

References

Bruegger, U. and Knorr Cetina, K. (2002), 'Global Microstructures: the Virtual Societies of Financial Markets'. *American Journal of Sociology*, 107(4): 905–50.

Calhoun, C. (1991), 'Indirect Relationships and Imagined Communities: Large-Scale Integration and the Transformation of Everyday Life', in P. Bourdieu and J. S. Coleman (eds), *Social Theory for a Changing Society*, Boulder, CO: Westview.

—— (1992), 'The Infrastucture of Modernity: Indirect Social Relationships, Information Technology, and Social Integration', in H. Haferkamp and N. J.

New Technologies at Work

Smelser (eds), *Social Change and Modernity*, Berkeley: University of California Press.

Carrier, J.G. (1998), 'Introduction', in J. G. Carrier and D. Miller (eds), *Virtualism: a New Political Economy*, Oxford: Berg.

Castells, M. (1996), *The Rise of the Network Society*, Oxford: Blackwell.

—— (1997), *The Power of Identity*, Oxford: Blackwell.

—— (1998), *End of Millennium*, Oxford: Blackwell.

Comaroff, J. and Comaroff J.L. (2000), 'Millennial Capitalism: First Thoughts on a Second Coming', in *Public Culture*, 12(2): 291–343.

Coronil, F. (2000), 'Towards a Critique of Globalcentrism: Speculations on Capitalism's Nature', in *Public Culture*, 12(2): 351–74.

Dilley, R. 1992. 'Contesting Markets: a General Introduction to Market Ideology, Imagery and Discourse' in R. Dilley (ed.), *Contesting Markets: Analyses of Ideology, Discourse and Practice*, Edinburgh: Edinburgh University Press.

Downey, G.L. and Dumit, J. (1997), 'Locating and Intervening: an Introduction', in G. L. Downey and J. Dumit (eds), *Cyborgs and Citadels: Anthropological Interventions in Emerging Sciences and Technologies*, Santa Fe, NM: School of American Research Press.

Eriksen, T.H. (2001), *Ögonblickets tyranni: Snabb och långsam tid i informationssamhället*, Nora: Nya Doxa.

Friedman, T.L. (1999), *The Lexus and the Olive Tree: Understanding Globalization*, New York: Farrar, Straus & Giroux.

Garsten, C. (1994), *Apple World: Core and Periphery in a Transnational Organizational Culture*, Stockholm Studies in Social Anthropology, 33, Stockholm: Almqvist & Wiksell.

Hannerz, U. (1996), *Transnational Connections*, London: Routledge.

Hasselström, A. (2000), '"Can't buy me love": Negotiating Ideas of Trust, Business and Friendship in Financial Markets', in H. Kalthoff, R. Rottenburg and H-J Wagener (eds), *Ökonomie und Geschellschaft, Jahrbuch 16 – Facts and Figures: Economic Representations and practices*, Marburg: Metropolis Verlag.

Jameson, F. (1998), *The Cultural Turn: Selected Writings on the Postmodern, 1983–1998*, London: Verso.

Knorr Cetina, K. and Bruegger, U. (2000), 'The Market as an Object of Attachment: Exploring Postsocial Relations in Financial Markets', *Canadian Journal of Sociology*, 25(2): 141–68.

Lash, S. and Urry, J. (1994), *Economies of Signs and Space*, London: SAGE.

Lave, J. and Wenger, E. (1991), *Situated Learning: Legitimate Peripheral Participation*, Cambridge: Cambridge University Press.

Lyon, D. (2001), *Surveillance Society: Monitoring Everyday Life*, Buckingham: Open University Press.

Martin, H.-P. and Schumann, H. (1996), *Globaliseringsfällan: Angreppet på demokrati och välfärd*, Stockholm/Stehag: Brutus Östlings Bokförlag Symposion.

Maurer, B. (2000), 'A Fish Story: Rethinking Globalization on Virgin Gorda, British Virgin Islands', *American Ethnologist*, 27(3): 670–701.

Miller, D. and Slater, D. (2000), *The Internet: an Ethnographic Approach*. Oxford: Berg.

Norberg, P. (2001), 'Finansmarknadens amoralitet och det kalvinska kyrko-rummet: en studie i ekonomisk mentalitet och etik', Doctoral Dissertation. Stockholm: EFI, Stockholm School of Economics.

Pauly, L.W. (1997), *Who Elected the Bankers? Surveillance and Control in the World Economy*, New York: Cornell University Press.

Sassen, S. (1999), 'Embedding the Global in the National: Implications for the Role of the State', in A.I. Samatar (ed.), *Globalization and Economic Space*, St. Paul: Macalester College.

—— (2000), 'Spatialities and Temporalities of the Global: Elements for a Theorization', *Public Culture*, 12(1): 215–32.

Strange, S. (1988), *States and Markets*, London: Pinter.

—— (1998), *Mad Money*, Manchester: Manchester University Press.

Thrift, N. (1998), 'Virtual Capitalism: The Globalization of Reflexive Business Knowledge', in J.G. Carrier and D. Miller (eds), *Virtualism: a New Political Economy*, Oxford: Berg.

Trouillot, M.-R. (2001), 'The Anthropology of the State in the Age of Globalization: Close Encounters of the Deceptive Kind', *Current Anthropology*, 42(1): 125–38).

Tsing, A. (2000), 'The Global Situation', *Cultural Anthropology*, 15(3): 327–60.

Whimster, S. and Budd, L. (1992), 'Introduction', in L. Budd and S. Whimster (eds), *Global Finance and Urban Living: A Study of Metropolitan Change*, London: Routledge.

Wulff, H. (1994), 'Moratorium på Manhattan: Unga svenskar och globalizering', in J. Fornäs, U. Boethius, M. Forsman, H. Ganetz and B. Reimer (eds), *Ungdomskultur i Sverige*, FUS-rapport nr 6, Stockholm: Brutus Östlings Bokförlag Symposion.

—— (1998), *Ballet across Borders: Career and Culture in the World of Dancers*, Oxford: Berg.

Young, P. and Theys, T. (1999), *The Capital Market Revolution: the Future of Markets in an Online World*, London: Financial Times, Prentice Hall.

–5–

Mobile Workplacing: Office Design, Space and Technology[1]

Heinrich Schwarz

The office, a certain idea what the office is, remains very valuable. Because it's a place where you meet people, and you just get together and work together and have interaction with people. (Office consultant Larry Alton)

The flexible office implies that people are moving around all the time. (Office consultant Connie Nord)

Introduction

'This is the club.'[2] The architect leads the group of visitors, young architecture students from a nearby university, into the office of the international architecture and consulting firm JFC.[3] The students find themselves in a big loft-like space; the large metal-framed windows suggest the floor of a former warehouse. A few feet past the entrance the group comes to a halt in a central open space, roughly 80 feet wide, in front of an area that could be a café with its round tables and comfortable soft blue chairs. All the tables are occupied by people with laptops sitting in front of them. As the visitors enter, a few heads are raised and workers glance briefly at the intruders before they turn their attention back to the screens in front of them or the mobile phones held against their ears. The sound of voices, keyboards and the distinct singsong of ringing phones, dialing modems, and alerting e-mail programs melt into a busy but not unpleasant sound carpet.

The tour guide, an energetic man in a suit in his sixties, explains to the visitors that these tables in the 'club' in front of them are not 'owned' by anyone but are meant to be used on a first-come first-serve basis, especially by those employees who have no office or desk of their own. The club, he emphasizes, is purely 'touch-down', it cannot be booked. This is also true, he continues, for some of the other shared areas in the office; for example, the two rows of wall-mounted bar-height workplaces next to the club. Along the windows are more traditional-looking desk arrangements equipped with computers, monitors and telephones. Most of these are occupied as well. The guide identifies them as the 'home-base' of design teams that are collocated in close proximity while working together on a project. Turning around, he points toward a small cluster of desks opposite the club in the middle of the open space and explains that these are the 'semi-permanent workplaces' for the support staff. Behind the group, left of the entrance – the students spin around following his arm pointing from place to place – there are four tiny cell-like rooms just big enough to hold a work surface and a chair for one person that the guide identifies as 'quiet booths'. In one, a woman is sitting behind the glass door busily typing away at her laptop; a man is talking on the phone in another. While the students try to map the verbal description onto what they see, the guide moves on following the main walking corridor deeper into the office.

In tours like this, the architecture firm JFC routinely presented their head-quarters to clients, media representatives, students, and other architects as a living example of their approach to new office and workplace design. In these tours visitors were introduced to both this firm's specific work and, more generally, to a changing understanding of office work. Yet, some visitors may have asked themselves whether the office really worked as claimed, whether the public spaces and the advocated mobility functioned as the design intended. They may have wondered what the rationale was for reorganizing offices in a way that eliminated personal workplaces. They may have speculated what it may mean to work in such an office on a daily basis and how such a design may affect individual work processes and the social fabric of the office.

Guided by similar questions, I take the mobile and non-territorial office of JFC as a fascinating example of how new technologies, spatial designs, and current visions of work converge to substantially reshape office environments and through them the experience of work. Drawing on fieldwork in the office, I examine what larger ideas inspired this office's design and how, as a result, the organizational and social reality of the office may be transformed. I will argue that JFC's office is informed by two competing visions of work that employ distinct design strategies in order to achieve particular forms of organization and sociality. The first design vision promotes a more social, interactive and collective organization of work. The second aims at increasing mobility and flexibility to build a more responsive, dynamic and mobile organization, yet in practice tends to generate also transience and anonymity. Based on my empirical research I suggest that in practice these two goals exist in tension in the office.

To illustrate the close relationship between spatial strategies and forms of sociality and to illuminate further the nature of the tension between the two competing organizational visions, I discuss the notions of *place* and *space* as concepts indicating both social and spatial orders. In the context of the office, *place* and *space* appear less, as some social theorists in recent debates have proposed, as progressive systems of order in history, but rather as simultaneously existing and conflicting ways of organizing work relations.

Technology is implicated in the design of both visions in ways different from space. While distinct spatial strategies underpin both the communicative office and the mobile office, technology has a less balanced role. Although technology is also often about connecting people, I argue that it is its alignment with mobility that threatens to strengthen the office's temporary and transient aspects, widen the gap between the two visions, and so further individualize work. Thus, the workplaces and workspaces in the office need to be conceptualized as techno-spatial hybrids facilitating different social formations, reformatted by electronic technologies.

These conflicting visions of the organization of work and the strategic role of technology in them, I propose, are not just a characteristic of this particular office or this firm's design approach. I believe the tension between the need for people to work together and the difficulty to connect in the context of moving and transient organizational forms is a pivotal one, running through contemporary strivings to organize and transform work more generally.

Alternative Officing: the Trend and the Study

The office design discussed in this chapter is part of a larger trend to reaccommodate offices to the changing needs and challenges of an allegedly more competitive, global and faster business reality. Gathering momentum in the 1990s, this trend has sometimes been referred to as the *alternative workplace* movement or *alternative officing*.[4] With AT&T, IBM, Ernst & Young, Anderson Worldwide, and the advertising agency Chiat-Day among the early pioneers, it has been predominantly but not exclusively large and medium-sized companies in fields such as computers and telecommunications, insurance, financial services and consulting, and advertising and media that have experimented with new workplace configurations, technological infrastructures and organizational forms.[5] This trend to reconceptualize offices is linked to and motivated by larger transformations affecting work, such as perceived shifts to a new information economy, flexible forms of production, and post-Fordist models of accumulation, the alleged rise of post-bureaucratic and virtual organizations, and the seeming spread of globalization. Although used for many different types of work, the redesign of work environments has been applied most frequently and successfully to service professionals and knowledge workers.[6]

Reorganizing work both within and outside of the office, alternative office concepts range from open plan to mobile or non-territorial solutions and from telecommuting to virtual offices. Alternative officing solutions are generally built on the belief that spatial and technological arrangements ought to be altered to improve work productivity. In some cases the shift is about removing barriers between people by tearing down office or cubicle walls. Other solutions center on putting wheels on desks and chairs to quickly reassemble work groups by pushing around furniture.[7] The more controversial and most publicized schemes, sometimes called *hoteling*, *hot-desking* or the *non-territorial office*, abolish individually assigned workplaces altogether and encourage the sharing or 'renting' of workspace when needed.

The following discussion draws on participant observation in the main office of JFC in London during seven weeks at the end of 1999. JFC is an international architecture and consulting firm with headquarters in England and other offices in Europe, North America, and Australia. It was founded in 1973 by two US-educated British architects. In 1999 the firm had more than 200 employees, about 120 of them in their main office. The firm had acquired a reputation for their research-based office design approach that emphasized open and non-territorial solutions. Since its redesign during 1997 and 1998, their own office, in addition to its regular function as innovative work environment, had also served them as a test bed for their ideas and as a showcase for clients. I observed the mechanics of the office and sought to understand the design and consulting work of the firm. I chose the company for their reputation in the field of innovative office design and for the opportunity to simultaneously investigate the designers' design practice and their own office use.

The Non-territorial Office

Perhaps not unlike that of some tour visitors, my first impression when I entered JFC's main office on the second floor of a refurbished Edwardian warehouse was quite positive: it seemed friendly and lively, open and light. The atmosphere was busy but not frantic. People were sitting, standing or walking, either working quietly by themselves, talking on the phone or engaged in conversation with others. The movement and degree of interaction generated a certain energizing dynamism, what office workers liked to call the 'buzz'. Portable pieces of technology seemed ubiquitous, especially in the central area. Connected to the nearest wall or floor jack, laptops occupied most of the desks and tables unless already equipped with a desktop computer, while identical-looking mobile phones either lay next to the computers or, almost as often, were in use.

Henry had been with the firm for more than ten years and was now a partner and head of its small research division. He was articulate about the firm's design philosophy and had been involved in the whole process of redesign. Walking with me through the office, he told me the current office design's origin story which I would hear in different versions at various occasions during my stay, including during the frequent public tours. JFC had a strong reputation for their user-centred design approach that combined workers' subjective preferences with observational data on their work practices and space use. Thus, a few years ago, when faced with the task to redesign their own office, Henry explained, the internal planning team began by researching their own work habits.

Looking at how and where people worked, the planners decided that the firm's employees could be divided into four categories defined by their daily working patterns or work styles, technology requirements and space use. The first two groups, about 40 per cent of the office staff, included those who were highly mobile and spent a good portion of their time away from their desks. This 'mobile office population' consisted, first, of the so-called 'nomads', mainly consultants and senior management who a majority of their time were outside of the office working with clients, visiting other offices or giving presentations. The other category of mobile workers was dubbed 'independents' and consisted of managers of multiple teams and researchers who worked mostly in the office but away from their desks. Since, according to their research, these two groups spent 60 per cent and more of their time away from their desks, personal and permanent work places seemed wasted on them. An internal study conducted after the redesign, a so-called 'post occupancy evaluation', quoted the original reasoning: 'It was felt that giving everyone a dedicated desk that would be empty for a large part of the time was not an effective use of space.'[8] Consequently, these two groups had to relinquish their desks and instead received mobile technologies, a laptop and a mobile phone, and one metre (i.e. three feet) of fixed filing space in a general-use cabinet near the entrance area.

Henry, as researcher, was determined an 'independent'. The idea was that he and other independents, nomads or outside visitors would work at one of the new 'shared' workplaces that were scattered around the new office layout and were not owned by anyone but to be used only temporarily. They could choose between different work or 'activity settings' depending on what kind of work they had to do: the enclosed 'quiet booths', for example, when they needed to be without disturbance, single open workplaces in quieter zones of the office for quick use, or the lively central club with its more dense population and café-like styling. Henry told me that he would usually arrive in the morning, take his laptop from his lockable filing space, get his mobile phone from the recharge rack, and pick a desk or table in the club that was still available. If he had to go to a meeting during the day, he was supposed to take his things with him or put them back into his locker, and most likely would need to find a new table afterward. If he needed to write he would choose a quiet booth instead. An internal discussion document at JFC explained the rationale behind the principle of multiple settings:

> The premise of the activity setting is that a single workspace – an all purpose workstation – is no longer sufficient. The aim is to design a variety of spaces to accommodate

the range of specialist activities undertaken within an organization. Staff are then at liberty to move between these, rather than doing all their work at a single workstation.[9]

The other two categories of office workers were determined to be less mobile. Since they worked on design projects with others and needed large computer screens and desk spaces, many architects and designers were seated together in team areas, called 'home bases'. The workspaces of these 'team residents' were still not considered permanent since the team was meant to occupy its home base only for the duration of a project. The support staff, the fourth category of 'work styles', were supposed to be easily locatable and thus were given what Henry called 'semi-permanent' workplaces typically arranged in small groups. Sheila, the secretary supporting Henry and other senior employees, for example, sat among four others near the central entrance area and in direct view of the club. Like the team architects and designers, the support staff had desk phones and desk computers; in difference to them, they commanded some extra filing space.

Enclosed or *open*, *owned* or *shared, bookable* or *touch-down* were the primary operative qualifiers for the new office design. A promotional brochure presented the conceptual plan of the new office with the different zones colour-coded according to the degree of ownership, enclosure and bookability. It visually represented the mix of open or enclosed, owned or shared work settings that characterized the office concept. The illustration graphically revealed how much the office redesign had pushed the environment toward the side of 'open' and 'shared', that is, a lack of enclosed private office space and the drastic reduction of permanent individually owned workplaces. An article on office design describes the difference between such a zoned non-territorial office and conventional designs:

> Taking the place of the one-person-to-an-office-or-desk stereotype, an assumption that has driven office design and planning for a century, is the idea of the office as a series of spaces designed to support a wide range of different tasks and activities. These task-based settings are only used on an as-needed basis.[10]

Not all significant qualities of JFC's headquarters were manifest in space. As we will see below, the technological aspects of the design were a prerequisite for the office to function as intended. Other aspects of the office design consisted of what the designers called 'space policies': behavioural rules telling employees how to use the new work environment, what to do and what to abstain from. A 'clear desk' rule, for example, required that all workplaces be cleaned up at the end of the work day in order to 'allow a more fluid use of non-proprietary space'. Another rule instructed not to occupy a work space when not needed. These policies strove to outlaw territorial behaviour.

In the following I want to show that what might seem to be a variety of different design aspects in fact converges into two distinct and fairly coherent design narratives. Seen from the intent of the designers but also from the reality of office use, one can distinguish two competing visions of work that informed JFC's office design and shaped the office and the way it worked.[11]

The Collaborative Community Vision

The first of the two visions of work to shape the office aimed at a more communication-intensive, social, or even communal organization where work was done together with others and tasks accomplished through collective efforts, where people knew each other, talked to each other, and learned from each other. The goals were to increase communication, collaboration and social interaction, deemphasize individualized work patterns, and stress collectivity and community.

The idea behind the open-plan, for example, was that communication was easier and collaboration better in an open environment without separating walls or closed doors. With about fifteen work spaces in close proximity the club was one such open area. Whoever worked in the club sat close to others, saw them come and go, noticed their visitors, and overheard pieces of conversations, willingly or involuntarily. The reasoning was that this gave useful background information about the work of others and offered opportunities to talk with co-workers who worked on different projects. This kind of partial involvement did not only occur in the club. In fact, the whole office contributed to a certain peripheral awareness of what was going on, since no workplace was solidly cut off from the others – except of course the cells and meeting rooms. The club's density, however, intensified the effect, as more people were merely an arm's length away and so more encounters and potential interactions might occur.[12] According to one of the firm's directors, the belief in density as desirable workplace strategy went back to research studies of stock brokers in New York City which the firm had conducted many years ago. While at one of the more successful companies the ratio was down to 3.8 square feet of workplace per person, she explained, other less successful firms had a much lower density. The difference was noticeable: at ten square feet per person there was 'no buzz, no energy, no sense of market conditions in that space'.

Henry drew the connection between communication and the firm's own work environment. He stated:

We probably do have a very clear vision as an organization of what we think an effective workplace is – Interviewer: tell me about that – I think it is exactly the same thing. We are living it in a way, it is about interaction, it is about communication, and it is about choice ... Therefore the club environment works for us, the quiet booths work, so that's what we think is a really good environment for any organization dealing in ideas and knowledge, – Interviewer: because? – because its about the only way you develop knowledge and talk about it and communicate and work in teams. So the environment should support those processes, compared to the traditional environment which segments the organization a lot more.

Connie was a consultant in a group at JFC called 'change management' that, rather than designing new workplaces, helped organizations with the transition to their newly designed environments. She gave an example from her own experience of one of the desired effects of an open environment on communication:

I think the [open environment] can create that [more communication] very well. I mean [our] space is quite a nice example, we cluster people in project areas because they are going on for quite some time. But recently we had some project areas broke up because the project was finished and suddenly the configuration had moved, and you, suddenly, you see somebody working on something new because it is open, and, I noticed, the project team had changed. It means I go up and ask what is going on … The open environment [does that] … It's got to make our communication quicker, make our knowledge transfer quicker, so that we deliver faster and better products – as a general rule.

And the discussion document quoted earlier summarizes the advantages of open plan as follows:

An open plan office is easier to scan in order to see whether colleagues are available for a formal or informal work communication, to discuss briefly an e-mail that has been sent, or arrange the time and place of a later meeting … Open plan working is intended to encourage spontaneous communication.

The office concept also reflected the high value put on informal forms of interaction. The office, said another study the practice was involved in, should be 'a more likely place for spontaneous, informal face-to-face contacts.'[13] For many years researchers of organizations have proposed that informal communication, as for example around the infamous water cooler, is essential for a healthy and productive organization in that it not only helps workers to get to know each other but also forms the basis for business-related information exchanges that may not occur otherwise. Following this insight, JFC's office was designed with a range of spaces and places in order to promote informal interaction. For example, the 'hub', a set of large round tables located near the central walkway and next to a kitchen-nook, was to be used for coffee-breaks as well as for spontaneous informal meetings (in difference to the club which was mainly a work area). There were of course also always short conversations going on around the espresso machine. Such 'functional spaces' offered 'an excuse for casual encounters', the internal discussion document suggested.[14] Since 'popular gathering places are those which have pleasant settings', as the document also claimed,[15] living-room-style seating arrangements at both sides of the club were meant to encourage office employees to sit down with visitors and colleagues. Wide walkways were to make it easy to stop and chat for a moment, or even to have conversations while walking. And in fact, employees acknowledged the positive effect that 'bumping into people' and subsequent 'informal chats' had for creating a 'friendly atmosphere' which, they said, was also good for business.

Project teams were an essential component for JFC, and team collaboration was supported by specific spatial arrangements. 'We assume that people work in teams', researcher Wendy confirmed. 'Part of the structure that is assumed by [JFC] is that the work is done by teams and that teams have to sit together.' The discussion paper explained why:

> It makes sense to promote spontaneous information sharing, while people are working at their desks. This is particularly beneficial for team working, when people need regular access to shared information.[16]

Therefore project teams worked in 'home-bases', relatively small collaborative areas with workplaces grouped together that were expected to support the constant exchange necessary during team work, to co-ordinate work, answer quick questions, have brief meetings and so on. According to the same document, these collaborative seating arrangements may have also provided 'an opportunity to create group identities'.[17] The name *home-base* suggests that the designers saw them as places to return to from client visits, meetings and other work spaces within the office, a home for the project and the team.

The objective to facilitate collaboration and boost communication also had fairly specific goals. As knowledge management had become an industry-wide concern, changes in work environments were looked at for improving the flow of information and the exchange of knowledge across functional areas. Larry, senior consultant in the firm's North American office, said:

> People recognize the workplace isn't about processing information, it is about creating ideas or sharing knowledge or creating something new.

JFC's planning philosophy considered knowledge exchange a growing challenge for businesses which their own office designs should address. Connie, the consultant, confirmed the focus on knowledge sharing. She stated:

> Increase in communication – I think of it as knowledge transfer, more than anything … Now that we can get hold of everybody all the time, and we realize that business is

becoming more competitive, it always is, becoming more competitive, and every company is trying to push forward, we realize the use, the value in sucking as much information from everybody as much as possible. We encourage information, so we cut down on the time it takes for me to find out who my main contact at [a client] is, and for a partner to share information with me about how to write a report, so I do it in half the time. It is more about knowledge sharing than actually producing work in teams.

Knowledge exchange was especially significant because JFC's own expertise was predicated on the productive exchange among each of its three functional areas: design, consulting and research.

In addition to the emphasis on communication, team work, and knowledge sharing, an equally important goal of the office environment was to generate a sense of community. Within the open environment some areas were more public than others. At the heart of the office, the entrance area with the club was the busiest and most lively work area and the most visible and public space. Like a town marketplace being the centre of activity, traffic and public happenings, the club served an important community function. Not just during extraordinary events, such as company meetings or event days, but also during regular working hours it served as the central nervous system of the office.

The notion of sharing was deeply embedded in the firm's approach to office design and the elimination of permanent workplaces. No longer owned by individuals, designers at JFC maintained, the new temporary workplaces were 'shared' and the office was based on the concept of collective ownership. Henry explained:

> For our organization we largely divorced the idea that [more communication, interaction and choice] need to be combined with individual ownership; we are a collective organization and space is owned collectively, and there are benefits attached to that.

Thus, the elimination of permanent individual desks was rendered as a shift from individual to collective space ownership. The label 'non-territorial' for these kinds of office concepts therefore denotes the end of *individual* territory. Although it may appear as a rhetorical trick, the language of sharing and collective ownership expressed a conviction that was central to JFC's design work. When I asked one of the senior planners of JFC whether he ever missed coming home to his own private office after all his travelling, his answer, perhaps in his voice as official representative, conveyed this sentiment as well. He did not miss anything, he said, since he felt he did come home to his private office, the whole office was his and was his home; hanging out in the shared areas of the office was more relaxing to him than staying in any enclosed room could be.

These notions of sharing and collectivity were not just embedded in the layout of the office: resources were organized communally as well. The reduction of individual filing space to a mere metre in a central location may have saved room, but a major rationale was to organize filing collectively rather than individually. The objective was to have most work material not owned by individuals and only accessible to them but organized in a common place where everybody could get to it, either physically in a shared filing area in the office or electronically on the electronic file servers that were part of the firm's network accessible via ubiquitous network drops.

The community notion was further promoted through the way space was allocated in a supposedly less hierarchical way. One of the tacit foundations of traditional office environments has been to assign space to employees on the basis of rank, position or status. Assigning work space according to need or task rather than status, JFC's office scheme broke with that 'estatism', as one consultant called that traditional view. Need-based space allocation sought to highlight equality between employees of varied titles and status and to de-emphasize rigid hierarchical structures that could hinder exchange and communication. The spatial 'flattening' was intended to create a less divided and more equal social structure.[18]

Reviewing these design characteristics, it becomes apparent that the goal of JFC's new office concept was a different kind of organization with a different social structure and distinct social forms – an organization with a different kind of sociality of work. The aspired sociality of the office was a more open, collaborative and social one, one less individualistic and isolating, a sociality based on a collective organization with a sense of community.

The Mobility and Flexibility Vision

Not all aspects of JFC's office worked toward this vision of a communicative and collective office. A number of design characteristics seemed to bolster a different kind of office and organization, one at odds with the previous vision. The goals were a more flexible organization able to quickly adjust to change. The office design also aimed at supporting mobile work patterns for a growing mobile work force.

The designers at JFC encouraged mobility through a number of measures. Mobile work was facilitated, for example, through the collective resource and filing system. As a strategy to minimize individual ownership, collective resourcing made mobility viable by reducing employees' dependence on personal files. The filing system in its physical instantiation promoted intra-office mobility while its electronic aspect also encouraged extra-office mobility.

But more centrally, one of the office's most outstanding features, its non-territoriality, was an attempt to make mobility work. The new design eliminated underused personal and permanent desks and office spaces and promoted instead the temporary use of a number of shared work spaces. Varying in the amount of space and degree of protection from disruption they provided, from the highly controllable cells to the less controllable club, these activity settings provided both employees in the office and those who returned from outside locations with a choice of work settings according to their varying needs. One of the specific needs of mobile workers was expressed in a quote by a senior executive from another European branch office:

> The nomadic worker has a real sense of belonging that must be nurtured and helped. It is important for these people to be able to go back to 'the Office' at any time and to know that there are specific spaces that they can use and informal areas where they can interact and meet with their colleagues.[19]

Although there was an interest in space saving, the design predominantly added to the ease of mobile working. Mobility and flexibility were also closely inter-twined as goals. As the consultant Connie reflected on the different meanings of the notion of the flexible office, she pointed to the way mobility, flexibility in location, and organizational adaptability could be closely interrelated:

> The flexible office is one where the work settings support the work practices. It is as simple as that. The flexible office implies that people are moving around all the time, in that kind of short term basis. The flexible word is about adapting to the company as it grows and flexes and ebbs and moves, and teams change all the time and projects come and go. That's the way it is flexible. – *Interviewer: So it is not about people moving?* – Not necessarily. It could be I move around a lot, I consider myself flexible. But it is not always what it means. People think a flexible office means we are not getting desks, we are all getting a laptop. Not necessarily, it may be flexible in a sense it is easily reconfigurable as your projects change, and they may change every year or every week, we don't know. And also flexible in terms of location. We're going to question the whole ethic of working in the office. It is not always appropriate, maybe you could work with your clients, in the car, on the plane, at home. That is flexible.

Although she rejected the perception that a flexible solution needs to imply a non-territorial or mobile design, this was the path JFC's designers chose for their own office. In an office context, flexibility could mean both organizational and individual flexibility. The design fostered individual flexibility in terms of where, when and how office employees worked. Given a choice of work spaces, easy access to collaboratively organized resources, and a ubiquitous technological infrastructure, workers faced fewer constraints on how they worked, from where and when than they would in an office with permanent office spaces. Assumed changes in the nature of work made this kind of flexibility appear desirable or even necessary.

The design also sought to enable a more flexible and responsive organization in terms of its size and adaptability. Change was considered 'the greatest challenge, aesthetic as well as programmatic, of contemporary architecture', and the firm was said to be more 'interested in the social phenomena of change than the chimera of a fixed and definitive style'.[20] Both of the design principles in their own office, open-plan and shared work spaces were thought to ease the effort to rearrange the layout, for example to make room for a number of new employees or to reseat people in order to accommodate a newly started project team. No walls, or even furniture in most cases, had to be moved. And since workplaces were not customized to the position or taste of individuals, fewer adjustments were necessary to move people around for new projects. This sort of change flexibility is one of the often-quoted rationales for a universal plan. JFC's office had in fact proven highly adaptable in that it had been able to absorb a large contingent of unexpected users. Originally designed for 75 people, it housed nearly 130 by the time I conducted my research. And although the overcrowding showed its unwanted side effects, the fact that the same space could take so many extra workers without major rearrangements was proof of its adaptability in the eyes of the firm. The *Post Occupancy Evaluation* study mentioned earlier commented not without pride:

> It is, though, one of the impressive qualities of the new office that it has succeeded in accommodating such an unanticipated increase in staff without seriously reducing productivity and quality of work.[21]

The architects strove for an organization of porous boundaries. The will to let in outsiders and visitors reflected the needs of an aspiring multi-national organization. What made the office attractive to nomads and independents was similarly inviting to outside visitors, whether they were from other branch offices of the firm, from clients or from the new parent company that had acquired JFC not too long before. The design not only provided space for travelers and visitors, it also made it easy for them to blend in with the full-time employees of the London office. For a spreading company like JFC, such permeability was predominantly positive as it was desirable to break down the borders between different offices and to open up relationships with clients.

Related to the office's mobility and flexibility, a certain dynamism was designed into the office as well. Due to its density and the constant movement and sound of people, the club especially was supposed to exhibit a kind of stimulating atmosphere. Like an engine meant to drive the organization, the 'buzz' of the club was supposed to energize the workers in the office. Talking about office workers, a senior partner put it this way:

They need to feel they are in this super exciting, demanding, pressured environment because that is when they do their best work.

In addition, a dynamic work environment was also a welcome image to be projected to outsiders. The same partner remembered his first contact with the company long before the latest redesign:

I knew when I waited in the reception that it was really an interesting organization, I just knew, because the level of activity, the running in and out of the organization, people coming in and out, I could tell instantly that it was a fun interesting organization, and I think, people instantly get those feelings when they go into an organization.

Like the previous design vision of a more communicative and social organization, this vision was about a different kind of organization and sociality of work: in this case a more mobile, flexible, transparent and dynamic one. But what was the rationale behind all this? In part, JFC's design approach resulted from specific organizational requirements, such as the work styles and space needs a particular organization had. Yet, in addition, their approach was predicated on a set of assumptions about larger changes in work and the economy. More flexible, mobile, adaptable and fluid organizations, for example, have been the aspiration of the business world for some time now.[22] The cluster of adjectives has pervaded the language of business people and popular media alike, expressing what is deemed necessary to survive in a world of global competition, accelerated change and evolving new business structures. JFC's flexible, mobile, diverse, permeable and dynamic office was an effort to create a similar type of organization, or more precisely, create an environment where such an organization could thrive. The same was true for the vision of a more collaborative and communal organization. More teamwork, knowledge exchange and interactive behaviour ought to respond to roughly the same set of challenges.

Tensions in the Office

Overall, the design was considered a success by the designers and planners at JFC. The open and shared work places seemed to increase communication and interaction among office users, access to senior executives had become somewhat easier, the choice among work settings provided stimulation and change to mobile employees, visitors found places to work, space was more flexible, and the majority of employees seemed to enjoy the dynamism and buzz of the office and, in particular, the central club area. Accordingly, in their *Post occupancy evaluation* study conducted to evaluate the results of the implementation of the new environment, JFC reports that:

Team working has increased, communication within the office has improved and project groups are able to form, evolve and disband much more easily as the projects in the office change.[23]

The nomadic and office-less existence had its advocates as well. A consultant explained that she would 'hate to have my own office'. Other mobile employees favored the constant change the non-territorial concept entailed. Evidently not appreciating regularity and routine, Joanne, a senior designer and project manager without a desk, asserted that she would not want to sit next to the same person every day.

However, despite this seeming success I suggest that in practice the mobile and flexible office aspirations had consequences that not only went beyond their intended goals but also revealed an underlying tension between the two main design schemes. As the work environment pushed mobility and flexible structures, potentially problematic results reshaped the social organization of the office and its culture as well. The ongoing movement of people and the temporary nature of structures introduced a certain transience and instability to the social fabric. Demanded by the pursuit of flexibility, the choice among a number of workplaces potentially weakened ties between people and to specific locations. As a consequence, the actual work dynamic, rather than supporting more collaboration and community threatened to individualize work.

One of the club's rationales, to strengthen social ties by exposing workers to colleagues sitting at neighboring tables, for instance, was potentially offset by the shortlivedness of such constellations. The design also helped little to integrate new employees. Newcomers did not attract much attention in an office with open borders and constant flux, and the environment made it difficult for new hires to orient themselves, to learn who is who, and to get to know people. As a result, an employee complained that it was often 'hard to get hold of people.'[24] And the internal evaluation study concedes that even 'support staff found it difficult to locate people as they could be sitting anywhere in the building'. Transience was a direct result of the principle of non-dedicated work spaces, but its effects might have been less pronounced, were it not for an office culture that, in adapting to the conditions of mobility and temporality, had developed an attitude of tolerance that paid little attention to strangers.

Efforts to design an office environment that would enable and promote an organization more mobile and flexible in its work practices, office arrangements, and locations threatened to result in short-term interactions and a transient office culture. Some of these goals were intended. Fast and brief exchanges and increased discretion about how to work on the side of individual workers was part of the new organizational model. Yet, the resulting transience of work relations was not a stated goal of the office architects but a partly implicit, partly unrecognized, and partly unwanted side-effect of their carefully designed flexible work environment. The outcome was in tension with the other major design vision behind the office. Constant movement and relocation and permeable office boundaries all weakened, if not undermined, the original intent of an open club environment.

Technology, Flexibility and Mobility

So far the description of JFC's office and the tension between the two organizational visions has more or less focused on the role of space. Yet, technology was a crucial element in the office planners' approach, part of the firm's self-understanding, and a central research effort: the firm had produced, for example, a number of published studies on the interaction between people, places and technology.[25]

Technology played a central part in their own office, both visible as computing and communication devices and invisible as part of an advanced infrastructure. In addition to the more traditional array of desktop computers and desktop phones, the office featured a system of technologies of mobility consisting of laptops and mobile phones; an intricate infrastructure of power plugs, phone and network drops protruding from walls above desk surfaces and hidden in the floor-carpet near tables; wireless transmitter stations in strategic locations on the ceiling serving the office internal mobile phone system; a set of public workstations; and a small computer-support staff responsible for maintaining the system. Pretty much all of the various workplaces and workstation, formal or informal, were equipped with power, Intranet access and occasionally analog phone lines for modem access for visitors.[26]

At first sight technology's role appeared fairly even-handed: on the one hand technologies supported communication and the sharing of resources, on the other they were a necessary part of the mobile and flexible organizational design. Yet in practice, the more effectively technology served as agent for a mobile organization, the more it could foster individualized ways of working in the office.

Although technology facilitated and encouraged communication and the exchange of information in the office through phones and e-mail and the external file server, the electronic aspect of a system of resource sharing, the goal to make the office a more communicative and collaborative environment drew to a large degree on physical attributes and the layout of the office, as I showed earlier. As it were, the forging of social ties and of a communal spirit relied more strongly on the organization of physical space than on technology.[27]

Yet technology was particularly central to mobile employees. Without the system of mobile technologies the vision of the mobile and flexible office would not have worked. Providing continuous means for work and communication despite all the movement, the wired (and wireless) office was a prerequisite for the principle of non-permanent workplaces. The nomads' ability, for instance, to move from workspace to workspace, from the club to a cell to a team space, relied on a system consisting of technological infrastructure and portable devices. Asked what the role of technology was for changes in office design, Henry explained:

> Absolutely fundamental ... First of all it was mobile technology that allowed the breakup of space within buildings, the fact that you could through structured cabling reconfigure your infrastructure very easily, plug in your computer at any port, that has been fundamental, because it means that you are not limited by the layout you have. And then mobile telephony, meaning that you have free address, it breaks up, it gives you the freedom to move.

The decision to give a good part of employees mobile technologies in exchange for assigned desks (or cubicles or offices) was, after all, based on the assumption that these technologies would enable their users to get their work done independently from their location – offering 'freedom to move'. It assumed that they could always communicate via phone or e-mail and would be able to design or write on their laptops as productively as if they were staying in one and the same place.[28]

Mobile technologies were not just a necessary requirement for the mobile and flexible office, they could be seen as a means to mitigate the potentially problematic effects of a mobile design and to keep the office from becoming too transient and temporary. Furnishing a kind of permanent workplace independent from physical locations, they made non-territorial solutions appear tolerable. Taking away from mobile office workers their personal and permanent desks appeared less extreme if one believed that the real workplace for mobile office workers was generated by their laptops and mobile phones and thus was carried along wherever they went. Constantly changing locations appeared less unstable if the mobile employees were seen to take their workplace with them in the form of their devices. Since interactions were assumed to take place in the communication spaces generated by e-mail or mobile phones, neighborly conversations mattered less when seemingly replaceable by electronic proximity. And, in fact, office internal phone calls to other employees were frequent, if not always successful, as calling them appeared to be the quickest way to find any of the mobile or nomadic employees, despite the limited size of the office.

Embedded in JFC's design concept was the premise that technologically generated workplaces and mediated communication and collaboration spaces could provide some of the continuity, permanency, customization, and personal ownership that the now temporary physical workplaces could no longer supply.

As a result, what was permanent for the nomads at JFC were their mobile technologies and the electronically mediated work spaces these made possible. And while they no longer owned any physical space, they now did own technology. Personal equipment carried around in shoulder bags or spread out on desks was a ubiquitous marker of the nomads and independents, the designated mobile workers. The phones even displayed the initials of their owners. As space had become collectively owned and shared, technology was owned individually, even more than before.[29] [30] By stressing individual ownership, mobile technologies, although in charge of mitigating the transience and autonomy of a mobile office, at the same time weakened collective ways and reintroduced individual ones.

The return to more individualized work patterns could also be observed in electronic filing. As discussed earlier, the strategy of collective filing was meant to reduce individual filing. Yet, in practice the idea could backfire. Garry, an architect who had joined the firm about a year ago, told me that in his experience, resources such as documents, exchanges and other important project information often wound up further dispersed over individuals and out of reach for others. According to him, the main reason was that project communication increasingly took place electronically and ended up sitting in e-mail and document folders on individual computers. While the discouragement of paper use was thus relatively successful, the effort to store electronic information collectively lagged behind. The requirements of high mobility made reliance on their own portable device more attractive to mobile workers than the use of the file server, which after all needed to be accessed in order to give away its information.[31] Although not hiding in individual desks any longer, vital project files could now reside on individual laptops, even harder to access by colleagues. Thus, despite intentions to the contrary, resources could end up even more individualized.

To summarize: even if we accept that the mobile-office vision attained some stability and gained some permanency via personal technologies and the electronic work spaces that these offered, the tension between the two design visions remained. In the end, technology in the office mainly emphasized and strengthened the mobile and flexible aspirations of the office concept. Aligned with the individual (employed as individual tool and resource), technology had the potential to weaken lasting social relations. Instead of furthering a more communicative, collaborative, and communal feel with a more intense and enduring social texture, the office was pulled in a different direction: towards a social order made of potentially anonymous individuals who moved around busily and conducted transactions in short-term encounters in a transient environment without rigid boundaries, permanent configurations, and stable social relations.

Technology, Place and Space

Linking forms of sociality with particular spatial orders, the two visions of work – the social, communicative organization and the mobile, flexible organization – evoke the concepts of *place* and *space* that have become central in social theory discussions on modernity and historical change, as they identify near paradigms for the organization of social life through periods of history. In these accounts the concept of *place* is seen as the governing principle of societies where social structures are anchored in fixed locales with firm boundaries. A society based on *place* is a local society where places function as common contexts and provide a sense of belonging to groups of individuals. In contrast, the order of modernity is founded on a notion of *space* that is dissociated from specific locations, is universal or global, and de-situates social life.[32]

Borrowing this distinction, the two organizational design visions can be described in a language where the first vision of an interactive and communal office rests on a principle of *place* and employs places of residency and situated interaction, while the design efforts towards a mobile and flexible office draw on the principle of *space* utilizing spaces of movement and temporary use, such as the single-person cells and the principle of non-territoriality. However, rather than following a historical progression from *place* to *space*, from the local and situated to the disembedded, or from the social to the individual, as theorists have often conceptualized the relation between the two principles, in the office both spaces and places co-existed. For it was the designers' intent to mix the two competing visions and to thereby combine and perhaps reconcile two different social and organizational forms; community and dynamism, collectivity and mobility, communication and autonomy.

Although a description in terms of a mix of place and space reveals the underlying socio-spatial principles of the office, it is not sufficient to understand the social dynamics of the office environment at JFC. Technology is key to understanding why the mixing of the two design visions was not as successful in blending forms of sociality as it was in combining types of spatiality. In fact, for some theorists, technology plays an explicit role in their spatial theorizing. Manuel Castells' perception of the shift from what he calls a *space of places* to a *space of flows*, for instance, is based on technology.[33] His notion of flows and their technological underpinning sheds some light on the functioning of the office, since the design vision of a mobile and flexible organization in many ways was a vision of flows, linking information flows to flows of human bodies. Yet, Castells' depiction of the role of technology on spatial and social relations, like that of other theorists of modernity, mainly focuses on its delocalising effect and pays not enough attention to the more complex intermixing that I found in the mobile non-territorial office.[34] Somewhat closer to the office reality but in a similar vein, architect and technology forecaster William Mitchell sees technology responsible mainly for dissolving spatial relationships in the workplace. Induced by technology, he observes processes of fragmentation and recombination into new patterns, resulting in the 'recombinant workplace' that eradicates *place.*[35]

Yet with its intricate combination and deliberate integration of electronic and physical work spaces, the office environment is becoming not just a fragmented and recombinant, but also a hybrid space.[36] Such hybridity in the office does not have to mean big wall-mounted video screens and augmented reality conference rooms. It can refer to the way physical spaces and places are technologically mediated, technologically motivated, and technologically meaningful; that is, they make sense predominantly in the presence of information and communication technologies. Let us be reminded that electronic spaces served a crucial function for JFC's office, not just for helping people communicate but also as indispensable part of mobile ways of working and the flexible and temporary use of physical spaces by mobile employees. In the office technologically mediated work spaces, ranging from individual computers to communication spaces and electronic resources, were closely linked to physical architectures of mobility. In that sense the office is an instructive example how technological infrastructures and electronic spaces are not just 'superimposed' on physical landscapes, but are closely and logically interlinked. The physical and the electronic were not separate and did not replace each other, but were deeply interrelated and formed and informed each other in fundamental and multiple ways. Thus, to use a slightly problematic terminology, the virtual was thoroughly plowed into the soil of the real.

However, it is important to recognize that technology is not universally synonymous with the principles of *space* or *flows*, nor fragmentation, nor with the individualization of work. Recent work in technology studies on the use of on-line communities has vividly demonstrated that digital technologies can create on-line spaces that display all characteristics of places and help form social organizations and communities.[37] To understand 'localized affiliation enabled by new media networks', anthropologist Mizuko Ito, for example, suggests the term 'network localities' to describe technologically mediated social places that foster communities, such as on-line multi-user environments or even networks of mass-mediated consumers.[38]

Technology, like space, can emphasize different organizational and social forms: it can stress individualized structures or social ones, can push *space* or *place* – or both. Crucially, the outcome depends on the details of the spatial, technological and social interventions. In the case of JFC's office, technologies were involved in both of the design strategies; they fostered local interactions as well as flexibility and mobile flows. Yet, due to the specifics of the design and use of technologies in the office, the results tended to weaken the more collaborative and team-based social forms and strengthen the flows of people and individual-ized forms. In JFC's office design, technology privileged transience and anonymity, re-established individual resource handling, and reintroduced indi-vidual ownership. Yet, it could have been otherwise.

Conclusion

Interwoven in this chapter were two interconnected lines of inquiry: a close analysis of a particular office design that included a reflection on the dialectic tension between individualized and social ways of working, and an exploration of the pivotal role of technology and spatial principles for forms of social organ-ization at work.

The central topic was the description and analysis of the self-experiment of innovative office designers who developed for themselves what they considered a showcase state-of-the-art office. I presented this experiment as an informative case of organizational engineering, where spatial and technological design strate-gies together with certain behavioural rules were meant to enable, encourage, or even enforce specific work styles, social structures and organizational character-istics. I argued that there were not one but two distinct organizational visions embedded in the design. Built around principles of proximity, open space and informal encounters, one vision aimed at increasing communication, teamwork, collective ways of organizing work, and a communal and social climate. The other design vision deployed principles of non-territoriality and multiple work settings together with an elaborate system of mobile technologies to achieve flex-ible work patterns, mobile ways of working and a more fluid, dynamic and responsive organization. I argued that in practice these two visions could be in conflict, where the mobile and flexible design efforts worked against some of the goals of a more communicative and collaborative organization.

I demonstrated how technologies were central in this process, particularly in shifting the balance between the two visions. Although part of both organiza-tional goals, helping to create places for communication as well as spaces for individual work, it appeared to weaken a more stable social texture and collec-tive philosophy, because its particular design and use was centrally linked to mobile and flexible ways. The mobile technologies in the office pushed mobile social forms and further reinforced individualized patterns of work. This was a story of contradictory organizational visions guiding office design that generated heterogeneous social realities, which differed in interesting ways from the designers' original intentions.

A related line of inquiry explored the close relation between space, tech-nology, and social forms. Borrowing the theoretical distinction of the notions of place and space shed some light on the interrelation between conflicting spatial, social, and technological orders at work in the office. But this worked only so far. With its co-existing spatial principles, physical and electronic spaces, and competing social forms the office was neither based solely on *place* nor on *space*. Rather it demonstrated that flows and social places do intersect and that hybrid physical and electronic environments have specific social consequences that depend highly on the particularities of technology design and use.

The inherent conflict in the office model between wanting people to work together more closely and the growing difficulty to connect brought about by constant movement and temporariness, identifies a pivotal contradiction in today's approach to office work that goes beyond this particular case. The tension between more individualizing and, if one can use this term, more socializing tendencies seems to be at the core of current transformations of office work. Yet, whether the organization of work is becoming more social or further individualized depends in part on the informed design and use of technology. Looking at the office at JFC it appears that both tendencies occur simultaneously, work getting more intensely individual and more intensely social at the same time.

Despite its contradictions, I see the particular office design I studied as a highly productive attempt to reinvent what it means to work in an organization in the shifting economic landscapes and cultural worlds of today. In their experimentation with new office environments the planners, designers and consultants at JFC helped to articulate the range of design elements, such as communication, knowledge exchange, collectivity, autonomy, transparency, space, place, technology, flexibility, mobility, ownership, choice, and change that work places and spaces of the future – and their users – will have to negotiate.

Notes

1. The following text is adopted from chapter three of my Ph.D. dissertation, 'Techno-Territories: the Technological, Spatial and Social Reorganization of Office Work' (Schwarz 2002).

2. The following narrative is not a true depiction of one single event, rather it is what could be called factional fiction, a composition assembled and condensed from different tours I watched. Office features, their presentation, and the character of the event, however, are faithful to how I saw the tours taking place.

3. This and other names are altered to protect the anonymity of people and organizations.

4. The terminology of 'alternative' workplaces and offices started to be more widely used in the mid 1990s and came probably to its peak around 1998/99; see as examples (Apgar 1998) and (Becker 1999). The phrase 'officing' became fashionable around the same time. Journalist Kerry

Jacobs observed in 1994 that the development towards mobile and virtual offices was no longer about 'offices' but about 'officing'. Perceiving a trend from stability to mobility both in practice and in language she characterized it as 'nouns become verbs' (Jacobs 1994).

5. For an overview of alternative workplace solutions including a number of case studies see Apgar (1998), Becker (1999), Davenport (1998), Illingworth (1994), Lieber (1996), Sims et al. (1996).

6. The terms 'knowledge worker' and 'knowledge industries' were coined by Peter Drucker and economist Fritz Machlup in the late 1950s (Drucker 1959).

7. An example of a flexible and mobile design where the furniture has 'big obvious wheels' is KPMG Peat Marvick's Silicon Valley plant; see Davy (1999).

8. The study was conducted within a year of the redesign to evaluate the new office ([JFC] 1998: 1).

9. The document was a discussion document intended to 'assist our clients in their thinking about the new office design.' ([JFC] 1999) This and other references are anonymized to protect the identity of the organization.

10. Laing (1998)

11. Although I will present examples and quotes from the designers to underpin my claims, I want to be clear that the specific formulation of these two organizational visions – including calling them that – is my analysis and not the firm's. The firm's designers may not perceive them as two separate strategies and may not entirely share my assessment of a tension between them.

12. See Kraut et al. (2002) on the effects of proximity on the likelihood of communication among co-workers.

13. [STUDY–2] (1985: 40) The study was the second in a series that investigated the relation between people, technology and work environments.

14. [JFC] (1999: 10)

15. Ibid.: 10

16. Ibid.: 9

17. Ibid.: 3

18. Similarly, Garsten notes the same idea of manifesting the ideal of a flat organization spatially in her study of Apple Computer (1994).

19. [Bente Group] (1998: 4)

20. [JFC] (1998: 11)

21. [JFC] (1998: 4)

22. See anthropologist Emily Martin for a discussion on the spread and significance of the concept of flexibility in contemporary culture, including its own flexibility (1994).

23. [JFC] (1998)

24. There were mobile phones to reach mobile employees in the office, but this was apparently not as reliable a method to get in touch with people as one would assume. The use of technology in the office will be discussed later.

25. In a presentation given to a mostly academic audience, a senior partner presented his view on the dual role of information technology. On the one hand it had substantially transformed work processes in the recent past requiring firms to react to these changes, he explained, but technology also offered new opportunities for design in that it could support new ways of working and enable more group, creative, distributed, and nomadic work. The presentation took place at MIT, Cambridge, USA, in March 1999.

26. Not all of the jacks and plugs were always functioning, however. Some employees complained that their mobility was impeded by the failure of parts of the infrastructure. It marked the insider to know which of the network plugs were not working properly and selecting their seating accordingly.

27. This is only true for office internal interactions. For communicating with clients or for nomads away from the office, communication technologies were of course crucial.

28. In other office concepts the mobile phones are sometimes replaced by a 'smart' desktop phone system that 'knows' who is using the desk at what time and routes incoming calls to the right phone and person. Such systems require log-in by users and therefore work best when employees switch desks not more than about once a day. Anderson Consulting, now Accenture, had installed such a system in their Boston/Wellesley office.

29. Although desktop computers and desktop phones in regular offices are also somehow owned by their users, they are usually not constantly with them, nor do they, for that matter, have officially provided name tags.

30. For a discussion of how technology came to replace space also as status symbol and marker of hierarchy in the office, see chapter four of my dissertation (Schwarz 2002).

31. Other reasons for the imperfect use of electronic filing may be found in design. To make people use an electronic file server diligently the interface needs to be transparent, visually appealing, and easy to use, and rules and conventions of organizing information collectively have to be established that can balance the need for standards on the one hand and flexibility on the other. Otherwise, electronic file servers quickly turn into a place nobody wants to visit or use.

32. See, for example, Castells (1996), Giddens (1990; 1991), or Harvey (1989).

33. See Castells (1996) and verbal comment during a presentation at MIT, Cambridge, MA, USA, March 5, 2002.

34. And perhaps not just in the office: a number of social geographers and

anthropologists insist that such concurrence of space and place should be seen as the defining characteristic of late modern societies more generally. Doreen Massey's rejection of the traditional definition of place in difference to space, or of the local in difference to the global, is a good example. Places are not defined by boundaries, she suggests, but through the interrelation with other places and their relation to the outside. 'The view of place advocated here […] stresses the construction of specificity through interrelations rather than through the imposition of boundaries and the counter position of one identity against an other.' (1994: 7) Places, therefore should not be 'counterposed to spaces as flows.' Translated into the language I have used here, it is the relation among the various places in the office that give them their quality, not their difference to the movement of people and flow of information or the spaces of flexibility. See also Pred and Watts (1992).

35. Mitchell describes the recombinant workplace as follows: 'In offices, electronic interconnection dissolves the traditionally tight spatial relationships among private workspaces such as office cubicles, group workspaces such as meeting rooms, informal social spaces, and resources such as files and copying machines. When files are online, and office workers have personal computers and printers, there is no longer much need to cluster private workspaces around central resources; these spaces can migrate to the home or to satellite locations, they can follow employees on the road, or they can transform into 'hot cubicles' that are not permanently allocated to particular employees but are reserved and occupied as needed.' (Mitchell 1999: 107f)

36. Verbal comment by William Mitchell during a presentation at MIT, Cambridge, MA, USA, March 5, 2002.

37. Jones (1995), Mynatt et al. (1998), Smith & Kollock (1998), Turkle (1995).

38. Ito (1999).

References

Anderson, Katherine (1995), 'Alternative Officing: Revolution or Merely Redesign'? *Journal of Property Management*, (January/February): 32–5.

Apgar, Mahlon (1998), 'The Alternative Workplace: Changing Where and How People Work'. *Harvard Business Review*, May-June: 121–136.

Becker, Franklin (1999), 'Beyond Alternative Officing: Infrastructure On-demand', *Journal of Corporate Real Estate*, 1(2): 154–68.

[Bente Group] (1998), *Annual Review 98*, Internal document.

Castells, Manuel (1996), *The Information Age: Economy, Society and Culture. Volume 1: The Rise of the Network Society*, Cambridge, MA: Blackwell.

Davenport, H. Thomas & Pearlson, Keri (1998) 'Two Cheers for the Virtual Office', *Sloan Management Review*, Summer: 51–65.

Davy, Jo Ann (1999), 'The Office of the Future: Technology and Workspace are Limited only by your Imagination', *Office Systems*, (June): 23–6.

Drucker, Peter (1959), *Landmarks of Tomorrow*, New York: Harper.

Garsten, Christina (1994), *Apple World: Core and Periphery in a Transnational Organizational Culture*, Stockholm Studies in Social Anthropology, 33, Stockholm: Almqvist & Wiksell International.

Giddens, Anthony (1990), *The Consequences of Modernity*, Cambridge: Polity.

Giddens, Anthony (1991), *Modernity and Self-Identity: Self and Society in the Late Modern Age*, Stanford, Stanford University Press.

Harvey, David (1989), *The Condition of Postmodernity*, Oxford: Blackwell.

Illingworth, Montieth (1994), 'Virtual Managers', *Information Week*, June 13: 42–58.

Ito, Mizuko (1999), 'Network Localities', unpublished manuscript.

Jacobs, Karrie (1994), 'Waiting for the Millennium: Part 1: The Box along the Information Highway, there is No Difference between Metaphor and Reality', *Metropolis*, (May): 76–79, 109–115.

Jones, Steven (1995), *Cybersociety. Computer-mediated Communication and Community,* Thousand Oaks: Sage.

[JFC] (1998*), [JFC]: Post Occupancy Evaluation* (Internal document).

[JFC] (1999), *Open Plan: Issues & Considerations: An Overview of History, Trends, and Issues* (Internal document).

Kraut, Robert, Fussell, Susan, Brennan, Susan and Siegel, Jane (2002), 'Understanding Effects of Proximity on Collaboration: Implications for Technologies to Support Remote Collaborative Work', in P. Hinds and S. Kiesler (eds), *Distributed Work*, Cambridge, MA: MIT Press.

Laing, Andrew (1998), *New Environments for Working: the Re-design of Offices and Environmental Systems for New Ways of Working*, London: Construction Research Communications Ltd.

Lieber, Ronald (1996), 'Cool Offices', *Fortune*, December 9.

Martin, Emily (1994), *Flexible Bodies: Tracking Immunity in American Culture,* Boston: Beacon Press.

Massey, Doreen (1994), 'A Global Sense of Place', in D. Massey, *Space, Place, and Gender,* Minneapolis: University of Minnesota Press.

Mitchell, William (1999), *E-topia: Urban Life, Jim – but Not as We Know It*, Cambridge, MA: MIT Press.

Mynatt, Elizabeth, O'Day, V., Adler, A. and Ho, A. (1998), 'Network Communities: Something Old, Something New, Something Borrowed', *Computer Supported Cooperative Work*, 6: 1–35.

Pred, Allan and Watts, Michael (1992), *Reworking Modernity Capitalism and Symbolic Discontent*, New Brunswick, NJ: Rutgers University Press.

Russell, James (1998), 'Alternative Workplace: the Way We Work,' *Architectural*

Record (June): 137–142.

Schwarz, Heinrich (2002). *Techno-Territories: The Technological, Spatial and Social Reorganization of Office Work*. Ph.D. Dissertation, Massachusetts Institute of Technology, Cambridge, MA, USA.

Sims, William, Joroff, Michael and Becker, Franklin (1996), *Managing the Reinvented Workplace: IDRC's Corporate Real Estate Project*, Atlanta, GA: International Development Research Council.

Smith, Marc and Kollock, Peter (1998), *Communities in Cyberspace*, New York: Routledge.

[STUDY–2] (1985), *Executive Overview*, Internal document.

Turkle, Sherry (1995), *Life on the Screen: Identity in the Age of the Internet*, New York: Simon & Schuster.

–6–

Claiming the Future: Speed, Business Rhetoric and Computer Practice

Robert Willim

Introduction

In the last years of the twentieth century, it was said that we in the Western world had entered a new economic era, the new economy. It was a time when new economic laws were to prevail, particularly arising from the potential that could be offered by network-linked electronics.

Work in trade and industry, according to many influential voices, would be different in the new economy. One of these voices was that of Kevin Kelly, a key person in the rhetoric about the new economic reality. In the book *New Rules for the New Economy: Ten Radical Strategies for a Connected World* (1999) he summed up some of the guidelines for a future economy based on electronic networks, a network economy (cf. Evans and Wurster 1999: 13).

> This new economy represents a tectonic upheaval in our commonwealth, a far more turbulent reordering than mere digital hardware has produced. The new economic order has its own distinct opportunities and pitfalls. If past economic transformations are any guide, those who play by the new rules will prosper, while those who ignore them will not. We have seen only the beginnings of the anxiety, loss, excitement, and gains that many people will experience as our world shifts to a new highly technical planetary economy.
>
> This new economy has three distinguishing characteristics: It is global. It favours intangible things – ideas, information, and relationships. And it is intensely interlinked. These three attributes produce a new type of marketplace and society, one that is rooted in ubiquitous electronic networks (Kelly 1999: 1f).

Kelly stresses the significance of networks, which he regards as the central metaphor for the organization of our thinking and our economy. Everything encompassed by a network is potentially linked together. A typical characteristic of a network-based world and economy is supposed to be the demand for high speed: rapid change and quick action. The importance of speed was a crucial idea for many of the actors who said that they were acting within the new economy. The focus on speed is nicely illustrated by the successful American magazine of lifestyle and management, *Fast Company*, which wrote about the new economy in forms resembling a manifesto. It was essential to become one with change, to be a high-speed actor in order to survive in the emerging network society (see *Fast Company*, April/May 1997).[1] One of the companies in Sweden which placed great emphasis on the need for being fast was the Internet consultancy Framfab (short for Framtidsfabriken, meaning 'Factory of the Future'). Over a short period of time measured in years, the company grew from a handful of people to a corporation with well over two thousand employees. The corporation came to produce mainly Internet applications and business solutions to clients such as Ericsson, Nike and Volvo. Framfab often used the slogan 'Creating the future'. The company tried to picture itself as a pioneer, as a company of the future, which was different from older industrial companies. The company rhetoric was concentrated around ideas about newness (Strannegård 2002: Willim 2002). Framfab should be an entirely new kind of enterprise. But how should the company retain a image of newness for a longer time (Strannegård 2002: 233)? One strategy was to embrace quick changes and to let high speed became a leitmotiv for the corporation. Framfab should never stand still, but instead always be one step ahead. The logotype chosen for the company was the fast-forward symbol, known from various electronic products. In the rhetoric about the company that was put forward by the tone-setting CEO, Jonas Birgersson, speed frequently recurred as a key word.

Purpose

Within the new economy high-flown rhetoric exclamations held a strong position. But the future wasn't to be created from merely words, the rhetoric should also be coupled with practices within companies such as Framfab. Therefore, I will continue with examining how rhetorical images of technology and technical development have been related to concrete computer-based practices in Framfab.[2] My central argument is that conceptions of the need for speed and the idea about 'creating the future' within the company and within the new economy were enforced when the business rhetorics converged with certain aspects of computer practices.

The material for my discussion is drawn from a ethnographic study I did at Framfab during the period 1999 to 2001. In my fieldwork I focused on one of the company's offices, the so-called Ideon-office, located in the Ideon Science Park in Lund, Sweden. I did interviews with the employees and observed the practices in the office. I also took part in different company-related events and looked at how the Framfab image was communicated.

Conjuring up the Future

Framfabs' image was to a large extent derived from the CEO's visions. Jonas Birgersson often spoke about his own and the company's vision. It was toward this vision that the company was to hasten. How was this vision to be attained? In a discussion of changing conditions in company organization, Per Olof Berg (2000) has stressed the significance of invocations for staking out the road to the future. He sees how a process that is unpredictable and difficult to grasp is collectively designed in interaction between concrete actions and invocations of a desired future.

Berg views invocation as a deliberate, purposeful strategy for change. A group of people have a collective faith that something will take shape in the future; one can speak of a shared vision. The vision coincides with an image of a goal, a projection of the future which guides what the various actors invest in the process. The whole process, which is difficult to grasp in its entirety, is dependent on the notions the different players have of a future goal – a goal that is to be conjured forth, choices that have to be made to harness, or rather to appease, reality, all in order to materialize the vision.

Companies created visions of a future which was to be invoked within the framework of the new economy. Many people, for example, viewed Kevin Kelly's predictions as beacons on the journey toward the future. According to Kelly, companies would be obligated to become one with change. They would be forced to become a new type of company if they wanted to survive. In the blurb to the Swedish edition of Kevin Kelly's book (1999), his rules for the new society are said to 'go far beyond business administration. Not just companies but everyone – politicians, organizations, media – ignore them at their peril'. According to the rhetoric, new laws would begin to apply, changing all existing industrial and economic practices as high-speed new companies, in an almost evolutionistic scenario, eliminated older actors. This development was affirmed by companies such as Framfab.

Conceptual Congruity

To make an analytical link between computer use at the Ideon office and wider trends in the IT business, a term used by the media researcher Lev Manovich may be fruitful. In his study of digital media he talks about *conceptual transfer*. According to Manovich, the cultural significance of digital media goes beyond the situations where a user is sitting at a computer trying to understand and use the technology. Since digital media have had such an impact on society, the concepts and distinctive features that characterize these media are also transferred to other spheres of society. Manovich says that this transfer takes place as cultural categories and concepts are substituted, on the level of meaning and/or language, by new ones that derive from the computer's ontology, epistemology, and pragmatics. New media thus acts as a forerunner of this more general process of cultural reconceptualization (Manovich 2001: 47).

It remains to be seen how correct Manovich is in his ideas about a broad cultural reconceptualization with an impact on society. In any case it may be noted that in certain contexts the concept of the computer has been more important for an understanding of processes and activities than in others. One such context was Framfab's Ideon office, where the computer was a central artefact. Its significance and its peculiarities were related to the understanding both of the nature of work in the company and of the employees' own role. Framfab's motto was 'to acknowledge and challenge the unknown', and the unknown was presupposed to lie within the framework of digital media. It was an electronic world, or a world in an electronic borderland, which was to be explored by the employees of the company. Framfab portrayed itself as a pioneer. The ground broken by the company was located within the electronic networks. It can thus be said that the world that was central for work at Framfab was dominated by the concepts, conditions and distinctive features of digital media. Framfab's focus on high speed was conceptually rooted in electronics, as was made visible by the fast-forward symbol in the company's logotype. The acceleration and change advocated by Framfab was in itself dependent on electronics. It was with electronics and digital media that rapid progress could be assured. Ideas about what the world was like and could be like were linked to digital media and to the potential of computers. The basic features characterizing computers, and the electronic systems of which they were part, could thus be interpreted as also guiding how an enterprise such as Framfab, and by extension the world as a whole, should function.

However, I do not want to see the process solely as a conceptual transfer from digital media to the world as a whole. Some of the distinctive conceptual features of the digital media harmonized with broader societal processes for a period of time. Framfab's growth and the positive forecasts of the new economy about accelerated processes, which would give us a better world, did not just arise out of conceptual transfers from digital media, but the phenomena were not isolated from each other either. During a period they found themselves in a field of shared associations, which may be seen as a concentration of cultural ideas shaped both by rhetoric and by material practices. On the basis of this field of associations, the direction of development might have seemed self-evident: forward and upward, change as upgrading.

Framfab focused on what they saw would happen in the new network society. It was thus not the old desktop computers, standing isolated in homes and offices, that were the technology of the future; instead, the fruits of success would be harvested with the aid of future network-connected electronic equipment. There is a congruity here between how Framfab as an organization profiled itself against older companies and how new generations of digital technology were contrasted to earlier technology.

Through the years, a desktop computer with an operative system like Windows had had a graphical interface consisting of a hierarchical file system: a structure of folders containing more folders, and so on. This visual way of representing information had been popularized by Apple Computer during the 1980s and then become increasingly common. It gave the illusion that reality could be reduced in a logical way, whereby each object had a distinct, well-defined place. In the 1990s, as more and more computers were linked up to networks and the Internet, another way of organizing data became significant. The main relational structure was then based on hyperlinks. The Web builds on a non-hierarchical system of links between objects, and it is unclear which object is most important. Any object is expected to be linkable to any other object by means of hyperlinks (Manovich 2001: 16).

We see a correspondence here between the form of the hyperlink structure and the way in which the Ideon office was organized. For several years Framfab's organization had a relatively loose, non-hierarchical structure. Earlier rigid corporate structures could be compared with the earlier hierarchical file system.[3] I am not trying to say that those who worked with Internet products at the Ideon office had been conceptually affected by the structure of the Internet. What is interesting is the correspondence between the non-hierarchical structure and the dynamic relations in digital network environments, and what the organization, the work and the social relations in the office looked like. In a way, Framfab reflected itself in the distinctive features that characterized the digital environments that they created and that they hoped would dominate in the future. Here we may speak of, not conceptual transfers, but *conceptual congruity*. The office was built up around hyperlinks rather than in a hierarchical structure.[4] The network replaced the hierarchy as the main metaphor for understanding the IT world of which Framfab was part.[5]

The conceptual congruity with electronic network patterns in the office was noticeable, for instance, in the diffuse command structure and in how projects at the office were organized in a relatively loose way. In addition, most of the employees were incorporated in extensive electronic networks of mailing lists, newsgroups and chat forums which extended outside the office and also outside the company. These networks could be significant for work in Framfab, since important work-related information and knowledge were communicated in the networks. There were thus no watertight bulkheads between the employees in the office and their acquaintances, who could very well be working for rival companies. It was just a question of keeping the information in the different channels separate. Details about products and commissions, for example, could not be discussed with acquaintances in other companies, but other matters concerning computers and work-related issues could very well be discussed. Working for Framfab thus became an integral part of the employees' lives, which led to difficulties in drawing clear dividing lines.

The networked electronic equipment were thus involved in a field of associations that concurred in large measure with ideas about the high-speed company Framfab. The talk of the new economy and of how IT would first create a network society and then enhance its importance within this society was a collection of associations. What arose can be seen as a field of associations in which a conceptual congruity was shaped with speed as the common denominator: faster technology, companies, growth and upgrading. In this field, change became synonymous with quick upgrading.

The S-curve

Framfab internal company seminar, Malmö Stock Exchange, May 2000. Along with a two-figure number of Framfab employees, I am listening to a member of the Framfab board. It is Paul Saffo, or Paul L. Saffo III, as he is properly called. He lives in California, works with business-oriented research at the Institute for the Future, and is Framfab's real future guru. Jonas Birgersson has transformed several of Saffo's ideas and presented them to various listeners. Now Saffo begins to talk about something I have heard Birgersson speaking enthusiastically about: the S-curve. It is about the breakthrough of new technology. He draws the curve for us. At first the line runs almost horizontal and then it soars dramatically, finally leveling out to become almost horizontal again, like an S. He then draws another line. It rises obliquely to the left, at an angle of 45 degrees, and cuts through the S-curve. He says that these lines illustrate how the Framfab employees can envisage the development of the Internet, and the type of services and products produced by the company.

According to Saffo, new technology tends to be overvalued in the short term but undervalued in the long term. The S-curve corresponds to the impact of the technology in reality; the straight line, on the other hand, corresponds to our expectations of the impact of the technology. We believe that the interest in and need for new technology, and hence technological change, increases in a linear fashion. In fact, development takes the form of an S-curve. Just now, Saffo says, we are at the point where it is starting to gain momentum in earnest. When it comes to the Internet, Framfab can reckon that, at the beginning where we are now, the market is not ripe. In the future, however, the need for Net-based products will increase; Framfab's future thus looks bright. Soon the exponential growth will take off, forward and above all upward.

What lies behind a rhetorical example like the S-curve, as used by Saffo, Birgersson and others?[6] When Saffo appeared at the Malmö Stock Exchange he was speaking of a broad phenomenon, the Internet. In this connection both the problem with and the advantage of the S-curve are its vagueness. He said that it usually takes more than twenty years for new technology to catch on in earnest. How could Framfab create a strategy based solely on the knowledge or the hope that the Internet would grow in popularity, and was the time now ripe for the exponential growth? The vague scope of the S-curve scenario was in itself a problem if the curve was to be an aid to the creation of concrete strategies in the company.

The advantage of the example was its rhetorical simplicity. It was effective for CEO Jonas Birgersson to draw the curve on a whiteboard, and based on Saffo's arguments he could claim that it would soon be time for a large-scale change. The curve could serve to send signals to the employees, to potential customers, analysts, share buyers and the general public: Do you want to join us on the upward journey, or will you remain on the sidelines of development? It was a rhetorical simplification, with the S-curve used as an ingredient in the formula for conjuring up the future. In several ways the S-curve suited Framfab's profile and Birgersson's simplifying rhetoric about being the biggest in the future. The S-curve also harmonized with the rhetoric about computers and IT in general at this time.

Faster

'It must go incredibly fast – at an incredibly good price. Welcome to the future! The latest Intel Pentium III processor, 600 MHz, awaits you. Beat the speed record on the Net.' These promises were made in an advertisement by the computer manufacturer Gateway in 1999. This was one of the many companies that used increased speed as a marketing argument for computer equipment. Another of these companies was Apple, which in 1999 marketed its G4 computers in a brochure which claimed on the front cover that the company produced technology that was beyond all speed limits. With its processor containing a 'velocity engine', the company made supercomputers: 'A computer is transformed into a supercomputer when it can perform at least one billion floating-point operations per second. An almost unreal unit of speed better known as a gigaflop'.

The focus on both speed and the future has gone hand in hand with computers for decades (see Johansson 1997: 214), but it seemed to be particularly widespread around 2000. The clearest examples can be found in various computer magazines, such as the Swedish *Mikrodatorn* and *PC för alla,* which cover computers and other kinds of IT. They print advertisements and reviews, and report on tests of new technology in which the speed aspect is stressed.[7] The focus on the speed of the computer as an artefact should be compared with the use of the technology. How did employees perceive the computers in the Framfab offices, and how did people perceive their home computers in their daily use of them?

Waiting

Lund, 20 June 2000. I push a square button on the front of my computer. Some lights come on. A green light shows that the power supply to the computer is on. A red one indicates that the hard disk is being searched. There is a hiss and a buzz as the hard disk increases in speed. After a few seconds the light on the front of the floppy disk drive comes on. A rattling sound is heard when the computer checks whether a disk is inserted. Then the start-up process continues, or 'booting up', as people often say. This is a metaphorical expression based on a way of pulling on one's boots – 'bootstrapping' (see Norman 1999: 70).

Just before the rattle from the disk drive is heard, I can read on the screen, in white text on a black background, the basic configuration of the computer, the performance of the processor in MHz, and so on. The amount of internal memory is counted figure by figure for a few seconds. The larger the memory, the longer the count takes. When the computer's basic functions have been started, the introductory screen showing the logotype of the operative system is shown – Microsoft Windows 98. In the ensuing seconds the Windows image of white clouds against a blue sky disappears, and white text against a black screen shows technical data. The Windows picture returns and disappears, replaced by a background picture – the desktop. An hourglass is seen in the middle of the screen. After a moment a number of icons pop up. For a further few seconds I can hear the hard disk still working, whizzing away. After a few seconds the sound falls silent and all that is left is the hum of the fan. The computer has started and is ready to use. The whole process took 2 minutes and 34 seconds.

Starting a PC in the year 2000 took several minutes. As soon as one pushed the 'on' button, one was faced with a wait. This applied to people using computers at home and people using computers in companies such as Framfab. There were various strategies for handling the computer's start-up time. Many people at the Framfab office in the Ideon science park in Lund, where I did my fieldwork, did not switch off their computers when they went home, partly so that they would not need to start them in the morning. Some people used the start-up time to fetch a bowl of cereal. There were several strategies to avoid unnecessary waiting. In most cases the start-up time could be coped with and entailed no great problem for people's work.

Several of the people I spoke with agreed that it was rather absurd that it should take so long to start a computer. In the infancy of television it took several minutes for the tube to warm up before a picture appeared. As television sets became more common, however, development eliminated the warm-up time. As computers have developed, the long waiting times at start-up have remained, despite all the talk of increased speed and revolutions.

Besides the relatively long start-up time, computer use still entails a number of other situations in which the computer takes time to carry out a task. In such cases the screen usually shows some kind of progress indicator, for example, a gray rectangle or a horizontal bar which is filled with colour as the process is completed. The indicator is to ensure the user that the system is still working, that the computer has not crashed. In addition, it shows how long the remainder of the process will take.

At these moments the computer sets the pace of the work. When a gray rectangle has appeared on the screen, it is impossible to hasten the process (cf. Thrift 1996: 177). Some people find this time frustrating, as a stage during which the user is waiting, involved but denied participation in the performance of the process (Bayley 1999). However, the time of the gray rectangles can also be seen as an opportunity for a micropause. Jakob Nielsen, who together with Donald Norman is one of the influential debaters in matters of IT-related usability, has therefore stressed the importance of a pleasing design for these progress indicators. They should be attractive for the user to look at (www.useit.com/papers/responsetime.html).

In many cases the computer's interface used to be unavailable to the user while gray squares drew attention to themselves on the screen. Technological development later made it possible for the user to perform other jobs on the computer while waiting; this is known as multitasking. Despite this possibility, the gray rectangles, often flanked by figures showing the percentage of processed data or the remaining time needed for the ongoing process in minutes and seconds, have an almost hypnotic attraction. This is reinforced by the way that the manufacturers, in line with Nielsen's recommendations, have tried to find pleasing graphic representations to show the progress. The user's attention is easily fixed on observing the course of the process. This can be regarded as an accentuation of the waiting time, of the process whereby the counted-down seconds or the rising percentages promise impending completion, that the end is in sight, that something will soon be over, so that one can proceed.

In these situations the user is a supervisor of the computer's work. This supervision does not necessarily require any great involvement. For example, in long processes such as copying of large amounts of data or compiling code,[8] the users in the Ideon office rarely sat watching the progress. Other tasks, such as reading e-mail, could be done at the same time, and one could still keep an eye on the process so that everything went as it was supposed to. The time of the grey rectangles may be viewed as a more or less acceptable part of the conditions for interacting with personal computers. However, the user is confronted with other types of waiting which are harder to explain. I call them delayed responses.

Lund, 29 June 2000. The cursor in the word-processing program Microsoft Word flashes rhythmically. Just under once a second, the vertical bar vanishes and reappears, showing the point in the document where input or editing can take place. I feed in the characters with the aid of the keyboard, and at the same moment electronic representations of the letters on the keys become visible on the screen. It all flows, it feels synchronized. When I type in a word on the keyboard, the vertical bar, the cursor, suddenly stops blinking. The letters that I have summoned up do not appear. Nothing happens on the screen. After a second or two the keyed-in characters, the word, can be seen on the screen. But for a few seconds I received no response to my actions.

This description of a prosaic moment in work in front of the computer can tell us something. Delayed responses are defects in the computer equipment. They are often due to defects in one of the components that make up a computer. For example, contributory causes can be too little internal memory, or too little graphic card memory, or too low performance in the processor or the hard disk, or compatibility problems between different components. Delayed responses occur particularly in the use of software which is more recent than the hardware components (cf. Norman 1999).

Computer-based work is a process that depends on constant synchronization between the user and the computer. The user often expects an immediate response to his or her actions. When my fingers meet the keys I expect something to happen directly on the screen. As a user I want my relationship to the computer to be one of seamless flow (cf. Ristilammi 1997: 22). Just as the pressing of the keys on a mechanical typewriter is accompanied by a direct response, the printing of letters and characters on a page, so the user of a word-processing program expects the press of a key to produce a character on the screen immediately. When there is no delay between a physical call on the services of a technology and its response, the user can feel a transparency in the computer. Delayed responses, like other delays in computer use, on the other hand, can lead to a feeling of the flow being interrupted. Instead the user becomes aware of the limitations of the equipment. The medium becomes a barrier between the user and what is represented on the screen.

What a user expects of a computer depends on the context. At Framfab, where there was a great demand for speed, where people were expected to have what is called a performance personality (Dyson 1997) and not to be slow-coaches, there was a high degree of sensitivity to delays in the technology. The people I spoke with thought that the jerkiness or undesirable delays in the use of computers could be frustrating, and that if one was under the slightest stress the waiting times could drive a person crazy. In an environment where people claimed to be making the products of the future, the vital technical equipment was expected to function without any friction. But it did not always do so. Delayed responses occurred at the Ideon office just as they did in Aunt Greta's home, at Ericsson, in the Cabinet Office, in schools, at Lund University Hospital and so on. Delays and waits, despite the rhetoric about the speed of computers, have been intimately associated with the use of computers. These two aspects – waiting and the lack of synchronization in everyday use, and the rhetoric about new, faster artefacts, and promises regarding future acceleration – stand in relation to present situations of waiting. The marketing rhetoric promises that future quicker products will 'erase themselves' as media, and that today's lack of immediacy will be replaced by more direct experiences. This dynamic, along with the waiting and the promises of greater speed, is dependent on a third ingredient, namely ...

Expectations

At the time of my study, computers had been used in networks in Sweden for several years, and networking had become increasingly common. A network card or a modem to link up with other computers or other electronics via the Internet was almost automatically included in a computer configuration. Network links were used to send electronic mail, to do bank business, book tickets, find information and search for entertainment of various kinds. The material available on websites developed from consisting of mainly text to become increasingly sophisticated graphically. Soon there was quite a lot of audiovisual material available.

The Internet and the Web, according to the rhetoric, would make computer use even faster. In a way, many applications actually did become faster. Or to put it more exactly, things which had formerly been impossible became possible. Examples are searching for various types of music via the Web and listening to songs stored on some computer on the other side of the world, or being able to download software components from a distant website. The Internet was expected to offer a temporal immediacy and a compression of geographical distances (cf. Castells 1996). However, connection in networks also meant longer delays. The short delayed responses and waiting times increased in number when computers interacted with the Internet.

The Internet yields both seeming temporal instantaneity and spatial compression. We can be everywhere all at once, all the time; but what of the inevitable slippage of time involved? The World Wide Web has created a life of dead moments, of moments spent waiting for the instantaneous to happen. (www.api-network.com/mc/0006/instanta-neity.html)

Unexpected delays and strange blockages in the technology took place more often when the computer was hooked up. The possibility to be connected also contains the risk of disconnection from a system which has become vital for the organization. In her study of the organizational culture at Apple, Christina Garsten has written about how blockages of the used technology was experienced at the company.

> It has been said that the new level of interconnectivity afforded by the electronic media heightens the fragility of social networks in various ways ... If the electronic network suddenly shuts down, nearness easily turns into absence, and the sense of controlling time changes into a feeling of impatience and frustration when important information is no longer available and one is disconnected from the rest of the organizational world (Garsten 1994: 162).

Apart from unexpected disruptions and delays, there were also more expected ones occurring at Framfab. Web browsers such as Internet Explorer or Netscape Navigator, with the aid of which information from various websites can be downloaded, had been furnished with their own progress indicators. In the top right-hand corner is a little box showing an animation of a revolving globe, or flying stars and planets combined with the producer's logotype, while the computer downloads information. Together with the hourglass and the gray rectangles, these small images have become tone-setting icons of waiting in computer contexts.

Down in the left-hand corner of the Web browser the program shows information about what happens during the download, the percentage already downloaded, the names of the files that are loaded and so on. Web documents are downloaded in stages, thus making the user attentive to the medium itself (see Manovich 2001: 207). When the download is complete, the user can concentrate on the content of the document or the web page. A click on a hyperlink and the waiting starts again. The medium once again becomes visible. This gives an oscillation between what the medium represents and the medium itself.

Waiting is in large measure related to the equipment that is used. For employees at Framfab there were relatively fast connections at work. In most homes at the same time, connection was by modem, which could mean rather long waiting times (cf. Nielsen 2000: 363–5). Many of the people who had a quick connection at work therefore felt a resistance to going home and switching on their computers, dialing up via a modem and connecting to the Internet. One of the employees said, for example, that he could never imagine sitting at home and being online with just a slow modem connection; he would prefer not to bother at all. One reason why many people at the Ideon office spent a lot of time at work, over and above their normal working hours, was that they could take advantage of the fast network connections. The company's equipment enticed the staff to stay on at the workplace; the network connections enabled activities that would not have been possible at home. Yet it was envisaged that homes too would get quick connections … in the future.

Around the year 2000 there was a great deal of talk about broadband connections, high-speed Internet and the rapid electronic networks of the future. About connecting Sweden. Or about 'the fast new country', as one of Ericsson's advertising campaigns said. In the future people would forget all about slow modem connections, as waiting times would be eliminated with the aid of new technology.[9] Jonas Birgersson marketed Framfab's subsidiary, Bredbandsbolaget, with the arguments that it was for a faster Sweden and that it would provide the country with high-speed broadband connections. Proper broadband, he said, faster than, say, what was being offered by Telia, the former state-owned telecom company. Birgersson proclaimed that the Net was dead, long live the Net (*CultureMag* 2000: 34), and in the Swedish mass media he was given the epithet 'The Broadband Jesus'.[10]

These promises should be seen in relation to the widespread waiting at computers. In the launching of new products this was a good seedbed in which to plant expectations that future technology would be able to eliminate unwelcome waiting times. These expectations of future products eliminating long waits meant that today's waits seemed even longer.

Hopes of an escape from waiting times were aroused in conjunction with the broadband mission, but as I have shown earlier, the promises were commonly heard in other parts of the computer market. An issue of the magazine *PC Extra* (4/1999) presented what were then the fastest processors for portable computers. The article was entitled 'Fastest' and was based on a test of different computers fitted with Intel's latest product. Symptomatically, the article began with an account of how Intel, a month previously, had demonstrated for the first time its as yet unlaunched processor with the code name 'Geyserville'. It would, of course, have a higher capacity than earlier processors and would therefore be classed in future tests as faster than existing products. By starting the article with the focus on technology that was not yet on the market, the magazine put a 'best before' stamp on the most recent products currently available. Rhetorical shifts between the present and the future in this type of article and in various types of marketing may be confusing (cf. Zorkoczy and Heap 1995: 13).[11] Tomorrow's artefacts, which were presented in prototypes and incomplete versions at electronic trade shows all over the world, promised desirable new products and constantly improved potential for the user. Mostly, however, the really hot technology was still not yet available in the shops; it was just out of reach. It can all be summed up in the phrase 'not now, but soon'.

Vaporware

People speak of software and hardware in connection with IT. There is a third, more elusive, category, namely *vaporware*; Vapor as in steam or mist. Vaporware is technology that has not yet been launched. It is a future product on the shelves which is vaguely discernible as in a fog. In IT contexts it has become extremely important to give the market information about the type of products a company is focusing on for the future. John A. Hoxmeier writes about this phenomenon:

> Software companies use a market signaling technique called 'product preannouncing' – a deliberate communication before a firm performs a particular action. Software preannouncements are often called 'vaporware' (systems or features announced long before a ship date) and have existed in the software industry since the 1980s. In some cases the software product or feature may never even appear. The preannouncement is usually a market signal directed at consumers, competitors, investors, distributors, and the sales force (Hoxmeier 2000: 116).

It is thus with the aid of vaporware that presumptive consumers' expectations are aroused. Product preannouncements are communicated through various IT-oriented media, for example computer magazines. For producers of software (and hardware), this always involves the risk of announcing promises of future products before they are sure that the promises can be kept. When a company does not manage to satisfy the mist-shrouded hopes, it can incur a negative perception on the market (see Hoxmeier 2000). Despite this, vaporware production has become widespread, and it should be seen as an important part of the marketing dynamic surrounding IT. It may also be the case that this dynamic has had a conserving effect on the market. Big companies like Microsoft, IBM or Intel have often obtained huge space in the media. They therefore have good chances of putting their preannouncements across, and thus being able to influence people's notions about the way development is headed.

As an example, in autumn 2001 a major preannouncement campaign was started by Microsoft. *Computer Sweden*, one of Sweden's largest IT magazines, then presented a great many articles about Microsoft's coming product called .NET. When the product later began to take more concrete shape, the technical evangelists from Microsoft appeared at meetings in different parts of the country to preach their message about the new technology. In September they came to People's Hall in Malmö, where they presented Microsoft's vision of .NET and the framework to representatives of various companies and organizations in the region. The phenomenon of vaporware has become an important part of the IT industry, although it is certainly not without problems. 'There is a paradox in the software industry. Many people complain about vaporware, but at the same time would like to know about new product features and functions' (Hoxmeier 2000: 120). Consumers with an interest in technology, especially people working with IT, are generally interested in coming products, particularly if their livelihood is dependent on the direction taken by development. Microsoft's .NET plans were so significant for a large part of the IT industry that they could scarcely be ignored. A company like Framfab and its employees simply could not fail to be interested in coming products. Future projections and direction indicators were too important to be ignored, even if they should later prove to be false.

It was not only large players such as Microsoft that produced vaporware. New companies which were small by global standards, like Framfab, also produced vaporware. In February 2000 Jonas Birgersson stood on the stage of the Riviera cinema in Stockholm, dressed in the yellow and blue shirt of the Swedish national ice hockey team.[12] The company's accounts were presented. In addition, Birgersson put on a show in which the high point came when he dropped a brick through a pane of glass. This was a symbolic gesture. The meaning was 'Brikks breaks Windows'. One of Framfab's products, called Brikks, would oust the Windows operative system. According to this gesture, Brikks would be, if not an operative system, then at least a substitute for one, something new and revolutionary in the computer world with the potential to eliminate market leaders such as Microsoft.[13]

From the cinema stage the CEO pointed to the desired picture of Brikks in the future. Brikks was something new that would put Windows in a peripheral position. For analysts, competitors and customers, the company presented a product that was not available on the market in its imagined form, but which it thought would be important. Framfab could thereby claim that the future was already being produced within the company's walls.

Vaporware was an ingredient in the formula for conjuring up a future. The 'Brikks breaks Windows' gesture should also be seen in relation to another such ingredient: the S-curve. Both vaporware and the S-curve were part of the company's strategic invocations (Berg 2000). A visionary direction was called up by means of allusions to a one-way course of development (think: the S-curve) and by hazy, mysterious assurances of promising future products (think: vaporware).[14]

How It Could Be

Ideas about vaporware create an intricate relationship between previous, present and future technology. When new technology comes into use it changes the user's relationship to earlier technology, and the technology that is not yet available is also part of the dynamics. Ideas about artefacts that have not yet been launched on the market help to change perceptions of the products that are currently in use. Notions about what other new technology will enable put the focus on what is being used at the moment. It can be regarded as a kind of 'the grass is greener on the other side' logic, in a temporal rather than a spatial sense.

The significance of expectations and the production of vaporware can also be associated with a driving force in connection with consumption which the sociologist Colin Campbell calls 'the desire for the new' (1992). It denotes the desire to lay one's hands on new gadgets which one hopes will feel better than the old ones. The new things that may possibly come in the future virtually transform the things that currently surround us. Fantasies and notions of *how it could be* shape and become part of everyday practices in relation to technology. The marketing rhetoric invokes new products as consumption's equivalent to utopias (cf. Ritzer 1999). The ethnologist Magnus Bergquist (1999) has written about the cultural significance of utopias. He stresses the importance of the dissonances that arise when we compare what we have around us at present with notions of what it might be like in the future.

The dissonances may be seen as a tension between experience and the longing for what is not present. In connection with recurrent practices such as upgrading, fantasy is always juxtaposed with experiences of the concrete use of artefacts. It can be seen as an interplay between absence and presence. The artist Paul Hertz describes a similar dynamic in an article about the longing for new artistic and sensory experiences. He writes that '... the power inheres in the symbol, not in the experience' (1999: 400). He believes that it is in fact the absence of a special experience that gives it the power to serve as an ideal.[15] It is easy to project a multitude of negative phenomena on one's material surroundings. In fantasies about future products, the image of escape routes takes shape: not now, but soon, we will avoid the problems. We will become more orderly, creative, positive, effective, will have more time and feel less stressed. If only we get that new product and can throw away this old one. Then we can attain our ideal, keep up with the times in technology, or even be ahead of our time.

Ideas about technology-related improvement seem to be powered in large measure by an optimistic faith in progress, based on the conviction that new technology will give us increasing opportunities to create a better world. This can be viewed as an *ethos of upgrading*, according to which technology brings constant improvements to humanity. With this ethos it is just a matter of stepping out and directing our gaze forward.

Technology-driven change could not only be seen as something positive in an ethical sense, but also as something aesthetically attractive. It would be possible to speak of a merger of ethics and aesthetics, of how what is perceived as aesthetically appealing can also be ethically correct. Beauty as goodness. An example of this merger can be found in the Italian futurists at the start of the twentieth century. They advocated speed as the (brutal but in their eyes necessary) way to a better world, a viewpoint that was articulated both in works of art and in (ethical) manifestos (cf. Schnapp 1999).[16] There are parallels between the futurists' cult of acceleration and the concentration of the IT world on upgrading and turnover (Johnson 1997).

If technological change, financial turnover and consumption are regarded as something which sustains a society and which therefore should take place to as high a degree as possible, ephemerality also becomes something potentially positive. Ephemerality is the other side of acquisition. Arjun Appadurai has used the term *the aesthetic of ephemerality* to illustrate the aestheticizing of the changeable (1997: 84). He links the aesthetic of ephemerality to consumption, arguing that the search for novelty actually has to do with a view of change as something intrinsically beautiful and appealing. The ephemerality of commodities is linked to sensations of pleasure.

It can be pleasurable to obtain something new, and also to get rid of something. Relegating outdated electronics to cupboards or attics and, after a period of interim storage there, cutting the ties with them by taking them to a rubbish dump can give a pleasing sense of renewal. Yet the great sense of pleasure is perhaps associated chiefly with fantasies about the artefacts that one may soon acquire.

Upgrading and Connecting

Knowing what type of technology was expected within the near future was crucial for Framfab's operations. However, it was not the case that everyone who worked in the office felt an unconsidered longing for the next version of a program and then upgraded as quickly as possible. One of the positive details stressed by some of the employees was that they had admittedly been given a large budget with which to buy equipment. It could be perceived as a dreamlike situation, where it was suddenly possible to lay one's hands on expensive new apparatus. To escape the sluggish old technology in favour of new devices would make work easier and also dramatically improve the chances of producing that new product. At the same time, there was considerable discussion of the advantages and disadvantages of technology. The old was not always worse than the new.

The upgrade ethos which has been such a prominent feature of the computer market should be contrasted with an interest cultivated by some people at the Ideon office; a fondness for old computers and electronics. Old Atari or

Commodore computers, early video games and analog synthesizers were regarded by many people as treasures. Some of the distinctive features of these early artefacts were perceived as excellent, despite subsequent years of computer development and upgrading.[17] However, this interest was not reflected within the framework of production at the Ideon office, where the focus was primarily on the future. But is it not the case that upgrading mostly means improvement? It is true, to some extent, that upgrading has led to better products. New functions have generally been added to the latest versions, errors in the code may have been corrected, the appearance may have changed, and so on. New versions, however, are usually more demanding than the old ones. A criticism levelled against the software industry is that the programs have swollen in size, although it is not certain that the users always want bigger programs. Donald Norman has put his finger on part of the problem by speaking of 'creeping featurism' (1999: 80f.). The term denotes how new versions of programs are primarily given a multitude of new functions, which inevitably makes them much more complex and resource-demanding.[18] This means that the requirements of the other equipment are also greater. In computer contexts this increase in requirements has had the result that the delays in the use of the technology that I described above have accompanied the development of technology, despite constantly increasing performance. Software upgrades have generally not been able to eliminate the delays; the reverse is more likely the case. Phenomena which can be classified as defects and as a source of irritation have thus been reproduced through generations of upgrades.

At intervals of a couple of years, Microsoft has released extensive upgrades of its Windows operative system. If a consumer (whether a private person or company) has bought the new version and puts the installation CD in the computer, there follows a pedagogical step-by-step guide to the installation. Boxes show pictures of happy people flanked by short messages about the opportunities provided by the new operative system. After half an hour or so, the upgrade is, one hopes, installed. Let us say that you now wish, for some reason, to change back to your old version of the operative system. There is then a way back. This, however, is far from being the pedagogical delight that the upgrade process was. It rather gives the feeling of giving back a present you have just received. The term downgrade is rarely used. Moreover, going back to an earlier version often involves technical complications. Where changes in software are concerned, they primarily concern upgrading; anything else is an unfortunate exception. Movement is one-way, the standards are set. As a computer user you are supposed to agree that upgrading is synonymous with improvement.[19]

From the point of view of IT companies there are some laggards in society who refuse to upgrade software and hardware. But there are few who switch back to older equipment. The whole system is built around upgrading and the ephemeralization of older equipment. Electronic products are supposed to be throw-away articles. In the summer of 1999 I visited Sysav's centre for the recycling of electronics in Malmö. It gave me a clear picture of the other side of upgrading: discarding. Sysav receives huge quantities of computer components and accessories, still in their unopened wrappers, which have been discarded by companies that frequently upgrade their equipment.

The motive force behind the upgrading is reinforced when people become connected. As computer use has increasingly meant communicating with other computers in networks, or with other users via their computers, there have been increasing demands for common systems and compatibility between products. It is thus essential to have a computer, a system, which is compatible with that of other users. As a user wishing to communicate with the world via your computer, you are in principle not allowed to decide for yourself at what speed you want to upgrade programs and hardware. Being connected to a network also means being synchronized with the network. If other computer users with whom you communicate upgrade, then you must upgrade too. This leads to an upgrade spiral with the constant renewal of products as the central logic. Linking up means to some extent being tied up.[20]

Outro

As part of the IT business Framfab was far from having an autonomous relationship to the prevailing movements of upgrading. Framfab and its employees were included in the IT world as both producers and consumers, and the direction indicated by the Framfab management also concurred with the direction followed by the IT business as a whole. It was just a matter of going with the flow.

The talk of the new economy and of how IT would first create a network society and then enhance its importance within this society formed a field of associations in which a conceptual congruity was shaped with speed as the common denominator: faster technology, companies, growth and upgrading. In this field, change became synonymous with quick upgrading. Paradoxes, contradictions and problems could be overcome by further increasing the speed. As the site manager at the Ideon office put it: 'What we do is to find a number of functions that exist at this speed. You can use that, not to solve problems but to get away from them.'

This mindset seemed to be fruitful for a couple of years. But the companies of the new economy soon ran into problems. From the spring of 2000 and onward the happy and optimistic years at Framfab turned into a more sombre reality. The stock-exchange rate declined and the company was decimated as office after office was quickly removed from the organization. The scenario was similar in a lot of the

IT companies at the time. The high valuations of the brave new visions put forward by companies such as Framfab turned out to be far too optimistic. So what happened to be a bubble of economic speculation burst (cf. *Kulturella Perspektiv* 3/2001; Thrift 2001). In spite of the downturn in the IT business, IT per se certainly hadn't played out its role. New electronics are still being spread around the globe and are integrated in people's everyday lives in a lot of different contexts. New IT products are being launched, sold and used, upgraded and eagerly compared with future releases and vaporware. Therefore, many of the processes pertaining to the new economy that I have described in this article still have an actuality. Several important research themes are certainly waiting to be found in the meeting point of business rhetoric, marketing and computer practices. Possible future research projects in this field are vaguely discernible as in a fog, a bit like vaporware.

Acknowledgements

This article has been made possible with financial help from the Swedish Research Council for the Humanities and Social Sciences, the Swedish Research Council and Öforsk.

Notes

1. The magazine *Fast Company* served as a model or at least a source of inspiration for several Swedish magazines geared to the new economy. Other examples are *Guru* and *Kapital*.
2. The discussion in this article is based on more detailed analyses in Willim 2002 (see www.framtid.nu).
3. The hierarchical file system is still used in the computers in the office, but the crucial point in my argument is that the hyperlink organization was a later invention, and to some extent a substitute for the hierarchy of the computer's isolated desktop.
4. If there is any ranking system, it is informal and characterized more by the hacker movement's competence-based ranking, for example (see Willim 2002; cf. Raymond 2001).
5. The term *conceptual congruity* harmonizes with the dynamics in organizations described by Karin Knorr-Cetina (1999). She sees how knowledge in an organization grows in a combination of social relations and the distinctive features of the objects that are central to the work of the organization; in Framfab's case this would be websites and computer components (see Strannegård and Friberg 2001: 60; cf. Salomonsson 2001). The objects and the people's relations to them become crucial for the way in which people relate to reality. The objects help to shape the human being.

Claiming the Future

6. I find the S-curve in a Swedish introduction to ethnology from 1976/1986, written by Nils-Arvid Bringéus. The curve is included to illustrate how innovations are received in a society. Bringéus writes about the spread of such things as television and tuberculosis check-ups, but he also writes about how horse-drawn rakes and other agricultural implements were adopted by people in different places.

7. In the ranking and awarding of points to different types of equipment, reviewers have often proceeded from measurements of speed. Measuring speed in computers, however, is not always relevant, or it really does not say very much about how the equipment might work in concrete user situations (see Norman 1999).

8. A translation between different programming languages, from high-level language to machine code (see Lunell 1994: 96).

9. The rhetoric about gains in time in future communication was not specific to IT, however; it was also found in connection with physical movement. Around the Öresund, the straits between Denmark and Sweden, there was much talk of future speed and time savings in connection with the construction of the Fixed Link (cf. Idvall 2000). The telling title of Fredrik Nilsson's study, *När en timme blir tio minuter* ('When an Hour Becomes Ten Minutes', 1999), which is about expectations concerning the Öresund region, comes from the rhetoric about time gains in connection with the construction of the future infrastructure, technology, and communications in the southernmost Swedish province of Skåne. In the debate about the Öresund Bridge, some people claimed that it was a 'dinosaur project' which was not necessary in a future of increased IT communication.

10. When the Swedish Broadcasting Corporation's economic news, *A-ekonomi*, summed up the past year on 27 December 2001, Jonas Birgersson was referred to as the 'Broadband Jesus'.

11. Rhetorical shifts between past, present, and future occur in several contexts. The ethnologist Malin Ideland, for example, has pointed out how mass-media narratives about gene technology are often illustrated with the aid of metaphorical excursions to the past and the future (Ideland 2000).

12. Unfortunately, I was not able to attend the presentation. I have obtained a view of the event via accounts in the media and what Framfab employees have told me about the situation.

13. This was the rhetorical image that was conveyed. It was intended to show that there were certain discrepancies between this description and the real potential of the product. I consider these discrepancies in Willim 2002.

14. This indication of a company's direction should be viewed in relation to the fact that a great many other actors portrayed the future as complex and in large measure unpredictable (Bergquist 2001).

15. Paul Théberge writes about the same type of processes in connection with electronic musical instruments: 'This constant forward looking – this deferral of pleasure and satisfaction into the future – is what contributes to the sense of desire and need that is necessary to maximize the pace of technical innovation and profit' (Théberge 1997: 119).

16. Richard Shusterman (2000: 236) has looked at the fusion of aesthetics with ethics, proceeding from a claim to this effect by Ludwig Wittgenstein. Shusterman shows how aesthetics combine with ethics chiefly in postmodernity. With the example of the Italian futurists in mind, however, it is worth asking how postmodern the merger of aesthetics and ethics really is.

17. One of the clearest examples of how older technology is perceived as being more valuable than new technology can be found in connection with electronic musical instruments, which are related to computers and can be encompassed in the term IT (Willim 1997).

18. Donald Norman illustrates the problem of creeping featurism with the aid of Microsoft Word. The number of commands in the program rose from 311 in 1988 to 1,033 in 1998. Norman says that this increase in commands and complexity does not correspond to the real requirements or needs of the user, but is instead a sign that something is 'sick' in the computer business (1999: 80f.).

19. The abbreviation ASP (Application Service Provider) flourished in the debate around 2000. It meant that companies could offer customers subscriptions to software. The product would thus become more of a service. Purchase of the product/service would thus mean a lasting commitment rather than a one-time event. Subscribing to a product/service is fully congruent with a focus on upgrading.

20. Ties and dependence are the negative sides of being part of a system, as becomes clear in many contexts. It is naive to think, for example, that it is primarily the consumer that influences which products are launched. The media researcher Mika Pantzar shows how Intel is concentrating on creating new uses and new users in order to keep up with the rhythm of development, and how representatives of Philips admit that there really is no need for some of the products they are about to launch – the challenge lies in creating a need for them (Pantzar 2000: 3; cf. Williams 2000).

References

Literature

Appadurai, Arjun (1997 [1996]), *Modernity at Large: Cultural Dimensions of Globalization*, New Delhi: Oxford University Press.

Apple's G4 computers, 1999. Unpublished brochure.

Bayley, Stephen (1999), 'The Speed of Life', *New Statesman*, 25 October.

Berg, Per Olof (2000), 'Dreaming up a Region? Strategic Management as Invocation', in Per Olof Berg, Anders Linde-Laursen and Orvar Löfgren (eds), *Invoking a Transnational Metropolis: the Making of the Öresund Region*, Lund: Studentlitteratur.

Bergquist, Magnus (1999), 'Framtiden går på utställning: Om utopins lätthet och materiens tröghet', in Eva Fägerborg and Christina Westergren (eds), *Mus och människa: Om IT som kulturellt fenomen*, Stockholm: Nordiska museets förlag.

—— (2001), 'Framtidsfixarna', *Kulturella perspektiv*, 3.

Bringéus, Nils-Arvid (1986 [1976]), *Människan som kulturvarelse*, Malmö: Liber förlag.

Campbell, Colin (1992), 'The Desire for the New: its Nature and Social Location as Presented in Theories of Fashion and Modern Consumerism', in Roger Silverstone and Eric Hirsch (eds), *Consuming Technologies: Media and Information in Domestic Spaces*, London: Routledge.

Castells, Manuel (1996), *The Rise of the Network Society*, Oxford: Blackwell.

CultureMag, May 2000.

Dahle, Cheryl (2000), 'Mind Games', *Fast Company*, January/February 2000.

Dyson, Esther (1997), *Release 2.0: a Design for Living in the Digital Age*, London: Viking.

Evans, Philip B. and Wurster, Thomas S. (1999), 'Strategy and the New Economics of Information', in Don Tapscott (ed.), *Creating Value in the Network Economy*, Boston: Harvard Business School Press.

Fast Company, April/May.

Garsten, Christina (1994), *Apple World: Core and Periphery in a Transnational Organizational Culture*, Stockholm Studies in Social Anthropology, 33, Stockholm: Almqvist & Wiksell.

Gateway 1999. Unpublished brochure.

Hertz, Paul (1999), 'Synesthetic Art – An Imaginary Number?' *Leonardo*, 5.

Hoxmeier, John A. (2000), 'Software Preannouncements and Their Impact on Customers' Perceptions and Vendor Reputation', *Journal of Management Information Systems*, 17(1), Summer.

Ideland, Malin (2000), 'Från grottmänniska till cyborg', in Susanne Lundin and Lynn Åkesson (eds), *Arvets kultur: Essäer om genetik och samhälle,* Lund: Nordic Academic Press.

Idvall, Markus (2000), *Kartors kraft: Regionen som samhällsvision i Öresundsbrons tid*, Lund: Nordic Academic Press.

Johansson, Magnus (1997), *Smart, Fast and Beautiful: on Rhetoric of Technology and Computing Discourse in Sweden 1955–1995*, Linköping: Linköping University.

Johnson, Steven (1997), *Interface Culture: How New Technology Transforms the Way We Create and Communicate*, New York: Basic.

Kelly, Kevin (1999), *New Rules for the New Economy: Ten Radical Strategies for a Connected World*, New York: Penguin.

Knorr-Cetina, Karin (1999), *Epistemic Cultures: How the Sciences Make Knowledge*, Cambridge, MA: Harvard University Press.

Lunell, Hans (1994), *Datalogi: Begreppen och tekniken*, Lund: Studentlitteratur.

Manovich, Lev (2001), *The Language of New Media*, Cambridge, MA: MIT Press.

Nielsen, Jakob (2000), *Designing Web Usability: the Practice of Simplicity*, New York: New Riders.

Nilsson, Fredrik (1999), *När en timme blir tio minuter: En studie av förväntan inför Öresundsbron*, Lund: Historiska Media.

Norman, Donald A. (1999), *The Invisible Computer: Why Good Products Can Fail, the Personal Computer is so Complex, and Information Appliances are the Solution*, Cambridge, MA: MIT Press.

Pantzar, Mika (2000), 'Consumption as Work, Play, and Art: Representations of the Consumer in Future Scenarios', *Design Issues*, 16(3), Autumn.

PC Extra 4/1999.

Raymond, Eric S. (2001), *Katedralen och Basaren: En oavsiktlig revolutionärs tankar kring Linux och öppen källkod*, Nora: Nya Doxa. [see English-language version in Chapter 11 References, this volume.]

Ristilammi, Per-Markku (1997), 'En längtan bortom maskinen: Om virtuell kroppslighet', *Kulturella perspektiv*, 2.

Ritzer, George (1999), *Enchanting a Disenchanted World: Revolutionizing the Means of Consumption,* Thousand Oaks: Pine Forge Press.

Salomonsson, Karin (2001), 'Karriärens kropp', *Kulturella perspektiv*, 3.

Schnapp, Jeffrey T. (1999), 'Crash (Speed as Engine of Individuation)', *Modernism/Modernity*, 6(1).

Shusterman, Richard (2000), *Pragmatist Aesthetics: Living Beauty, Rethinking Art*, 2nd edn, Lanham, MD: Rowman & Littlefield.

Strannegård, Lars (2002), 'Nothing Compares to the New', in: Ingalill Holmberg, Miriam Salzer-Mörling and Lars Strannegård (eds), *Stuck in the Future? Tracing the 'New Economy'*, Stockholm: Bookhouse Publishing AB.

Strannegård, Lars and Friberg, Maria (2001), *Already Elsewhere: Om lek, iden-titet och hastighet i affärslivet*, Stockholm: Raster förlag.

Théberge, Paul (1997), *Any Sound You Can Imagine: Making Music/Consuming Technology,* Hanover: Wesleyan University Press.

Thrift, Nigel (1996), *Spatial Formations*, London: Sage.

—— (2001), '"It's the Romance, not the Finance, that Makes the Business Worth Pursuing": Disclosing a New Market Culture', *Economy and Society*, 30(4), November.

Williams, Rosalind (2000), '"All that is Solid Melts into Air": Historians of Technology in the Information Revolution', *Technology and Culture*, 41, October.

Willim, Robert. (1997), 'Tillbaka till framtiden: Om musiktrender och elektronik', *Kulturella perspektiv*, 2.

—— (2002), Framtid.nu – flyt och friktion i ett snabbt företag, Stockholm/ Stehag: Brutus Östlings Bokförlag Symposion.

www.apple.com, Accessed 21 February 2001.

www.brikks.com, Accessed 5 April 2001.

www.api-network.com/mc/0006/instantaneity.html, Accessed 2 August 2000.

www.framfab.se, Accessed 24 October 1999, 12 January 2000.

www.idg.se, Accessed 18 July 2000.

www.useit.com/papers/responsetime.html, Accessed 28 February 2001.

Zorkoczy, Peter and Heap, Nicholas (1995), *Information Technology: an Introduction*, 4th edn, London: Pitman.

7

Networking as a Form of Life: The Transnational Movement of Internet Pioneers

Paula Uimonen

On 5 June 2001, the Sheraton Hotel in Stockholm was a primary hub for people actively involved in the global expansion of the Internet. The hotel hosted the registration for the annual conference of the Internet Society (ISOC), INET 2001, which was held at the Stockholm International Fairs (Stockholmsmässan), the city's largest exhibition hall, on 6–8 June (http://www.isoc.org/inet2001). While at the Sheraton, conference participants could attend the technical tutorials arranged in conjunction with the event, along with the annual Developing Countries Networking Symposium. One of the most prestigious hotels in Stockholm, the Sheraton was also where the VIPs of INET 2001 were staying, and a conveniently short walk from the Stockholm City Hall where an opening reception was held.

As I walked through the doors of the Sheraton, I entered a familiar field scene. Making my way to the registration desk on the mezzanine floor, I encountered Internet pioneers whose life stories I had recorded on previous occasions, not to mention people whom I had met in a more informal manner. Throughout the day, the scene repeated itself as I attended some of the sessions on networking in developing countries and later in the evening, the reception at the City Hall. Representing a strategic node in the transnational and translocal networking that soon evolved into my main data-gathering method, I had attended these INET events since 1997, as part of my fieldwork for my doctoral research on the social dynamics of Internet development in developing countries (Uimonen 2001).

Hosted in different parts of the world, the annual INET conferences represent the materialization of the Internet community. The Internet community is a loose constellation of people, scattered around the world, who are devoted to the Internet and the spirit in which it has developed. One of the most prestigious manifestations of the Internet community, and especially its core of Internet pioneers, is the Internet Society. Founded in 1992 by some of the most well known American Internet pioneers, the Internet Society is headquartered in the United States. Nonetheless, reflecting the global expansion of the Internet, the organization has evolved accordingly. Today the Internet Society draws on a membership of some 8,600 people in over 170 countries and has chapters in some 50 countries around the world (see http://www.isoc.org).

In the following, I will discuss the networking activities of Internet pioneers, drawing on my Internet Society/INET ethnography. Combining anthropological network studies (Hannerz 1980) with the concept of cultural management (Hannerz 1992), I will focus on the ways in which Internet pioneers participate in the cultural process of Internet development. In terms of cultural management, the Internet pioneers embody two organizational frameworks of contemporary cultural flow, that of *form of life* and that of *movement* (Hannerz 1992: 46–50). Their participation in the production and reproduction of the meaning of the Internet is based on their everyday involvement with the Internet and their desire to extend access to this technology to other people.

An instance of decentralized, bottom-up type of cultural flow, the culture of the Internet pioneers reflects the boundary-crossing nature of networks (Hannerz 1980). Such boundary crossing translates into social relations demarcated by a considerable degree of fluidity, a prime example of which is the Internet community that many Internet pioneers subscribe to. Based on shared interests rather than physical proximity, the Internet community is above all a *community of interest* (Graham 1999; Rheingold 1994), a transnational community that cuts across organizational, national and continental boundaries. This community is but one example of the transnational social landscapes, what could be defined as *netscapes* (Uimonen 2001), that frame on-line social interaction. As exemplified by the Internet pioneers, these instances of global cultural flow combine a localized sense of belonging with a global, cosmopolitan outlook.

The experiences of the Internet pioneers allow us to appraise the linkages between virtual mediations and socially anchored practices that demarcate the Internet, their networked brokering reflecting some of the core characteristics of a media technology most commonly defined as the network of networks. In other words, representing the *social nodes of the Internet*, the Internet pioneers provide a vantage point from which to assess the social and cultural embeddedness of the Internet, or what I have elsewhere referred to as *the culture of networking* (Uimonen 2001).

Pioneering the Culture of Networking

To its pioneers, the Internet is not just a technology, but also a culture. The ethos of this culture is often referred to as 'the spirit of the Internet', important components of which are the 'sharing' and 'spreading' of knowledge of, and by way of, the Internet. This knowledge-sharing ethos of the Internet is traceable to the origins of its predecessor, the ARPANET, a program of the Advanced Research

Projects Agency (ARPA) of the US Department of Defense dating back to the late 1960s. The ARPANET was aimed at allowing researchers to share costly computing facilities and its development was characterized by collaborative pooling of resources and open dialogue (Hafner and Lyon 1996: 145). Knowledge-sharing is also characteristic of the communicative aspects of the Internet which have informed the development of some of the most important applications, including electronic mail and electronic discussions lists (Naughton 2000).

The perception that the Internet is a culture points toward the social and cultural embeddedness of technologies and technological artefacts. As much as technology tends to be viewed as something that affects societies from the outside, social-science treatments of technological development point to the inseparability of the technological and the social (e.g. Escobar 1994; Pfaffenberger 1992; Hakken 1999; Latour 1993; Miller and Slater 2000). I have argued elsewhere that the Internet represents a cultural construct, the characteristics of which I refer to as the culture of networking (Uimonen 2001). The culture of networking is both a reflection of the technical interfaces of computer networking and the ideas and values that have accompanied their development, patterns of meaning that in turn have been influenced by the wider social environment framing Internet development.

In terms of social distribution, the culture of networking is most prominently manifested in the Internet pioneers. Representing the social nodes of the Internet, these are the people who have actively contributed to its development around the world. Reflecting the multifaceted nature of the Internet, Internet pioneers form a heterogeneous category of people of different professional backgrounds, rather than a specific occupational type. Technical developers are of course well represented in this category of people, their skills being focused on the development and maintenance of the technical infrastructure of the Internet. But from the outset, the Internet has attracted people from a variety of professions. In tracing the networks of Internet pioneers, I have encountered legal experts, policy-makers, educators and librarians, to name but a few occupational categories one would not necessarily associate with a technology. Similarly, given the global reach of the Internet, its pioneers are drawn from various national backgrounds. In a national context, the introduction of the Internet is often attributable to the efforts of pioneering citizens of that country. Even so, their own introduction to the Internet, and their subsequent efforts to introduce it to their own country, tends to entail contacts with people in other countries, as will be further discussed below.

When it comes to the issue of social stratification, it should be acknowledged that Internet pioneers tend to belong to the relatively privileged social stratum of well-educated, well-travelled professionals. Again, the elitist nature of their social profile is typical of the social make-up of Internet users in general, most of whom continue to belong to the urban/suburban middle class. In this regard one could view the Internet Society as a rather elitist organization, its members being drawn from the wealthier social strata of societies around the world, whether classified as developed or developing countries.

To the Internet pioneers, the culture of networking is a form of life. Their perspectival constructs are informed by the 'everyday practicalities of production and reproduction' that an Internet-oriented 'form of life' entails, the orientation of which permeates their daily activities, be it in the workplace, at home or in their social circles (Hannerz 1992: 47). Not only do these people have the Internet as a significant component of their professional and personal activities, but also they have incorporated the ethos of the culture of networking into their daily lives. Regardless of what national or organizational environment these people work in, they subscribe to the knowledge-sharing ethos of the culture of networking, their own efforts being aimed at providing people around the world with access to decentralized, uninterrupted flows of information. In so doing, they rely on the principles of networking, including the participation in communities of interest that characterizes on-line social formations.

Let us return to INET 2001, the annual conference of the Internet Society, for a more detailed picture of the culture of networking in practice. One of the more visually striking characteristics of INET events is the presence of the Internet, as expressed in an abundance of computers and cables. At the Stockholm International Fairs, the main entrance lobby hosted a dozen computers connected to the Internet, allowing participants to check and send e-mails, and browse the Web. This area was almost as busy as the large tables placed in the corridors leading to the conference rooms where participants could plug in their own machines. In the conference rooms, the organizers provided a connected computer for the panelists, while some members of the audience took notes of the sessions on their laptops.

As is common in business and academic worlds in general, this connected environment, temporarily set up in the space of an exhibition centre, testifies to the desirability of being within easy reach of the Internet among people acculturated in the culture of networking. Accessibility to the Internet allows participants to carry on their daily activities, even in far-flung parts of the world. If anything, the conference participants expect connectivity to the Internet, at sufficiently high data-carrying capacity, and it is not uncommon that they log on to the Net at recurring intervals.

Although much of the essential infrastructure required for INET events is available at the conference sites selected for the hosting, this is not always the case. In 1997, INET 97 was held in Kuala Lumpur, Malaysia. The conference site, the Putra World Trade Centre, had all the amenities required of a modern conference facility, including such a chilled air-conditioned environment that one could easily forget being in the tropics. Add to this the ultra-modern cityscape of Kuala Lumpur, especially the famous Petronas Towers, and the host environments seemed a perfect match for the event. Except for connectivity. In order to provide sufficiently high levels of connectivity for the INET event, and the training workshops for developing country participants that preceded it, the government service provider upgraded the country's data-carrying capacity. Even so, unable to have high-speed access in their hotel rooms, some participants chose an early return to their better-connected home environments.

The presence of the Internet certifies the social capital of participants. Most panelists use computerized presentations, typically PowerPoint, when addressing the audience of a given session. It is not unusual that a panel of five speakers is accompanied by an equal amount of laptops lined up one next to the other. Once when giving a talk at an INET event, I chose not to use computerized visual aids. Following my session some participants offered to teach me how to use the tools. The fact that these people felt that my presentation suffered from its non-technical format, and their assumption that it was a result of my technical ignorance, indicated how much value is placed on technical competence when addressing an INET audience.

Although technical prowess and high-speed access to the Internet form important components of INET conferences, the main purpose of these events is, however, social networking. It is the ability to meet people face-to-face that is the primary attraction, as exemplified by the name itself, which stands for International Networking. Granted, participants typically use the Internet in preparation for INET, information on the event being posted on the Internet Society Web site and distributed through the organization's electronic bulletin. Submissions of abstracts for papers and panels, and registrations for the event, as well as accommodation and transportation are typically conducted on-line. Participants also use e-mail to check if particular friends and colleagues will be attending the event, as well as to organize meetings in advance. Even so, the Internet is used as a facilitator for a social, real-life get-together.

The opening reception is an informative example of the value placed on social networking. Catering to some 1,000–1,500 conference participants, this reception is hosted in a sufficiently large compound that also confirms the status of the event. In Stockholm, it was held at the Stockholm City Hall, a historical landmark where prestigious events such as the Nobel Prize dinners are hosted. On 5 June 2001, from 7 to 9 p.m., the Blue Hall of this historical site was devoted to the Internet community. Tables were laid out offering a selection of Swedish delicacies, accompanied by various refreshments. The room was teeming with activity, as individuals mingled through the crowd, greeting people they already knew, while introducing themselves or being introduced to new acquaintances.

Following the reception, some people coalesced in smaller groups and continued their interaction in nearby settings.

Given the size of INET events, certain techniques are used to facilitate the social networking. As at large conferences in other areas, participants wear badges denoting their name, organizational affiliation and country of residence. These badges are worn throughout the conference, allowing participants to identify one another at a glance. Sometimes the first name is displayed in larger letters, a tribute to the informal nature of the Internet, but often it is the full name that is enlarged. These badges are accompanied by business cards, which most participants carry with them. Etiquette dictates that if a person offers you his/her business card you must accept it and give one of yours in return.

This reciprocal exchange of cards facilitates networking during and after INET events. A participant can approach an individual with whom he or she is interested in interacting, offering his or her business card as a way of introduction. The exchange of cards is then accompanied by some introductory remarks, after which the individuals can engage in further conversation, or continue their networking with others. Following sessions, members of the audience often approach the panelists, exchanging their cards with speakers with whom they are interested in networking. After the conclusion of the INET event, participants are able to follow up through e-mail on the contacts made.

The emphasis placed on social networking reveals the extent to which networking serves as a primary modus operandi for members of the Internet community. Representing the materialization of a community of interest, in this case one that is devoted to the promotion of the Internet and the spirit in which it has been developed, the annual INET conferences allow community members to establish, maintain and expand their networks. Reflecting the subcultural characteristics of the culture of networking, the 'collectively held meanings' that participants share 'need not encompass every aspect of the flow of meaning within this relational segment', but is often 'an "in principle" variety' that in turn is related to the many ways in which subcultures are embedded in 'a larger whole' (Hannerz 1992: 71–5). At INET events, the overriding principle of a shared devotion to the Internet allows people of differing professional and cultural backgrounds to achieve a sense of shared values and commitments.

In the Internet community, networking also serves as a principal means for professional advancement. This is all too evident at INET events where networking is often carried out with a view to identifying people that can be called upon or collaborated with professionally, the individual ties forged also representing the linking of organizations and projects. This practice corresponds to the boundary-crossing nature of networks. From an anthropological perspective, networks represent a concept with which to appreciate the ways in which social agents cross and manipulate institutional boundaries, a process in which they actively use their roles rather than being constrained by them (Hannerz 1980).

The proficiency with which people are able to carry out networking is, just like the culture of networking, unevenly distributed. As much as networks represent boundary-crossing, decentralized social formations, they are not immune to principles of social stratification, as exemplified by the social profile of Internet pioneers discussed above. Similarly, the annual get-together of the Internet community is only accessible to people who have the resources required for registration fees, travel and accommodation. The elitist configuration of the Internet community is further diversified internally. There are Internet pioneers of great international repute, and there are Internet pioneers who are barely known, even in the Internet community.

At INET events, various status markers are in operation, some of them visible, others more intangible. One of the most visual status markers is the tags added to certain badges, denoting if the person is a speaker, an exhibitor, a member of the Internet Society's Board of Trustees or the INET Program Committee. These tags set apart the average participant from those playing a more active role, and one that is awarded a greater status. The plenary sessions represent another visible status marker. Organized in the mornings, they are hosted in the largest conference rooms available. The opening plenary session is usually devoted to the Internet Society, leading members of which report on the organization's various activities. This is followed by plenary sessions devoted to the themes of the conference, typically chaired by well-established members of the Society.

A more intangible, but more significant status marker is the nodal positioning of people in various networks. The ability to establish and manage contacts with strategically positioned people from around the world is not an easy task, yet it plays an important role in the establishment and maintenance of social capital. In the Internet community, the extent and composition of an individual's network serves as an important status marker. Here the axiom 'it is not what you know, but whom you know' is prominently manifested. In addition to facilitating professional advancement, an individual's network confirms his or her social status, the nodal positioning in a given network serving as a social signifier.

I recall an informal dinner with one of my INET contacts, let's call him Andrew, who attends these events mainly for their networking value. In explaining what he does for a living, Andrew explained his professional activities in terms of networking. Andrew spends a lot of his time travelling, meeting with visionary people around the world. He also attends a lot of conferences, again in order to identify interesting, and in many cases professionally valuable, people. This vast network allows Andrew to put people in touch with one another, people who have similar interests and/or objectives. In so doing, he hopes that people will acknowledge his assistance and make their own contacts available to him, if and when needed.

People with an extensive network are thus able to play a brokering role of considerable significance. In network studies, a broker is 'a person with a particular kind of network range' (Hannerz 1980: 190). Typically, the broker uses his or her network in such a way that he or she *facilitates* contacts among persons, groups, or institutions who are otherwise not within easy reach of one another' (ibid.: 191, emphasis in original). In the Internet community, those who are able to play this brokering role are generally awarded a higher status. Having access to a broad range of people, in different organizational and national settings, they are able to call upon the services of key people when needed. Similarly, they are also well placed to initiate or facilitate contacts between appropriate people, the undertaking of which solidifies their own network(s), while confirming the status of their nodal positioning.

Netscapes in the Developing World

Attracting Internet pioneers from around the world, INET events resemble something of a United Nations of the Internet community. Although the lingua franca of the event is English, it is spoken in a multitude of accents, and while most participants appear in casual professional attire, others choose more colourful garments in tribute to the traditions of their countries of origin. The global thrust of the event is also manifested in the conference program, which contains speakers from a multitude of countries. Even so, it would be a mistake to take this global orientation as an indicator of a community devoted to the replacement of the local and the national with a deterritorialized cyberspace. Quite the contrary, the very people involved in the promotion of the Internet, and with it the culture of networking, are actively linking the global and the local, the virtual and the real. This linking is achieved through the spread of Internet access around the world, providing people with opportunities to use a transnational medium that connects peoples in various places.

Internet development in developing countries is a good example of the transnational linkages and interactions that demarcate the global expansion of the culture of networking. The cast of characters involved in this process consists of people from both the developed and the developing world. We find people from the developed world who have devoted their time and effort to the expansion of the Internet in developing countries. We also find people from the developing world who have pioneered Internet development in their countries of origin. In the latter case, the Internet pioneers in question have typically been exposed to the Internet during their temporary residence in a developed country, often while undergoing higher education. Upon returning to their countries of origin they typically use their overseas contacts to introduce and spread the Internet in their own countries.

We also find concrete instances of transnational collaboration between people from the developed and developing world. The Network Training Workshops organized by the Internet Society is a prime example of a transnational node of technology transfer.[1] Initiated in 1993 by Dr George Sadowsky, an American with extensive experience of working with developing countries, the Network Training Workshops provide training in Internet technology to professionals in developing countries. To date, some 2,500 people from over 130 developing countries have received training through these annual workshops. The trainers, most of whom originate from Europe, North America and Australia, are well-known and well-established Internet pioneers, usually based at universities.

These Internet Society workshops have played a catalytic role in Internet development in developing countries, workshop attendees often having pioneered the Internet in their countries of origin. For instance, one of the participants of the 1998 workshop set up the first Internet Service Provider (connectivity hub for local Internet access, usually known as ISP) in Timbuktu upon his return to Mali. And two other participants, who also attended the 1999 workshop, were involved in setting up the first Internet Service Provider in Bhutan in June 1999. Similarly, when the Internet was first established in Laos, three of the students who had access to this experimental e-mail service partook in the Internet Society workshops. The organizers who, according to George Sadowsky, select participants according to 'their ability to do something in their institutional and national framework' to recognize and encourage this pioneering role.[2]

Social networking complements the training provided during these workshops. During the 1998 workshop hosted in Geneva, the workshop tutorials, accommodation and cafeteria were all in adjacent buildings, forming something of an Internet enclave in the student facilities of Cité Universitaire. The physical environment of the workshop was thus highly tuned to social networking. Networking is further facilitated by the context in which the participants find themselves. Their shared interest in Internet development already provides them with a sense of commonality, despite their diverse national and organizational backgrounds, as does their shared experience of undergoing training.

The training and networking is further accentuated during the INET conference that succeeds the workshop. Here the workshop participants are given the opportunity to attend the numerous sessions and technical tutorials covered by the conference, as well as the social events organized in conjunction with the event. In addition to forging ties with fellow workshop participants, the conference provides the trainees with ample opportunities to network with a larger crowd of people, all of whom share their interest in the Internet.

The Internet Society training workshop is an example not only of technology transfer but also of acculturation into the culture of networking. When addressing INET 2000 in Yokohama, George Sadowsky underlined that spreading the Internet through the developing world was not just a question of technological development but also of 'passing on the spirit of the Internet', including 'sharing what you know and extending the Internet where it hasn't been before'.[3] At the training workshop, the spirit of the Internet is passed on to a multitude of Internet pioneers. Trained in network technology and exposed to the principles of networking, participants are acculturated in the culture of networking, the ethos of which is inseparable from the technology they are taught to master.

Internet development can thus be interpreted as an instance of cultural management, a process in which actors and networks of actors participate in the construction and reconstruction of culture (Hannerz 1992: 17). An outcome of culturally mediated social agency, the Internet is, like all technologies, a cultural invention, one that carries meaning (Escobar 1994; Mackay 1995). As such, the Internet is subject to cultural management, as different actors involved in the process of Internet development participate in the creation, maintenance and distribution of the meaning of the Internet.

In terms of a cultural process, Internet development is above all a movement. Like many movements, the culture of networking emerges from a form of life, in this case one that denotes a devotion to the spirit of the Internet (Hannerz 1992: 50). Similarly, Internet development is a movement in culture, one that is aimed at transforming meaning (ibid.: 49). In the case of the Internet pioneers, their culturally transformative objectives are inspired by the knowledge-sharing ethos of the culture of networking. Reflecting the Internet itself, this movement is particularly decentralized, and it relies very heavily on the voluntary efforts of individuals (ibid.: 50). The culture of networking is also demarcated by the 'outward-oriented missionizing' that characterizes movements; in this case a pronounced desire to extend the Internet and the spirit in which it has been developed around the world (ibid.). This missionizing thrust is also evident in the organizational culture of companies such as Apple Computer (Garsten 1994).

In this regard, it is worth interpreting the Internet Society as a transnational movement in culture. Although many of its members are drawn from state agencies and commercial enterprises, the structure of the Society is that of a volunteer organization, or as it describes itself 'a nonprofit professional membership organization' (see http://www.isoc.org). The Internet Society is thus structurally removed from the two dominant organizational frameworks of cultural process; the state and the market (Hannerz 1992: 46–50). If anything, the mission of the Internet Society is to be a movement in culture, the organization's mandate revolving around the spread of Internet technology and culture, as expressed in its mission statement: 'To assure the open development, evolution and use of the Internet for the benefit of all people throughout the world'.

Let us briefly return to INET 2001 for a sample of the missionizing work in which Internet pioneers engage. Entitled 'The Quest for Global Self-Regulation', the governance summit plenary panel of this event was devoted to one of the most hotly debated issues in the Internet community: the organization, allocation and management of domain names (domain names is the technical term for Web addresses). These functions are currently managed by ICANN, the Internet Corporation for Assigned Names and Numbers (http://www.icann.org), an organization formed in 1998 in response to a widely felt need to restructure the domain-name system (for background, see Abbate 2000: 189–90).

Perceived as a first attempt at Internet governance, the restructuring of the domain-name system has remained a focal issue for members of the Internet community, and their missionizing is largely inspired by the culture of networking. Insisting on a more participatory bottom-up approach, along with a more global representation, members of the Internet community have pushed for a consensus-building approach, while promoting a self-regulatory organizational framework (see for instance NGO and Academic ICANN Study (NAIS) Report, 2001). The meetings of the Internet Corporation for Assigned Names and Numbers are often held in conjunction with INET, as in the case of INET 2001 immediately prior to it, illustrating the importance of domain names for the Internet community. This is also why the INET 2001 governance summit plenary was devoted to the issue, drawing on established members of ICANN and the Internet community.

In terms of a movement, Internet development in developing countries is an expression of the construction of transnational social landscapes. The Internet pioneers form the social core of transnational networks that, paraphrasing one of the most common Internet browsers, can be termed 'netscapes' (Uimonen 1999, 2001). In using the term 'netscapes', I am building on Appadurai's (1990) concept of transnational social landscapes, while adding a category that is captured in neither his 'technoscapes' nor his 'mediascapes'. Seeing that the Internet is best viewed as a medium based on networking technologies, it traverses the 'global configuration and distribution of technology' of technoscapes as well as the 'capabilities to produce and disseminate information' of mediascapes (ibid.: 297–9).

The Internet pioneers represent the main navigators of the cultural flows of netscapes. A considerable part of their daily activities is carried out in the networked environments of the Internet. Moreover, they actively contribute to the very existence of these deterritorialized landscapes of cultural expression and experimentation, their pioneering efforts being aimed at making them available to people around the world. In so doing, they themselves use the translocal space of the Internet to co-ordinate their activities, the network of networks allowing them to carry out the transnational networking and brokering that Internet development entails.

Even so, as much as the Internet pioneers are devoted to the expansion of deterritorialized, boundary-crossing netscapes of global cultural flow, their activities remain anchored in existing social realities. In developing countries, Internet development is closely tied to nation building, a process in which Internet pioneers play an important brokering role as they seek to utilize the Internet as a tool for nationwide modernization (Uimonen 2001). In addition to being the very people who bring the Internet to a given country, it is Internet pioneers who bring the Internet to the attention of political decision-makers. This is also where the movement aspect of the culture of networking comes into play, as Internet pioneers target politicians and policy makers in order to raise their awareness of the significance and characteristics of the Internet.

Malaysia, host of INET 97, provides an example of the linkages between Internet development and nation building. Although a Malaysian chapter of the Internet Society has yet to be formed, Malaysian Internet pioneers were all too aware of the prestige awarded to INET events in the Internet community. Seeing that most INET events are hosted in the richer parts of the world – with the exception of INET 94 held in Prague, no other INET event has been hosted in a developing or emerging country – the opportunity to host INET 97 was particularly prestigious to Malaysia. In hosting the event, Malaysian Internet pioneers sought to ascertain Malaysia's place on the international Internet map, especially the country's ambitious Multimedia Super Corridor (MSC) project, which was featured in a special session.

Important as this international exposure was, INET 97 was also an imperative occasion to spread awareness of the Internet within Malaysia. Before, during and following the conference, the event was given extensive coverage in local media. The print media underlined the significance and timeliness of the event, encouraged readers to attend because 'Malaysians should not miss the opportunity to gain as much knowledge as possible from the conference', seeing that 'Internet experts, advocates and enthusiasts' would be discussing 'issues that have a significant bearing on future developments of the Internet' (Sani 1997). Similarly, against the backdrop of the Kuala Lumpur skyline, news reporters were highlighting the event on national TV broadcasts, along with the national slogan *IT boleh* (IT can) and a reiteration of the aims of the MSC to catapult the nation into a knowledge society.

INET events can also serve as a platform for minority advocacy efforts, as was the case with the 'Indigenous and Diaspora Groups and the Internet' panel at INET 2001. Organized by Steve Cisler, an American with a history of involvement in indigenous Internet usage, this was the first INET session ever to focus on cultural minorities and one of the few INET 2001 sessions that was Web cast. The panel consisted of a Forest Sami representative, a Maori representative and a member of the Tatar diaspora.

Networking as a Methodology

Conferences, workshops and meetings as field sites, discourse analysis as a means with which to appreciate the cultural construction of a technology, and interaction with members of a transnational community to identify strategic nodes of Internet pioneers are all examples of the methodological strategies I have employed to study the social dynamics of Internet development in developing countries. The focus of this investigation, and the multiple ways in which it has been carried out, is an example of networking. Not in the sense of formal network analysis (e.g. Garton, Haythornethwaite and Wellman 1999), in which the range of a given network is mapped and quantified, but in accordance with the principles of networking that demarcate the activities of the Internet pioneers. In anthropological terminology, this networking translates into 'multi-sited' and 'translocal' fieldwork, relying on 'polymorphous engagements' and 'circumstantial activism', rather than more traditional participant observation over an extended period in a specific locale.

Networking for the purpose of carrying out ethnographic research is an example of the 'polymorphous engagements' that my research has entailed (Gusterson 1997). Gusterson proposes the concept of polymorphous engagements to identify a methodology that involves interactions with informants across dispersed sites, while collecting data from a disparate range of sources in different ways (ibid.: 116). Representing an 'eclectic mix' of research techniques, polymorphous engagements can include conducting of formal interviews and extensive reading of newspapers as well as official documents while paying attention to popular culture and doing fieldwork over the telephone and by e-mail. Not surprisingly, these research strategies have a tendency to 'blur the disciplinary boundaries between anthropology, sociology, political science, cultural studies, and even journalism' (ibid.).

In this investigation, my polymorphous engagements have taken different forms, including and reaching beyond my Internet Society engagements. My interactions with informants have taken place in a variety of settings, ranging from the informant's professional office environment to international conferences. The data gathering has also extended well beyond engagements with informants. Since 1995, I have followed international and national television broadcasts about the Internet, read newspapers and magazines dealing with the subject, watched movies depicting the Internet, and paid attention to how the Internet has become integrated with various aspects of popular culture, including television series and advertisements. I have also gone through an extensive amount of textual material.

These polymorphous engagements have been carried out in various parts of the world, my investigation being an example of 'multi-sited fieldwork' (Marcus 1995). Born out of studies oriented toward world-system-based and interdisciplinary contexts, multi-sited fieldwork has become increasingly popular over the years (ibid.: 97), especially in the growing field of 'transnational anthropology' (Hannerz 1998, 2001). In my case, attending INET events has already involved a string of localities: Kuala Lumpur, Geneva, San José in California, Yokohama and Stockholm. Two of these sites, Kuala Lumpur and Geneva, have also served as nodal points for more extensive fieldwork, while the Geneva and Stockholm nodes also represent doing fieldwork at home.

To be expected, Internet use has played a crucial role in my investigation. Much of the networking pertaining to the development of the Internet takes place on-line, in the virtual environments of cyberspace. While cyberspace thus presents a 'site', it is not really a location, but rather a scene for various activities that by virtue of being mediated are removed from any specific place. The 'site' of cyberspace points to the need to acknowledge more 'translocal' sites, the existence of which are important components of the network/s of sites that multi-sited fieldwork aims to capture (Hannerz 1998).

The Internet has clearly facilitated my efforts in following the transnational Internet community, as well as providing a wealth of useful data in general (see also Uimonen 1999). I have relied heavily on e-mail to set up and follow up on interviews, and as a means to stay in touch with informants to follow developments taking place beyond the period of fieldwork. Even so, reflecting the practices of the Internet pioneers, most of the time I have used e-mail communication to complement rather than replace face-to-face meetings, the latter allowing for a smoother establishment of trust. By subscribing to electronic mailing lists, I have also participated in various on-line discussion groups. Web sites have provided me with a wealth of relevant material and I have also set up my own project web site to facilitate the dissemination of information to informants and other interested parties (http://www.i-connect.ch/uimonen).

Immersion into the virtual worlds of cyberspace has allowed me to get a better feel for the topic investigated, the importance of which cannot be overstated. My own exposure to the different interfaces that demarcate on-line interaction has facilitated my establishment of empathic relations with Internet pioneers. It has also allowed for a more interactive research process. At a time when many, if not most, anthropologists have incorporated the Internet into their professional and personal lives (representing as they do the academic community that first had access to it), my immersion into the network of networks has also allowed me to problematize what many take for granted. This holds particularly true for the historical and comparative scope of my study, which differs from the tendency to focus on specific applications (often Web sites), on-line constellations (virtual communities and chat rooms) or locales (Internet use in a specific country/community/group).

Carried out in a multitude of localities and settings, including the translocal site of cyberspace, my research has included playing the role of a 'circumstantial activist' (Marcus 1995). Faced with a situation characterized by cross-cutting and sometimes contradictory personal commitments, I have shared the feeling of 'doing more than just ethnography' that multi-sited research often entails (ibid.: 113–14). This holds particularly true for the circumstantial nature of my involvement, which has entailed my working *with* different subjects in certain sites, and in other sites *against* them (ibid.). I have appeared on conference panels with Internet pioneers, addressing issues of common concern. I have also joined Internet pioneers in their political struggles, using my expertise to lend additional weight to their efforts. But I have sometimes also played the role of the devil's advocate, insisting on issues and methodologies that are not common in these contexts, as exemplified by my non-use of PowerPoint on certain occasions, combined with deliberations on non-technical social issues.

All of these activities have relied on the principles of networking, and by extension, the crossing and blurring of boundaries. In my case, the topic of my investigation, the network of networks, is also my primary methodology. Moreover, in carrying out this investigation, I have played a pioneering role similar to that of my informants, my own experiences in doing so overlapping with theirs. And seeing that I have become an avid Internet user, I will always stay engaged with my field.

For anthropologists, such boundary crossing is only likely to become more commonplace as we engage in studies of our own cultures. When our subject matter is a medium that we also use in our daily lives and when our informants are fellow-professionals engaged in activities that are rather similar to our own, it becomes somewhat difficult to maintain a sense of clear boundaries between 'us' and 'them'. Yet, it is precisely by recognizing these similarities and overlaps that we can further the anthropological understanding of the world we live in, an interconnected world where the universal and the particular are intertwined rather than opposed.

Concluding Reflections: Blurring Boundaries

The local/national/global linkages that I have examined in this chapter suggest that far from erasing cultural identities, Internet development is closely linked to a grounded sense of belonging. Even the most transnational of communities, the Internet community, pays tribute to national identities, a symbolic expression of which is the inscription of the country of residence on the badges of INET participants. Nonetheless, this cultural identification is combined with a pronouncedly global outlook. Having interviewed numerous Internet pioneers from around the developing world, I have been struck by the cosmopolitan orientation of their visions of Internet development (Uimonen 2001).

In the case of Internet pioneers, cosmopolitanism is, however, by no means opposed to nationalism. Quite the contrary, as much as they appreciate the global reach and scope of the Internet, the pioneers of the Internet are very much concerned with the issue of national inclusion into a global whole. If anything, their preoccupation with spreading the Internet in developing countries suggests that the objectives of progress that underlie the 'myth of modernization', of which technological development forms an intrinsic part, are aimed at providing the means of 'inclusion' in modern 'world society' (Ferguson 1999). The desire for inclusion, and fear of exclusion, of developing countries in a world order in which access to the Internet is becoming a significant development factor is what motivates the Internet pioneers. This belief in the universal applicability of the Internet is also echoed in the Internet Society's mission, which in 1999 was adjusted to include the statement 'The Internet is for Everyone'.

What we find here is an example of cultural hybridity, of 'glocal' cultural forms in the making (Robertson 1995). It has already been ascertained that locals and cosmopolitans represent two interdependent perspectival categories (Hannerz 1990, 1996). We can use the term 'glocalization' to capture the interdependence between the global and the local, the universal and the particular, which demarcates global interconnectedness (Robertson 1995). This boundary-crossing hybridity is very much present in the perspectives of the Internet pioneers, their activities being aimed at linking together the local and national with the global. This is also comparable to Internet usage in Trinidad where participation in the 'cosmopolitan spaces' of cyberspace allows users to uncover their own differences in relation to 'others and elsewheres' (Miller and Slater 2000: 97–8).

In theoretical terms, in order to grasp the social and cultural embeddedness of the Internet, we need to go beyond binary oppositions between the virtual and the real, the global and the local, the universal and the particular. For instance, Castells's (1998: 350) postulation that the new social structure of the information age is a network society 'made up of networks of production, power, and experience, which construct a culture of virtuality in the global flows that transcend time and space' is somewhat misplaced. Ethnographic studies from around the world point to the continuation, elaboration, negotiation and reconceptualization of social boundaries in the virtual realm (e.g. Garsten 1994; Landzelius, forthcoming), rather than the emergence of a 'culture of real virtuality' (Castells 1998). In this regard, it is useful to assess the global scope of the Internet in terms of netscapes: transnational social landscapes that are constructed and recon-structed by social agents (Appadurai 1990; Hannerz 1992, 1996).

What we are dealing with is a phenomenon that mediates, translates and inter-twines, a network of networks that both crosses and blurs boundaries, stretching them without necessarily erasing them. The culture of networking, the social and cultural embeddedness of the Internet, is a transnational movement. But it is not a culture that hovers above the socially inhabited world. Rather, people like the Internet pioneers, to whom the creation of a space that intertwines different real-ities and activities represents a form of life, drive this culture. This practice of linking, of inter-connecting, is essentially a practice of relating, or what Latour refers to as 'relationism' (Latour 1993: 114). And it is through a better under-standing of the ways in which it relates peoples and places that we can appreciate the Internet.

Notes

1. The following account is based on interviews with George Sadowsky and participant observation at INET events. The account of the 1998 workshop draws on my own observations while doing volunteer work with the organ-izers.
2. Interview with George Sadowsky during INET 98 in Geneva, 26 July 1998.
3. Participant observation at INET 2000, Yokohama, July 2000.

References

Abbate, J. (2000), *Inventing the Internet,* Cambridge, MA: MIT Press.

Appadurai, A. (1990), 'Disjuncture and difference in the global cultural economy', in M. Featherstone (ed.), *Global Culture: Nationalism, Globalization and Modernity*, London: Sage.

Castells, M. (1998), *End of Millennium*, Oxford: Blackwell.

Escobar, A. (1994), 'Welcome to Cyberia: Notes on the Anthropology of Cyberculture', *Current Anthropology*, 35(3): 211–31.

Ferguson, J. (1999), *Expectations of Modernity. Myths and Meanings of Urban Life on the Zambian Copperbelt*, Berkeley: University of California Press.

Garsten, C. (1994), *Apple World: Core and Periphery in a Transnational Organizational Culture*, Stockholm Studies in Social Anthropology, No. 33, Stockholm: Almqvist & Wiksell.

Garton, L., Haythornethwaite, C. and Wellman, B. (1999), 'Studying On-line Social Networks', in S. Jones (ed.), *Doing Internet Research: Critical Issues and Methods for Examining the Net*, London: Sage.

Graham, G. (1999), *The Internet: A Philosophical Inquiry,* London: Routledge.

Gusterson, H. (1997), 'Studying Up Revisited', *PoLAR: Political and Legal Anthropology Review*, 20(1): 114–19.

Hafner, K. and Lyon, M. (1996), *Where Wizards Stay Up Late: the Origins of the Internet*, New York: Simon & Schuster.

Hakken, D. (1999), *CYBORGS@CYBERSPACE: an Ethnographer Looks to the Future*, London: Routledge.

Hannerz, U. (1980), *Exploring the City: Inquiries Toward an Urban Anthropology*, New York: Columbia University Press.

—— (1990), 'Cosmopolitans and Locals in World Culture', in M. Featherstone (ed.), *Global Culture. Nationalism, Globalization and Modernity*, London: Sage.

—— (1992), *Cultural Complexity: Studies in the Social Organization of Meaning*, New York: Columbia University Press.

—— (1996), *Transnational Connections: Culture, People, Places*, London: Routledge.

—— (1998), 'Transnational Research', in H.R. Bernard (ed.), *Handbook of Methods in Anthropology*, Walnut Creek, CA: Altamira Press.

—— (2001), 'Introduktion: när fältet blir translokalt', in U. Hannerz (ed.), *Flera fält i ett: socialantropologer om translokala fältstudier*, Stockholm: Carlsson Bokförlag.

Internet Society (2000), http://www.isoc.org

ICANN (1987), http://www.icann.org

Landzelius, K. (ed.) (forthcoming), *Going Native on the Net: Indigenous Cyberactivism and Virtual Diasporas over the World Wide Web*, London: Routledge.

Latour, B. (1993), *We Have Never Been Modern*, Cambridge, MA: Harvard University Press.

Mackay, H. (1995), 'Theorizing the IT/society relationship', in N. Heap, R. Thomas, G. Einon, R. Mason and H. Mackay (eds), *Information Technology and Society: A Reader*, London: Sage in association with the Open University.

Marcus, G. (1995), 'Ethnography in/of the World System: the Emergence of Multi-Sited Ethnography', *Annual Review of Anthropology*, 24: 95–117.

Miller, D. and Slater, D. (2000), *The Internet: an Ethnographic Approach*, Oxford: Berg.

NAIS Report (2001), *ICANN, Legitimacy, and the Public Voice: Making Global Participation and Representation Work*, Report of the NGO and Academic ICANN Study (NAIS), http://www.naisproject.org.

Naughton, J. (2000 [1999]), *A Brief History of the Future: the Origins of the Internet*, London: Orion.

Pfaffenberger, B. (1992), 'Social Anthropology of Technology', *Annual Review of Anthropology*, 21: 491–516.

Rheingold, H. (1994), *The Virtual Community: Homesteading on the Electronic Frontier*, New York: HarperCollins.

Robertson, R. (1995), 'Time-Space and Homogeneity-Heterogeneity', in M. Featherstone, S. Lash and R. Robertson (eds), *Global Modernities*, London: Sage.

Sani, R. (1997), 'Global Internet Conference Begins', *New Straits Times/ Computimes*, 23, June.

Uimonen, P. (1999), 'Technology, Modernity and Globalization: some Social Aspects of Internet Development', *Antropologiska Studier*, 62/63: 7–15.

—— (2001), *Transnational.Dynamics@Development.Net: Internet, Modernization and Globalization*, Stockholm Studies in Social Anthropology, 49, Stockholm: Almqvist & Wiksell.

8

Mainstream Rebels: Informalization and Regulation in a Virtual World

Christina Garsten and David Lerdell

Introduction: an Outlaw in Cyberspace

Becoming an outlaw in cyberspace is easy. All you have to do is try to adhere to established norms for social communication. And be ignorant. Christina's first encounter with netiquette was rather dramatic and threatened to stigmatize her for the duration of her fieldwork. It was one of the first days of fieldwork at Apple Computer. She was just getting acquainted with AppleLink, the corporate worldwide telecommunications system, and with the local Intranet system. It so happened that her very first electronic message composition was a reply to one of the hardware engineers – an energetic, speedy young man in his early twenties. Jim put most of his energy on technology and for him working at Apple was more of a lifestyle than of tedious work. Trained in a school system in which computers were largely absent from the curriculum, let alone netiquette rules, but in which the norms of letter writing were taught and inculcated as knowledge of great social and professional value, Christina replied by adhering to these norms. Her 'letter' was stylishly indented, and the style of writing was as formal as a normal letter would be. Jim's response, through the Intranet, of course, was agitated:

1.48 pm Jim
Diary

To: Christina

You are now set up in the Diary. Your password is xxx. Double-click on your name in the list on the right hand side, type in your password, and you may then enter information about yourself.

Jim

2.13 pm Christina
Re: Diary

To: Jim

HELLO JIM!

Thanks for your help!
I may be able to organize myself now!

Christina

2.19 pm Jim
Re: Diary

To: Christina

Sure. But why all these indentations?

2.53 pm Christina
'INDENTATIONS'

To: Jim

Hey you!

What kind of an 'aesthetic jerk' are you?
(*citing George*) [another Apple colleague, authors' remark]

Christina

2.55 pm Jim
Re: 'INDENTATIONS'

To: Christina

Stop indenting everything one centimetre.

This event, which occurred before electronic communication became widely spread and before the Web was established, taught her something important about Apple culture: the tone of voice should be informal, direct and free from the burden of traditional corporate mannerism or the stilted social style of educated middle-class society. It also taught her something about the wider culture of on-line communication. There were obviously norms and rules or codes of conduct for communicating on the Net which were not entirely the same as those of the 'real world'. But they were there, and before Christina could find her feet as an 'apple' in the field, as it were, she also had to learn how to navigate successfully on the Net. This meant learning the rules for Net communication.

The above example leads us astray from the idea that the virtual communicative space is one characterized by freedom from established codes of conduct and norms – a space within which the individual is free to reconstruct him- or herself according to spontaneous whims and fantasies. The anecdote focuses attention on the violation of a code. The agitated reactions of the hardware engineer show that there were indeed norms and codes of conduct to be adhered to, and that had been broken in the dialogue. Pointing to such 'failures' to act properly accentuates behaviours that may be relatively informalized or detraditionalized but which nevertheless serve to provide sustained voices of established authority. 'In practice', as Heelas (1995: 9) puts it, '– and despite the language of autonomy and choice – we are controlled by routines, rules, procedures, regulations, laws, duties, schedules, diaries, timetables and customs.'

What the growth of technology-mediated communication does, however, is to problematize social relations and the ways in which these are established and maintained, and challenged, for that matter. It makes us reflect on what constitutes a relation as well as what constitutes a community (cf Albrow et al. 1997). It places the norms and rules by which interaction in such communities is to be governed into the limelight. The fact that technology-mediated communication is often global or transnational emphasizes the problem of taking for granted a sharedness of rules and norms for interaction. As a newcomer on the Net, one is treading unsafe terrain.

This chapter problematizes the relation between informalization and regulation with respect to work-related social interaction on the Internet. The discourse of information technology raises hopes of transcending national, class and gender differences, and of empowering individuals and groups. It is said to facilitate creative network constellations and formation of organizational communities of belonging in and across organizational, national or other boundaries. There are strong connotations of democratic ideals and egalitarianism. On the other hand, we argue, the networked world is also a highly regulated environment. There are sets of preferred values, social and professional codes of conduct that shape and restrain communication. Hence, social interaction on the Internet has a double edge to it. While it opens up possibilities for swift, informal and potentially empowering communication, it also entails a specific kind of global structuration of ideas and practices.

We question the idea that virtual, mediated communication differs substantially from 'real' face-to-face communication. We argue that virtual and real communicative patterns interpenetrate each other and that virtual communication to a large extent is modelled upon face-to-face communication. Instead of building upon Manuel Castells's (1996: 358–75) division of the real and the virtual as separate units and a 'culture of real virtuality', we prefer to regard the two as integrated. Virtuality is not a 'new reality' but part of everyday life (see also Pfaffenberger 1992). Virtuality is social, and should be thought of in terms of 'social virtuality'. Following Miller and Slater (Miller and Slater 2000: 6–8) we suggest that on-line and off-line worlds penetrate each other deeply and in complex ways. Whether people are writing on-line or off-line, there are norms, codes of conduct and rules that shape the way in which people communicate. The distinction between the 'real' and the 'virtual' is thus misleading to the extent that it misses the degree to which communication on the Internet is modelled upon and embedded in communication off-line. In spite of the enchanting rhetoric of informalization in on-line communication, off-line rules tend to shape communication in cyberspace.

The chapter builds on Garsten and Lerdell's research into the practices of on-line interaction. It draws on Garsten's earlier fieldwork at Apple computer in Sweden, the United States and France, where she studied on-line and off-line communication among professional software engineers and other Apple employees (see Garsten 1994, 2001). This involved some degree of participant observation on the Net, as it were, being involved in and observing discussions mediated through information technology. This virtual fieldwork by no means exhausted or dominated everyday communication. Face-to-face communication and communication mediated by other kinds of technology were equally intense, providing a broad spectrum of social interaction. The chapter also draws on Lerdell's research on professionals in organizations and networks engaged in forming the basic structures of the Internet. As part of his research, Lerdell made participant observation at a meeting of the Internet Engineering Task Force (IETF), an organization that co-ordinates Internet standardizing procedures. During this meeting a number of interviews with attendees were conducted. Focus was set on how the participants in the IETF activities communicate with each other as more or less spatially distant colleagues. Much of the standardizing work takes places electronically through various mailing lists, which is why studying electronic communication was an important methodological approach. We also draw upon ongoing debates about libertarianism and related issues, among others media debates carried out in the magazine *Wired*.

Beyond the Conventional: the Tyranny of Informality

When entering into discussions about the different aspects of Internet communication we are operating in what Schneider (1993: 2) calls 'an enchanted milieu', characterized by libertarian ideals, a great portion of individualism and strong anti-regulation sentiments. The Internet is in this sense an example of what has been labelled 'technologies of freedom' (see Misztal 2000: 171). The rhetoric around the Internet invokes notions of a different, alternative kind of communication supposedly free from many of the normative constraints of face-to-face encounters. The enchanting power of Internet communication lies in the rhetoric of freedom, resisting domestication and escaping regulation.

The enchanted domain of the Internet, dominated as it has been by technolibertarian ideals, invites the idea that formal behaviour can be more relaxed and external constraints released. This may be described as a form of 'informalization' (Misztal 2000: 43). The process of informalization has been captured in Elias's notion of the civilizing process, which describes changes in the relation between external social constraints and individual self-constraints (Elias 1978). Following an increased division of labour, the growth of individualism, the deconventionalization of organized practices, the effects of new media communication and the pluralization of social life in general, 'modern' societies generally put less pressure on people to conform to the formalities of behaviour, it has been argued (Wagner 1994). By the same token, we are left with higher levels of structural insecurity as we have to work out for ourselves a variety of strategies for everyday interaction. Nowadays, the concept of informality is most frequently used in relation to forms of interaction on the Internet and in relation to forms of social life in communist and post-communist societies (Misztal 2000: 171).

In Internet communication, with people being to a greater extent decontextualized from formal office roles and with formal codes of behaviour no longer corresponding to the actual relationships, informality emerges as the main code of behaviour. There has been, and still is, a fashion for informality, whereby it is openly prescribed, sometimes leading to 'the tyranny of informality' where 'being informal' is the order of the day (cf. Misztal 2000: 44). This was the case at Apple, where the stilted corporate code of IBM and others was explicitly rejected and a more informal, relaxed code of behaviour was encouraged. Being a Net wiz was part of what it took to be a 'real apple'. This was something Christina had yet to learn and that was clearly communicated to her by Jim. Informality also has its implicit and taken-for-granted rules.

It is often argued that the liberation of communication from the constraints of time and space provides participants with an experience of informal and intimate interaction. Enthusiasts see the promise of a digital Utopia in an open, global forum to which anybody can contribute ideas and information in an informal way, and where democratic and virtual communities can form. The pioneering first generation of Net users, with their cyber-hippie romanticism, university-campus culture and counter-cultural impulses, left behind them for the next generation of users the informality and self-directedness of communication, and the idea that each individual has his or her own voice and expects an individual-ized answer (Castells 1996: 357). Contributing to the atmosphere of informality is the fact that the Internet can be used for just about anything; for printing, publishing, marketing, debating, entertainment, education, exchanging informa-tion and so on. Within Usenet one can join huge numbers of newsgroups or post a message at computer bulletin-board systems, participate in hosted conferences or play interactive computer games, send electronic mail or have an intimate chat within an Internet Chat zone. In Misztal's (2000: 178) words:

> Although the Net's openness, the informality and self-directedness of this form of communication as well as its enormous complexity and formlessness, together with its continuous evolution, make it difficult to evaluate the character of the Internet and the related networks that make up the greater Net, we have enough evidence to suggest that it can offer some new opportunities for more flexible, interactive, decentralized and democratic modes of communication.

Electronic communication has been claimed by many to differ from face-to-face encounters in a number of respects. For example, it has been described as less civil and more conflictual, less conventional, more risky, and more democratic (Misztal 2000: 183; Sproull and Kiesler 1991: 67). Not only does electronic mail broadcast organizational gossip or jokes, but also spreads organizational infor-mation, which may increase employees' commitment to corporate goals. Managers may also feel threatened by the flow of information, its lack of respect for hierarchies, and their lack of control over its content (Wellman et al. 1996). The ease with which recipients may be added to a message, messages can be distributed to large crowds through distribution lists and re-sent across organiza-tions makes it rather unpredictable and difficult to control. Electronic communi-cation is charged with many of the fears and hopes of alternative and comple-mentary forms of communication. It takes place before, after, and in between face-to-face encounters.

Technolibertarianism: the Rhetoric of Freedom

The world of high-tech and electronic communication brings to mind rationality, standardization and an engineered sterile kind of modernity. It is, however, a world in which flesh, blood and vivid ideas have given places. In the words of

Borsook (2000: 3), 'High-tech, like any human artefact is not culturally tasteless, odorless, colourless. It contains attitude, mind-set, philosophy; and with geeks, the attitude, mind-set, and philosophy is libertarianism, in many-blossomed efflorescence.' Libertarianism is often claimed to be the ideology of cyberspace (Kamiya 1997), and others claim that libertarianism makes up the underlying value system of most cyberpunks. In Borsook's words; 'Libertarianism is a computer-culture badge of belonging, and libertarians are the most vocal political thinkers and talkers in high tech' (2000: 7).

The term libertarianism is very vague in itself. It is often understood as a set of political and philosophical ideas, where freedom for the individual is at the centre of attention and where coercion from others – be it other individuals or the state – should not interfere with the individual's own rights. But the term is ambiguous, and the differences between libertarianism, liberalism and neo-liberalism are hard to define. One must therefore be careful not to use the term 'libertarianism' too loosely to describe more or less unorganized, erratic or anarchic behaviour of individuals. *Wired*, being one of the most influential magazines reporting on various aspects of the Internet, has been described as very libertarian in character (Agre 1995). *Wired*, Agre argues, is made up of 'narratives of individualism, rational progress, technological determinism, and the autonomous development of the market' (Agre 1995)[1]. As is noted by a *Wired* columnist, critics often translate libertarianism into 'anarchism, egoism, and plain selfishness and greed' (McCullagh and Singleton 1997).

Individualism is a central tenet of libertarianism. The freedom of the individual is central in discussions about how the Internet and the world at large ought to be organized. Self-government of individuals is advocated, as opposed to 'others-government' where other actors regulate the behaviour of the individual. In the Libertarian FAQ (Frequently Asked Questions), the following is said about self-government:

> Libertarians want a win-win world of peace and plenty. And we believe that the only way to get it is through self-government ... NOT others-government ('Frequently Asked Questions About Libertarianism' 1998).

Anti-regulation is another strong notion in libertarianism. Numerous are examples of loud-voiced more or less self-appointed advocates representing the 'Internet community', claiming that the way to govern the Internet is for the authorities to stay out of the Net. One well-known example is the opposition that was organized by the Electronic Frontier Foundation, among others, against a proposed bill criminalizing 'indecent' speech on the Internet, the Communication Decency Act (CDA). Thus, in the libertarian view, the way to 'govern' the Internet is through self-government. There is almost a moralistic character to the idea, formulating what to do and what not to do, but also *how to do it.*

It should be noted here that in spite of the relative dominance of the libertarian and related technology-friendly strands of thought, there are also other, more critical views. One such collection of thoughts is the neo-Luddite spectrum. Not yet an organized movement, the neo-Luddite approach contains multitudes of those who have in common an awakening from the technophilic dream and resistance to one aspect or other of the industrial monoculture (Sale 1996: 258). Drawing upon the history of often active and violent Luddite resistance to the introduction of large-scale machines into the cotton trade in late eighteenth century Britain, neo-Luddites argue that the technologies created and disseminated by modern Western societies of today are out of control and threaten the fabric of social life. The Luddites were the first victims of the Industrial revolution and the first to resist its impact. Two hundred years later, neo-Luddites resist the political agendas of late industrialization and the enslaving impact of computing technology on social and individual life. These rebels comprise environmentalists, religious movements, anti-globalization movements and a range of other groupings. Computers are polluting in their manufacture, the neo-Luddites argue; they increase the reach and power of transnational corporations, widen the gap between the wired-up rich and the computer-illiterate poor. The neo-Luddites argue against a world-view that sees rationality as the key to human potential and technological development as the key to social progress. According to the neo-Luddites, the political nature of technology should be recognized and technologies regulated (Sale 1996: Chapter 9).

Despite alternative views such as those represented by the neo-Luddites, technolibertarianism with its rhetoric of freedom has shaped communication on the Internet to a significant degree. Conversely, the rise of the Net was integral to the rise of technolibertarianism. It gave formerly isolated libertarians a place to find each other. As Borsook (2000: 216) has it, 'On the Net they found solidarity and a better land: They were not alone'.

Jargonizing it All

In the same way as anti-technology movements have their local and specific historical roots, the technolibertarianism of the Net enthusiasts stems in large part from the hippie culture of west-coast USA (see e.g. Levy 1984; Roszak 1986). It was here that a particular version of libertarianism took shape through the establishment of virtual communities of 'hackers' and 'crackers'. One of the first of many virtual communities to be established on the Internet was The Well, started by former hippies. From the 1960s onward, when computing – especially the networked kind of computing – spread around the departments of Computer Science at universities in North America and in Western Europe, the more advanced among users were named 'hackers' (Delio 2001; Saffo 1993). The term was originally a mark of respect for someone who excelled in the operation of computers and software. A hacker was conceived as a person who enjoyed exploring the details of programmable systems and how to stretch their capabilities, one who enjoyed the intellectual challenge of creatively overcoming or circumventing limitations (Raymond 2000).

But since this was a new world, it was not very clear how to behave in it. Even if most of the early hackers had some education in computer science, far from all had been socialized into a 'computer scientist', and as the use of the Net became more widespread so did social and cultural heterogeneity. In the course of time, the term hacker began to be used to connote a person breaking into computer systems, and has given rise to both apprehension and negative reactions from governments and other public agencies and to a particular kind of romanticism expressed in popular culture.

In 'the Jargon File', the following is stated concerning 'hacker':

:hacker: n. [originally, someone who makes furniture with an axe] 1. A person who enjoys exploring the details of programmable systems and how to stretch their capabilities, as opposed to most users, who prefer to learn only the minimum necessary. 2. One who programs enthusiastically (even obsessively) or who enjoys programming rather than just theorizing about programming. 3. A person capable of appreciating {hack value}. 4. A person who is good at programming quickly. 5. An expert at a particular program, or one who frequently does work using it or on it; as in 'a Unix hacker'. (Definitions 1 through 5 are correlated, and people who fit them congregate.) 6. An expert or enthusiast of any kind. One might be an astronomy hacker, for example. 7. One who enjoys the intellectual challenge of creatively overcoming or circumventing limitations. 8. [deprecated] A malicious meddler who tries to discover sensitive information by poking around. Hence 'password hacker', 'network hacker'. The correct term for this sense is {cracker} (Raymond 2000).

The Jargon File may be described as something similar to a dictionary. It is a result of a collective effort starting out in the early 1970s at the laboratories for artificial intelligence at MIT, Stanford University and other nodes in the computer-science community, involving among others some of the pioneers in the creation of the ARPA network (which later evolved into the Internet). The fact that the Jargon File distinguishes between the terms 'hacker' and 'cracker' is a reflection of a minority of computer-literate individuals starting to use their skills in rather dubious ways. At Apple, for example, employees and managers alike were careful never to use the term 'cracker' in relation to its software engineers. 'Hacker', however, was a commonly used term. Hackers embodied the ideals of a libertarian, informal, relaxed and democratic type of organization, in which 'power to the people' would be given through powerful computers and intelligent electronic-network connections. Crackers, however, worked only for themselves, against corporate goals.

However, as heterogeneity among actors increased, so did the abuse of computers and networks; an abuse that caused concern among hackers who believed in and fought for their own Utopia. And one way of counteracting 'bad' behaviour is to formulate some rules.

The ideas and beliefs behind the more artful expressions of hacker activity have also influenced the rules regarding behaviour on the Internet, as well as the organization of Internet itself. Life on the Internet is to some extent regulated by Netiquette. The Internet itself is regulated by technical standards. We will now look further into these different kinds of regulation.

Netiquette: the Dos and Don'ts of Cyberspace

Interestingly, what appears as a haven for freedom seekers and rebellions is in large part controlled by norms, rules and standards. Almost every Internet Service Provider (ISP) has some guidelines on how to behave on the Net, often under the label 'netiquette'. The largest Internet service provider in the world, America Online (AOL), provides information on proper behaviour when posting to a newsgroup ('Newsgroup Netiquette' 2001). When signing up as a user on one of the providers of 'free' e-mail, such as Microsoft Hotmail and Yahoo Mail, you are also introduced to membership rules and a certain set of codes. While the membership rules imply an agreement between you and the supplier to use the services in a civil and law-abiding manner, the set of codes, i.e. 'netiquette', is meant to facilitate and govern e-mail communication. The term netiquette itself suggests that we have to do with something partly new, partly old. Whereas the 'Net' part refers to the network of computers, such as the Internet, 'etiquette', on the other hand, is a:

> system of rules and conventions that regulate social and professional behaviour. In any social unit there are accepted rules of behaviour upheld and enforced by legal codes; there are also norms of behaviour mandated by custom and enforced by group pressure ('etiquette' 2000).

Much of the writings on netiquette can be traced to a discussion carried out in a discussion forum called the USENET. USENET News was created in 1979 as a small network consisting of a number of discussions, arranged by topic. These discussions were formed into so-called news groups, which was one of the most popular applications of the pre-Web Internet. Ten years later, there were already over 11,000 news groups (see e.g. Hauben and Hauben 1997; Herz 1995; Platt 1997; Randall 1997). Today, the number is significantly higher.

In discussions on how to behave properly on the USENET, phenomena such as 'flaming' and 'spamming' were heavily debated. For example, an impolite posting in a newsgroup could be labelled 'inflammatory' due to its strident and ill-mannered style – hence the notion 'flame' for this kind of behaviour. Dery (1993) defines a flame war as 'vitriolic on-line exchanges ... conducted publicly, in discussion groups clustered under thematic headings on electronic bulletin boards, or – less frequently – in the form of poison pen letters sent via E-mail to private mailboxes'.

'Spamming' refers to another kind of misuse: sending an e-mail to many recipients, often in order to sell something. The term 'spamming' comes from a certain variety of canned meat under the trademark of SPAM, whose claim to fame was assured in a Monty Python sketch, where the word was repeated over and over, driving people crazy (Cerf 1993; Gaffin 1999; Hauben and Hauben 1997; Naughton 1999; Zakon 1997).

So, what are the rules of the game on the Internet? Virginia Shea's book on how to use the English language in 'the digital age', *Netiquette* (1994), provides a good summary, and is often quoted when referring to 'the dos and don'ts of cyberworld'. Analogous to the Ten Commandments, ten core rules of netiquette are distinguished (ibid.):

Remember the human. Never forget that the person reading your mail or posting is, indeed, a person, with feelings that can be hurt.

Adhere to the same standards of behavior online that you follow in real life. Be ethical, and remember that breaking the law is bad Netiquette.

Know where you are in cyberspace. Netiquette varies from domain to domain.

Respect other people's time and bandwidth. Try not to ask stupid questions on discussion groups.

Make yourself look good online. Check grammar and spelling before you post. Know what you're talking about and make sense.

Share expert knowledge. Offer answers and help to people who ask questions on discussion.

Help keep flame wars under control.

Respect other people's privacy. Don't read other people's private e-mail.

Don't abuse your power. The more power you have, the more important it is that you use it well.

Be forgiving of other people's mistakes. You were a network newbie once too!

Almost all 'etiquettes' build upon adaptation and pleasantness (Ribbing 1991). Some traits from 'real' face-to-face life find their way into netiquette; you ought to remember that we are all humans, and that you should behave in a similar way on the Net as you do elsewhere. Other requirements, such as knowing in which domain on the Internet you find yourself, are more 'Net-specific'. There are also commandments that are more elitist in character, such as those appealing to sharing enlightenment with others who may be less computer literate, sharing expert knowledge, not abusing your own power, and being humble enough to forgive other people's mistakes.

In an attempt to investigate how netiquette is enforced in 'real life', we created a character named Mable Sartre-Mines whose *raison d'être* was to take part in discussions going on in a number of chat rooms devoted to computers in various ways. In a chat room on Microsoft's MSN Chat (<chat.msn.com>), the following conversation was recorded:

> Welcome to PcHelpHere! Please enjoy your stay. We do NOT condone piracy or bot/script talk here, thanks.
> Mable_SartreMines : what is bots?
> S£ayer : ZzzzZZZZZzzzZZzZzzzZZzZzZzzZZZZzzzzzz
> Mable_SartreMines : why CANT I ASK QUESTIONS ABOUT BOTS?
> FunBard : Mable_SartreMines , please Lower Your Caps! It is rude and considered shouting in chat. Thank You.
> Mable_SartreMines : Please tekk ne
> Mable_SartreMines : tell me
> Call_me_Ishmael1 : no bot talk in here
>
> You have been kicked out of the chat room by Host FunBard: Disruptive behaviour

We learnt two things from our chat experience. First, some thin layers of netiquette are important to know when trying to chat. For example, using capital letters is one of the more blunt and common breaches of the netiquette, as evinced above. Secondly, people taking part in chats like to show that they have experience, and they like policing as well. As one can tell from the excerpt above, some sort of a bouncer, if not a chat police, simply throws you out from the conversation if you prove to be too much of a newcomer and an illiterate.

Emoticons: Signs of Understanding

One apparent trait of on-line communication is the use of graphical signs called 'smileys', due to their grinning, smirking and smiling character. Here are some examples found in the Unofficial Smiley Dictionary in EFF's (Extended) Guide to the Internet (Gaffin and Heitkötter 1994):

:-) Your basic smiley. This smiley is used to inflect a sarcastic or joking statement since we can't hear voice inflection over e-mail.

;-) Winky smiley. User just made a flirtatious and/or sarcastic remark. More of a 'don't hit me for what I just said' smiley.

:-(Frowning smiley. User did not like that last statement or is upset or depressed about something.

:*) User is drunk.

:-)-8 User is a Big girl.

:-{) User has a mustache.

+-:-) User is the Pope or holds some other religious office.

These 'smileys' or 'emoticons' have gained huge popularity, diffused through e-mailing, chatting, and later on even between mobile phones in the form of short messages (SMS):

> Chatting to old friends and making new ones on your mobile 'phone, or on the Internet can be the best and cheapest way to make plans, have a row, start a romance or end an affair and it's discreet! But your messages can be open to misinterpretation when the person you are talking to can't see you or hear the inflection in your voice. The mood of your message is one of the hardest things to convey. 'Emoticons' are a shorthand way of explaining or elaborating on your meaning. Made from punctuation marks on your keypad, they take up very little space, can be keyed in seconds and make the difference between a lasting friendship and a social disaster ... The sub-text of your words, acronyms or abbreviations will become crystal clear to anyone reading them if you punctuate your message with emoticons, whenever and wherever you feel like it. (WAN2TLK? ltle bk of txt msgs 2000: 8–9).

Emoticons aim to convey feelings and moods in a context where they are less directly apprehended. When the human element in communication is missing, when fears and hopes of co-workers cannot be seen directly, there is an increased risk of misunderstanding and conflict. At Apple, one such incident involved a heated discussion among product managers, situated on different sides of the Atlantic. As the two, an American man and a Swedish woman, tried to resolve the conflict (which centred around the mandate for the local Swedish office to 'localize' a particular product), things escalated. After having had to involve their respective managers in the issue, the Swedish woman flew off to California to try to sort things out, in face-to-face interaction. Eventually, the conflict was solved and the woman could fly back to Sweden.

As we have seen, it is easy to be misunderstood when expressing oneself briefly in an e-mail message or when chatting. Emoticons can help make on-line communication 'thicker', by way of offering a stylized way of 'translating' accents found in facial expressions or gestures in an interpersonal meeting, or elaborated and well-formulated texts found in longer letters or books, into well-known standardized signs of understanding.

'Netizens' with Influence: the Case of the Internet Engineering Task Force

Quite contrary to what is often claimed, the Internet is not characterized by total anarchy or chaos, but is actually a rather organized and managed space. Management is not carried out by one single organization or a single person, but by several organizations. In parallel with the development of the Internet, a number of organizations came into existence, organizations that were set up with one particular and shared goal: standardization. The multitude of organizations and abbreviations thus developed may have contributed to the image of the Internet as something unorganized and anarchic in character.

The development of the specifications for the Internet's predecessor the ARPANET was quite informal and based on contributions from a number of individuals rather than the result of an organized activity. The documentation of the development process was often incomplete and rarely updated. However, since the different researchers involved in the development were located in different parts of the United States, a form of on-line documentation was created, the so-called Request for Comments-series (RFCs), to spread specifications and ideas among the researchers. As the Internet grew so did the standardization process, and several organizations and processes were formed. One of the acronyms that was repeated more often than others was the IETF, the Internet Engineering Task Force. In order to make some sense of how some of the basic rules for the functioning of the Net were created, David went to a meeting arranged by IETF in Memphis, Tennessee, in 1997. Prior to the meeting, he had followed the instructions to read a certain document, the so-called 'Tao of the IETF: A Guide for New Attendees of the Internet Engineering Task Force' (Malkin, 1994). This strong suggestion was posted on IETF's Web site in capital letters which, according to David's humble experience of how to behave on the Net, was the same as shouting at someone. So he took it very seriously and began reading the *Tao* on the delayed flight from Stockholm to Memphis.

What he learnt from reading this document was that he was to experience something very different, and that

> [n]ewcomers to IETF face-to-face meetings are often in a bit of shock. They expect them to be like other standards bodies, or like computer conferences. Fortunately, the shock wears off after a day or two, and many new attendees get quite animated about how much fun they are having.

Another topic in the *Tao* dealt with how the attendees were supposed to be dressed. He read: 'Since attendees must wear their name tags, they must also wear shirts or blouses. Pants or skirts are also highly recommended.' Well, that sounded reasonable. Reading on, he also understood that he would not make very much use of the suits that he had brought. 'There are those in the IETF who refuse to wear anything other than suits. Fortunately, they are well known (for other reasons) so they are forgiven this particular idiosyncrasy.' And since David was not known at all, even if he liked to see some similarities between himself and the typical 'IETFer', who was 'fiercely independent', he never unpacked his suits ... Not wearing a suit paradoxically meant that he was breaching another suggestion in the *Tao*, since one would do wise in not expecting an IETFer to follow orders. The rest of the document concerned more technical matters, and he did not understand all that much of it all, nor did it interest him to any great extent. But he was not too concerned about this lack of understanding and interest on his part, since he was informed that '[t]ao is sometimes translated "the way", but according to Taoist philosophy the true meaning of the word cannot be expressed in words'.

OK, David reckoned, so he was up for something shocking, fun and to some extent also unintelligible – and to top it off, it would all take place in Memphis, Tennessee. Besides the location being associated with two 'kings', no less (Elvis and Martin Luther), he had heard that the blues scene was supposed to be really cool. He admitted being quite excited about the whole idea of it. It did not begin very promisingly, however. He was welcomed by what looked like the mother of all thunderstorms. So, after David had been in the air or in various airports for about 24 hours, the weather had made sure that he did not get any rest at all before entering the conference venue, the most famous hotel in all Memphis: the 'Peabody', 'the South's Grand Hotel'.

Prior to the actual opening of the meeting, the IETF arranged a so-called 'newcomers' orientation' on-site for those attendees who were taking part for the very first time in the activities. The number of first-timers was 400, which made up 30 per cent of the total number of attendees.

The meeting was arranged by the secretariat of the IETF, and one of its officers opened it by telling the newcomers that an IETF-meeting was a 'very informal session', and that they would 'have no idea what the next week will be like. We will keep this very informal'. Furthermore, the newcomers were once again reminded that the IETF was very different compared to other standard bodies, and that he took for granted that they all had read the *Tao*, since it 'captures the flavour of the IETF; it's informal, we try to put humour in it as often as we can', besides being chaotic and hectic. Furthermore, they were to find 'the hallway conversation very informative', much more so than the actual meetings. They were also recommended not to ask any questions if they did not know what they were talking about, since the whole process was under a fierce time pressure. At the same time newcomers were told how to get themselves informed; and if they disagreed with what was proposed or discussed, they were not to complain but to prove it wrong and suggest another solution. This was all in the way of the IETF credo:

> We reject kings, presidents and voting
> We believe in rough consensus and running code.

If someone disagrees with an approach, the way to prove it is to write the code and demonstrate it, as opposed to just saying 'I don't like this approach'.

So, did David find the meetings fun, chaotic, hectic and down-to-business? Well, as far as he could judge the whole event was quite different from how standardization goes on in the much more formal International Organization for Standardization (ISO) (cf Tamm Hallström 2000). He had fun at the social event that was a 'Blues Brothers Party', followed by a night out in Memphis's blues district. The meetings were quite chaotic – certainly so to an outsider like himself – and not much more than the technical matters were discussed. Even at the social event when the attention of all the attendees were focused on the daily march of the ducks arranged by the Peabody, one of the attendees compared the marching of birds into a water fountain to the routing of Internet traffic. The meeting was very informal when it came to dress code and the not-so-polite way the attendees approached each other. The latter was quite problematic for some of the newcomers (if not outsiders). A delegation from the People's Republic of China, all dressed in suits, were listened to when they complained about a certain suggestion, but outright ignored by the more well-spoken and dominating attendees. A lasting impression of this meeting (and of other meetings David has attended over the years arranged by other Internet-related organizations) is that the process of standardizing the Internet may look very informal and open. However, for those who may want to influence the process, there are high informal barriers to entry.

The alleged openness is a claim that not everyone agrees with. On the contrary, when it comes to decision-making the IETF-process has been criticized for being less open than processes in more formal standardization bodies, due to the lack of voting rules. The opaque decision-making process in the IETF also makes it unclear who really has the decision-making power.

As the Internet itself grew, so did the number of participants in the standardization process. Many new participants began to visit at the IETF-meetings – people with different backgrounds, who had no prior experience of the ARPANET, and who might not have the same level of knowledge as the ARPANET pioneers.

Some of the people participating in the work of the IETF felt that the rules of the IETF, as well as the rules of the Internet as such, ought to be formalized. This eventually led to the publication of an RFC called 'Netiquette Guidelines' (Hambridge 1995):

> In the past, the population of people using the Internet had 'grown up' with the Internet, were technically minded, and understood the nature of the transport and the protocols. Today, the community of Internet users includes people who are new to the environment. These 'Newbies' are unfamiliar with the culture and don't need to know about transport and protocols. In order to bring these new users into the Internet culture quickly, this Guide offers a minimum set of behaviors which organizations and individuals may take and adapt for their own use.

Here, we find similarities to Shea's book in the view that the more experienced users ought to assist newer ones, but the RFC is much more detailed and more like a handbook than a description of proper behaviour. IETF's 'Netiquette Guidelines' also makes a distinction between 'one-to-one communication' such as mail and talk; and 'one-to-many communication', such as the World Wide Web, mailing lists, and MUDs.[2] It is implied that one-to-one communication differs in character from one-to-many communication.[3]

Furthermore, it is interesting to note the similarities and differences between IETF's Netiquette Guidelines and the so called 'hacker ethic' (Levy 1984). Levy means that there is among hackers a common philosophy which stems from the computer itself: 'It was a philosophy of sharing, openness, decentralization, and getting your hands on machines at any cost – to improve the machines, and to improve the world.' He further states that this ethic is seldom codified, which would differ from much that we have seen. As one famous hacker says: 'Freedom of speech! ... That's the whole basis for the hacker ethic. If you don't understand that, you've got no business here' (Levy 1984; Platt 1997).

As stated in the beginning, we argue that on- and off-line worlds are tightly interrelated. In the IETF case, this gives rise to a tension that becomes evident when comparing the discussions on the electronic mailing lists to discussions at face-to-face meetings. It is quite easy to be very upfront – if not plain rude – toward your 'colleagues' on the mailing lists. But it is not at all that easy to maintain that position when meeting face-to-face. This tension between on-line and off-line behaviour is most probably one important reason for the importance of arranging face-to-face meetings. These help keep on-line discussions fruitful and prevent them from being destroyed or hampered by off-the-point debates or time-consuming flame wars.

Concluding Comments: Socially Embedded Virtuality (or, What's so Informal, Anyway?)

In this chapter, we have aimed at problematizing the relation between informalization and regulation with respect to work-related social interaction on the Internet. We have suggested that while the discourse of information technology promises freedom from the normative constraints of face-to-face interaction, the networked world is also a highly regulated environment. There are sets of preferred values, social and professional codes of conduct, which shape and restrain communication. Hence, while social interaction on the Internet opens up possibilities for swift, informal and potentially empowering communication, it also entails a specific kind of global structuration of ideas and practices. We may expect more explicit forms of regulation and standardization of conduct to merge with increased organizational complexity and globalization (Brunsson et al. 2000).

The reaction that Christina encountered when trying to communicate on the Intranet at Apple Computer clearly signalled the presence of rules and norms of communication. She was urged to be less formal, less stilted, yet to adhere to certain normative expectations she did not yet know. Furthermore, this remark was presented in an agitated tone of voice. At a meeting of a standardization body that was drawing up the basic structures for the Internet, David saw that the more formal attendees – such as representatives from other parts of the world than North America – were more or less neglected since they were seen as too formal, too businesslike and too conservative in their manners. Also, less experienced and more formal participants were told many times over by more established attendees to read the *Tao* and behave accordingly.

These two experiences highlight an interesting paradox on and around the Internet. It is possible to see the often-claimed and fought-for informality as indeed very formal in character, especially if you do not know what is considered 'informal' in this domain. Even more conspicuous is the large number of self-appointed monitors, or police officers, that you meet when trying to communicate on the Internet as such, not to mention when you get yourself involved in trying to influence – or merely just discuss – the rules of the Net:

> Although much hyperbole maintains that everyone in cyberspace is equal, a study of online community reveals that this is not the case ... The traditional form of regulation in cyberspace has been through an informal set of customary laws. Online transactions have been policed through the consensual actions of users accessing and interacting in cyberspace (Dodge and Kitchen 2001: 79).

It is clear that these monitors, or police forces, are not appointed by anyone and that they are not acting on a mission from anyone other than themselves and their equals. The question that comes into mind is why so many 'netizens' feel they have the right to police over others? And who *are* these people requesting others to behave according to *their* rules?

The particular ways in which communication on the Internet is regulated speaks to the cultural, social, financial and political bias of the Internet. Communication patterns on the Net do not only reflect a particularly libertarian ideology, but a Western, middle-class way of life, including some and excluding others:

> Contrary to what academics, themselves members of the new global elite, tend to believe, the Internet and Web are not for anyone and unlikely ever to become open to universal use. Even those who get access are allowed to make their choices within the frame set by the suppliers, who invite them 'to spend time and money choosing between and in the numerous packages they offer (Bauman 1998: 53).

According to Wellman et al. (1996: 216), the average user of the Net is a 'largely politically conservative, white man, often single, English-speaking, affluent, residing in North America, professional, manager or student'. Although trends suggest an increasing participation of women, non-English speakers and people of lower socio-economic status, the dominance of a certain socio-economic and political category has had a great impact on netiquette rules. The do's and don'ts of cyberspace are to a large extent set up by the very same category that dominates communication on the Net. The wired neighbourhood or 'the third place', as the Internet is sometimes called, is a neighbourhood with particular cultural preferences, norms, and expectations. What at first hand looks quite informal, sub-cultural and to some extent even rebellious appears at closer scrutiny much more mainstream.

Acknowledgement

We would like to thank the Swedish Research Council for funding this project.

Notes

1. *Wired* itself conducted a reader survey resulting in a picture of its readership, in which the label 'libertarian' alongside labels such as 'anarchist', 'conservative' and 'progressive' could be used to describe its characteristics (Kinney 1995).
2. The Web refers to the graphics-intensive environment made up of zillions of so-called home pages filled with hyper-text. A mailing list is an ongoing e-mail discussion on a particular topic, a MUD – Multi-User Dungeon/

Domain/Dimension – is a virtual space on the Internet where users can interact socially.
3. See for example Calhoun (1992) for a sociological analysis of the implications of increased indirect social relationships.

References

Agre, P.E. (1995), 'Computing as a Social Practice', *Electronic Frontier Foundation (EFF)*, http://www.eff.org/Privacy/Security/Hacking_cracking_phreaking/Legal/social_computing_pagre.paper. Accessed 27 August 2001.

Albrow, Martin, Eade, John, Durrschmidt, Jörg and Washbourne, Neil (1997), 'The Impact of Globalization on Sociological Concepts: Community, Culture and Milieu', in John Eade (ed), *Living the Global City*, London: Routledge.

Bauman, Zygmunt (1998), *Globalization: the Human Consequences*, New York: Columbia University Press.

Borsook, Paulina (2000), *Cyberselfish: a Critical Romp Through the Terribly Libertarian Culture of High Tech*, New York: PublicAffairs.

Brunsson, Nils, Jacobsson, Bengt (2000), *A World of Standards*, Oxford: Oxford University Press.

Calhoun, Craig (1992), 'The Infrastructure of Modernity: Indirect Social Relationships, Information Technology, and Social Integration', in Hans Haferkamp and Neil J. Smelser (eds), *Social Change and Modernity*, Berkeley: University of California Press.

Castells, Manuel (1996), *The Rise of the Network Society*, Oxford: Blackwell.

Cerf, Vinton (1993), 'A Brief History of the Internet and Related Network', in Bernard Aboba (ed.), *The Online User's Encyclopedia: Bulletin Boards and Beyond*, Reading, MA: Addison-Wesley.

Delio, M. (2001), 'The Greatest Hacks of All Time', *Wired*. http://www.wired.com/news/technology/0,1282,41630,00.html. Accessed 26 August 2001.

Dery, Mark (1993), *Flame Wars: the Discourse of Cyberculture*, Durham, NC: Duke University Press.

Dodge, Martin and Kitchin, Rob (2001), *Mapping Cyberspace*, London: Routledge.

Elias, Norbert (1978), *The Civilizing Process*, Oxford: Blackwell.

Etiquette (2000), *Britannica*, http://www.britannica.com/bcom/eb/article/0/0,5716,33730+1+33150,00.html?query=etiquette. Accessed 7 March 2001.

Frequently Asked Questions About Libertarianism (1998), *Advocates for Self-Government*, http://www.cs.uu.nl/wais/html/nadir/libertarian/faq.html. Accessed 7 September 2002.

Gaffin, Adam (1999), 'EFF's Guide to the Internet, v. 3.21' (formerly 'The Big

Dummy's Guide to the Internet'), *Electronic Frontier Foundation (EFF)*, http://www.eff.org/pub/Net_info/EFF_Net_Guide/netguide_3.1.txt. Accessed 10 October 1999.

Gaffin, Adam and Heitkötter, Jörg. (1994), 'EFF's (Extended) Guide to the Internet. A round trip through Global Networks, Life in Cyberspace, and Everything … v 2.3', *Electronic Frontier Foundation (EFF)*, http://www. cosy.sbg.ac.at/doc/eegtti/eeg_toc.html. Accessed 7 September 2002.

Garsten, Christina (1994), *Apple World: Core and Periphery in a Transnational Organizational Culture*, Stockholm Studies in Social Anthropology, 33, Stockholm: Almqvist & Wiksell.

—— (2001), 'Play at Work: Contested Frames of Hacking', *Focaal*, 37: 89–101.

Hambridge, S. (1995), 'Netiquette Guidelines (RFC 1855)', *Request For Comments*, Internet Engineering Task Force (IETF).

Hauben, M. and Hauben, R. (1997), *Netizens: on the History and Impact of Usenet and the Internet*, Los Alamitos: IEEE Computer Society Press.

Heelas, Paul (1995), 'Introduction: Detraditionization and its Rivals', in P. Heedas, S. Lash and P. Morris (eds), *Detraditionalization: Critical Reflections on Authority and Identity*, Oxford: Blackwell.

Herz, J.C. (1995), *Surfing on the Internet: a Nethead's Adventure On-line*, New York: Abacus.

Kamiya, G. (1997), 'Smashing the State: the Strange Rise of Libertarianism', *Salon*, http://archive.salon.com/jan97/state970120.html. Accessed 26 August 2001.

Kinney, J. (1995) 'Anarcho-Emergentist-Republicans – Is There a New Politics Emerging in the Net/cyberspace/digital Culture?' *Wired Magazine*, 3(9).

Levy, Steven (1984), *Hackers: Heroes of the Computer Revolution*, New York: Bantam Doubleday Dell.

McCullagh, D. and Singleton, S. (1997), 'In Defense of Libertarianism', *Wired*, http://www.wired.com/news/print/0,1294,6864,00.html. Accessed 26 August 2001.

Malkin, G. (1994), 'The Tao of IETF: a Guide for New Attendees of the Internet Engineering Task Force (RFC 1718)' *Request For Comments*, Internet Engineering Task Force (IETF).

Miller, Daniel and Slater, Don (2000), *The Internet: an Ethnographic Approach*, Oxford: Berg.

Misztal, Barbara A. (2000), *Informality: Social Theory and Contemporary Practice*, London: Routledge.

Naughton, John (2000), *A Brief History of The Future: the Origins of the Internet*, London: Orion.

Newsgroup Netiquette (2001), *America Online (AOL)*, http://www.aol.com/nethelp/news/newsnetiquette.html. Accessed 7 March 2001.

Pfaffenberger, Brian (1992), 'The Social Anthropology of Technology', *Annual Review of Anthropology*, 21: 491–516.

Platt, C. (1997), *Anarchy Online*, New York: HarperPrism.

Randall, N. (1997), *The Soul of The Internet: Net Gods, Netizens and the Wiring of the World*, London: Thomson Computer.

Raymond, E.S. (ed.) (2000), 'The Jargon File' (4.2.3), http://tuxedo.org/jargon/jarg423.gz. Accessed 23 November 2000.

Ribbing, Magdalena (1991), *Nya etikettboken: spelregler för väluppfostrade*, Stockholm: DN.

Roszak, Theodore (1986*), The Cult of Information: the Folklore of Computers and the True Art of Thinking*, New York: Pantheon.

Saffo, P. (1993), 'Cyberpunk R.I.P.', *Wired Magazine*, 1(4).

Sale, Kirkpatrick (1996), *Rebels Against the Future: the Luddites and Their War on the Industrial Revolution: Lessons for the Computer Age*, Reading, MA. Addison-Wesley.

Schneider, Mark A. (1993), *Culture and Enchantment*, Chicago: University of Chicago Press.

Shea, Virginia (1994), *Netiquette*, San Francisco: Albion. http://in.on.ca/tutorial/netiquette.html. Accessed 30 March 2003.

Sproull, Lee and Kiesler, Sara (1991), *Connections: New Ways of Working in the Networked Organization*, Cambridge, MA: MIT Press.

Tamm Hallström, Kristina (2000), *Kampen för auktoritet: standardizeringsorganizationer i arbete*, Stockholm: The Economic Research Institute, Stockholm School of Economics.

Wagner, Peter (1994), *A Sociology of Modernity*, London: Routledge.

WAN2TLK? Ltle bk of txt msgs (2000), London: Michael O'Mara.

Wellman, Barry, Salaff, Janet and Haythornthwaite, Caroline (1996), 'Computer Networks as Social Networks: Collaborative Work, Telework and Virtual Community', *Annual Review of Sociology*, 22: 213–38.

Zakon, R. (1997), 'Hobbes' Internet Timeline (RFC 2235)', *Request For Comments*, Internet Engineering Task Force (IETF).

–9–

Steps on Screen: Technoscapes, Visualization and Globalization in Dance

Helena Wulff

The Internet is often thought of in terms of globalization and transnational connections, and this applies to dance installations and performances from across the globe that can be accessed on the Internet. There are also dance performances that take place in different countries, even in different continents, *at the same time* via the Internet.

This was the case with *Ghosts and Astronauts*, a telepresence work choreographed by Susan Kozel (1998a) and performed in 1997 at Riverside Studios in California and The Place Theatre in London via Internet's videoconference link.[1] Kozel herself performed in the dance piece. She starts her vertiginous *conte* about how bodies floating in (cyber)space suspend notions of time and place. Dancing across the Atlantic Ocean, or rather performing via videoconference, does entail a perception of 'here and now', yet this is a new and continuously changing 'here'. Kozel (ibid.: 84) describes this truly instant global experience:

> When I perform via videoconference link I do not think of the other performers and myself as occupying endpoints, instead I have a strong sense that we can slide into the grainy, two-dimensional image, down an imaginary tunnel that links the remote locations.

Most interestingly, Kozel (ibid.: 85) notes that 'the fragility of interaction across distances echoes the vulnerability of proximity.' Despite the physical distance of the performers in *Ghosts and Astronauts*, there was vulnerability as well as closeness in the piece. One important outcome of this cross-continental live screen performance is thus that distance does not have to be a hindrance to intimacy.

The two sites of *Ghosts and Astronauts* were quite different. In the Riverside Studios in California the projection of *Ghosts and Astronauts* was high up on a white cyclorama. The audience was seated, standing or walking around. The computers and camera people were on the white floor in full view with the dancers. The Place Theatre in London, on the other hand, was a more conventional theatre setting. The audience was directed to the seats. On the black stage space, a transparent cinema screen displayed the live dance from Riverside on both sides of the screen. The audience could choose to watch the projection with Kozel dancing through the screen, or change their perspective by getting up to walk behind the screen in order to watch Kozel dance in front of the screen.

The floating nature of *Ghosts and Astronauts* may appear to refer to an emotional state, or what it feels like to 'dance in space'. This was made possible by the dancers being suspended in harness on wires. Yet it was the camera that made them 'fly, float or fall' (ibid.: 89). Kozel explains that her idea of floating in space goes back to work with microgravity, which French choreographer Kitsou Dubois conducted when she was employed at the French National Centre for Space Research in order to train astronauts to adjust to weightlessness. So there were similarities between 1960s images of slow moonwalking and the movement quality of the performers in *Ghosts and Astronauts*.

This dance performance is an instance of the increasingly global nature of the modern Euro-American dance world. Based on long-term ethnographic studies of ballet, contemporary stage dance, Irish traditional dance, dance shows and dance installations (Wulff 1998a, b, 2002a, 2003) I will discuss the technoscapes of changing aesthetics and work practice that new technology has brought to the dance world, as well as visualization and globalization in dance. I am taking Arjun Appadurai's (1996: 34) concept of technoscape into the realm of dance because it highlights that:

> the global configuration, also ever fluid, both high and low, both mechanical and informational, now moves at high speeds across various kinds of previously impervious boundaries.

These technoscapes are unpredictable in relation to political dominance and the market, and include unskilled as well as highly skilled labour in a global cultural economy. The technologies that go into dance technoscapes are television, but primarily video, CD-ROM and the Internet. Since television, video and computer interface with each other it is relevant to include all three of them here. Dance video is available on the Internet, choreography that was made on animated choreography software is used in dance videos (as well as in live dance) and broadcast on television. Dance has been recorded and reproduced through technology for a long time, but in the 1990s new technology radically changed and expanded the aesthetic possibilities and thus the range of work practices in dance. Digital technology is a part of the growth of sophisticated dance performances both live and on screen, sometimes including both live dance and screen dance such as in *Ghost and Astronauts*, often with a global scope.

The fact that digital technology can easily and cheaply be copied in large quantities, raises urgent and contested issues over property rights and dance that are further complicated in a global context.[2] Property rights in relation to music on the Internet has received a lot of attention, such as the legal battle over Napster, because of the large sums of money that are involved in the music industry. This is not the situation with dance. There is, however, one recent case of remarkable economic success in dance: *Riverdance*, the Irish dance show, which made a splash as an interval diversion in the Eurovision Song Contest in 1994, and then skyrocketed into global success. With the success of *Riverdance* came conflicts over property rights. As I intend to show in this chapter, dance is good to think and compare with, both for similarity and difference, but above all dance and new technology crystallize wider processes of contemporary cultural concerns such as the increasing transnational nature of many work practices, the arts and democracy, reality versus virtuality, and the global marketplace.

Dance and the Democratizing Triumph of Technology

Technology and dance go as far back as the inventions of photography and film, including ritual dance in early flickering black-and-white ethnographic footage and Fred Astaire partnering Ginger Rogers in lighthearted romantic film. According to Judith Lynne Hanna (1988: 20–1) dance on television first appeared in the United States as early as 1931 with the dancer Maria Gambarelli. Penman (1993) also mentions her as the first dancer on British television, in 1932, in his account of the focus on dance, ballet and dance documentaries developed by the BBC over the decades. In the United States, dance on television came to mean 'spectacle and diversion' in the form of variety shows in the 1940s and 1950s. Although modern choreographers did work with television, Anna Kisselgoff, *The New York Times*'s legendary dance critic, talked to me in an interview about the problems of getting ballet and modern dance accepted on this wide-reaching medium in the 1950s. There was the view of ballet and modern dance as being indecent because these dance forms often featured tight-fitting and minimal costume, revealing body parts that normally would be hidden. But with the enormous expansion of television in the United States, there was also more dance on television, which gradually was reaching people who would not find their way to the theatre. Referring to a telephone survey in the 1970s, Hanna (1988) is able to show that the attendance figures at live performances grew for four dance companies after they had been on television. This was in the beginning of the so-called dance boom, which swept across North America and Europe carried by the economic expansion in the 1980s. One lasting result of the dance boom, as well as the growth and prominence of modern dance, was that dance audiences became more mixed socially. As Hanna suggests, dance on television has contributed to this.

The democratizing nature of technology for the mass distribution of art has been described by Walter Sorell (1981: 399) as 'the triumph of technology', a statement in the same spirit as Walter Benjamin's (1969 [1936]) article 'The Work of Art in the Age of Mechanical Reproduction'. Benjamin's famous argument was that the reproduction of art has a political potential of liberating people who were suppressed socially and economically. This idea was rejected by other scholars of the Frankfurt School in an equally famous critique. They saw mass media as a means of manipulating people and making them passive. In the 1950s, Raymond Williams (1975) combined the two camps suggesting that television could be used as a revolutionary force bringing education and democracy to the masses, but he also emphasized that in the wrong hands there was a danger that television might manipulate people. With the appearance of inexpensive media and technology that can be used and controlled more widely, such as the Internet, this debate has recently taken another turn (see the Introduction in this volume): one of the many uses of the Internet is as a grass-roots medium connecting people of lesser means and political agendas on a global level.

When dance first appeared on television it was not only a way to make ballet and dance accessible for a general public, but it also opened up a whole new world of making new choreographic effects. The American choreographer Merce Cunningham was a forerunner when it comes to choreographing dance for television and video. In *Blue Studio* he inserted five copies of himself dancing, on what was the blue part of the tape, which made it look as if he were partnering one 'Cunningham' after another (Cass 1993). Cunningham has also experimented with transposing dance, which was choreographed for film, television or video, to stage (Sorell 1981, Rubidge 1993). Now in his 80s, Cunningham continues his extraordinary creativity making cutting-edge dances also with new technology. The live dance piece titled *Biped* is made with so-called motion-capture computer technology. On stage 3D mega-dancers, in the form of coloured contours of animated cartoon-like computer dancers, appear together with real dancers. Dafova (1999) describes how Cunningham captured the motion of real dancers: first he had real dancers dancing short sections he had choreographed in a studio. The dancers, who wore sensors all over their bodies, were filmed by ten cameras that were connected to a computer, which registered the light that was made by the movements of the sensors. These movements were projected onto digitized drawings of contours of dancers – who then came on stage. When *Biped* was performed at the Abbey Theatre in Dublin as a part of the new International Dance Festival Ireland in May 2002, I did note that there was no direct interaction between the huge multi-coloured animated dancers and the real dancers. As the dance progressed the lines, or sticks, of the animated dancers were detached and slowly fell down on the screen where they continued to move around taking different shapes. The real dancers were all dressed in glittering metallic costumes reflecting the light in rainbow colours. One of the women dancers started shaking as if electricity were going through her body, as if she had suffered an electric shock. This abstract dance piece, especially the huge size of the animated dancers in contrast to that of the real dancers, seems to tell a story about the omnipresent powerful new technology and suggest that real people do not yet quite know how to handle this.

Dance Aesthetics and Work Practice

There is a traditional distrust of representations of dance in the Euro-American ballet and dance world. It is believed that dance on film, television and video is inaccurate, that the heart of live stage dance cannot be captured on a screen, on neither a still nor a canvas, let alone in words. 'People should come and watch us in the theatre', dancers tend to insist, referring to a sense of loss in the conveyance of live dance to screen dance. This loss consists of the challenge that the presence of the audience provides for dancers, which on a good night spurs them into unimagined spaces of dance artistry, but on a bad night can be quite disastrous. This unpredictability and excitement of every single live performance is addictive to many dancers. An important characteristic of live dance, contrary to screen dance, is that live dance is a multi-sensory experience both for dancers and audience. As dancers dance, they watch each other, they feel and touch each others' bodies, they listen to the music and they smell a combination of sweet theatre make-up, sweat and perfume, and dry rosin from the soles of their shoes.[3] The audience primarily watches and listens, and smells the theatre scents. Screen dance on the other hand is made to be watched and listened to – but it has no smell and it cannot be touched[4] – and it lacks the expectant atmosphere of live dance.[5]

When dancers are eager to point out that screen dance is 'not the same as live dance', e.g. not as 'real', their concern is that screen dance does not produce the same atmosphere as live dance. Still, the argument remains that screen dance can be categorized as a different dance form, a dance form in its own right, which creates other spaces than dance on stage.

There is yet another dance form, that of new technology being used in live performance such as in *The Secret Project*, a dance theatre performance, installation and Web site (www.timara.oberlin.edu/people~rpovall/secret/secret.htlm) by choreographer-writer Jools Gilson-Ellis and digital artist-composer Richard Povall. On a video of the hour-long performance in Cork City and in a post-performance discussion with the dancers and the audience, Gilson-Ellis (who is also one of the three dancers, all women) explains how the soundscape of the performance was designed: some sound was made by the dancers as they moved, their movements were videoed by a camera in the back of the auditorium. The video camera was connected to a computer (the BigEye motion-capture software) which was processing this information into sound, a pre-recorded piece of music or text. The only technology that was visible for the audience was the tiny microphones they carried close to their mouths. In this funny and moving multimedia performance, personal and political secrets of womanhood are explored through the relationship between text (poetry, song, dialogue), exquisite yet powerful movement and sound. The choreography is partly set, partly improvised. The spoken text, written by Gilson-Ellis, weaves into the soundscape as the dancers speak or sing in English with Irish and English accents, in French and in the Irish language. The rather abstract atmosphere of *The Secret Project* is broken in the middle of the piece by a story about a girl who shares her skipping-rope with her best friend until she takes it away from the girl and then tries to hit her with it. Perhaps an allusion to the fate of some secrets?

Reality versus Virtuality, Body versus Machine

Working with technology can lead to a closeness between one's body and machines, and for artists it can produce new aesthetics and creativity. It has been suggested that such creativity which comes out of social relationships between human and machine will have a feedback on the technology. It was the experience of virtual interaction with strangers through video cameras and monitors in the installation *Telematic Dreaming* that made Susan Kozel (1998b [1996]) agree with those who anticipate that artistic expressions of virtual reality will have an impact on technology.

In the article 'Spacemaking: Experiences of a Virtual Body' Kozel (1998b: 88) is interested in the double meaning of dance as spacemaking, both in how dancing can be said to 'make space' or structures in the air around the performer and also how dancing takes place in, 'makes the space', of virtual reality. According to Kozel:

> The collaboration between dance and VR technology is a new art form, or at least a hybrid made by uniting different ways of spacemaking.

In this article Kozel describes and discusses her experience of performing for hours each day during the course of a month in the installation *Telematic Dreaming* by Paul Sermon, at an exhibition for contemporary art in Amsterdam. People in different rooms were connected via telepresence technology: Kozel was lying on a bed in one room, on a floor above and far away from the visitors to the exhibition. Her image was projected on the bed in a room where visitors could interact with her. Their movements were videoed by cameras together with the image of Kozel and transmitted back to monitors in her room. This was how she related and responded to the person on the bed in the room downstairs. The virtual contact tended to start off with fingers touching each other by way of small and careful movements. But when the movements grew and included the whole body, emotions surfaced which made people both astounded and so uncomfortable that some people left. Kozel experienced moments of closeness and flow in the exchange with strangers, but was concerned that these intimacies with a succession of strangers would be harmful to her feelings of love in the real world.

Telematic Dreaming highlights notions of trust, sex and violence. There were some threatening incidents such as when someone produced a knife and someone else pushed an elbow in Kozel's virtual stomach. This upset her, which testifies to the vulnerability even of virtual interaction. The opposite also occurred: a tender interplay spurred a man to go and get a rose for Kozel, which he offered her in virtual space. Another sensual encounter with an attractive stranger was replaced by coarse cyber-sexual violence when two men in leather jackets attacked the image of Kozel's head and pelvic area. As she watched the horror of this 'back alley scenario' (ibid.: 84) on the monitor in her room, Kozel instinctively withdrew her real body and self from the image.

The act of virtual sex was 'a mimetic version' (ibid.) of real sex, an extension rather than a substitute. One of Kozel's virtual lovers came back many times, but when they met in person having coffee in the gallery cafeteria, they were inhibited and formal: their virtual rapport did not carry over to real life. This does raise the question of whether the extension of one's body into cyberspace through sex or any other activity there implies a change of the self on the way. It certainly seems as if Kozel and her lover were two different people when they had sex in cyberspace and when they had coffee in the real cafeteria.

The possibility of experimenting with identities, disguise and anonymity, as well as the ability to disappear, are prominent topics in discussions on virtuality. The complexity and scope of global connectivity – and especially the speed with which such connections are established – still appear mind-blowing to most of us (as does the risk of computer viruses closing down world-wide computer systems in seconds). Kozel (1998b: 86) argues that 'the ability to disappear is central to the experience of the body electric'. When she took part in the *Telematic Dreaming* installation she could have disappeared by moving away from the bed and out of the frames of the video camera or by hiding in the chromakey sheet (which would have made her merge into the background). She could also have left one part of her body such as a foot within reach of the camera. For Kozel does not investigate sudden and total virtual absence, but 'this now-you-see-me-now-you-don't quality', and the departure and the return to the body after having travelled in cyberspace. The social and political change of such journeys has a wider application far beyond the dance and arts world. This is one aspect of social virtuality.

With a Dancer's Eye

Although visual anthropologists have long been aware of the importance of vision and alternative ways of seeing, this interest is now making its way into other areas of anthropology as well. As Grimshaw (2001: 172) recently argued, 'vision is central to modern anthropology' especially in the production of ethnography (see also Ginsburg 1998 and MacDougall 1997, 1998). Banks and Morphy (1997: 5) have identified 'visual systems' and 'visible cultural forms' thereby opening up visual anthropology to the anthropology of art (Thomas 1997), aesthetics (cf. Banks 1997, Hendry 1997) and technology (Edwards 1997, Born 1997, Hughes-Freeland 1997, Wulff 2002b) among other fields.

It is a dancer's job to be looked at. Even though music and sound (also in the form of silence) is an important part of dance, and I will come back to the impact of sound on the visual in *Riverdance* below, dancers are without doubt the targets of visuality. How then do dancers, who are taught to be watched, watch dance themselves? One explanation for why dancers are uneasy about recorded dance on screen is that the same choreographic section looks different on stage than on a screen. It is an instance when the 'eye' of the camera, 'the third eye', registers other pictures than does the human eye. Screen dance inevitably has us watch dance through the camera.

Live dance performances are usually videoed for a number of reasons: dance productions need to be documented for future revivals, for choreographers' and dancers' curriculum vitae and for dance history records. But live dance is also importantly videoed for ongoing rehearsal work. If something went wrong in the performance – or unexpectedly well – the video can often explain why. It can be stopped, a certain section can be rewound over and over again and contemplated. It happens that dancers are summoned to watch the performance video when the performance has just ended, before they leave the theatre, but usually this viewing takes place the day after. One of the issues at stake, then, is what the audience saw and what it did not see. Most performance videos are recorded from a static position, they do not zoom in on solos or other parts of the proceedings on stage. The members of the audience, on the other hand, are able to move their heads and gazes from one side of the stage to the other and upward and downward across the proscenium arch. The difference between the static videoing and the moving gaze of the audience is especially noteworthy when there is a big stage with many dancers and a lot of stage properties and set design as well as an orchestra and a conductor (cf. Wulff 1999).

There are very few active dancers and choreographers left now who did not grow up with television and video. This means that dancers are used to screen images, they have been socialized into reading and responding to images on screens, into quickly making their own visual selections in a flow of pictures. Yet their dance training was oriented toward live dance, not toward dancing on or for screens. In live dance and ballet, bodily expressions, especially facial expressions, have to be clear and simple in order to reach out in theatre auditoria. This is obviously less of a problem in so-called chamber dance, featuring a few dancers for a small audience or experimental performance settings, than in big theatres such as opera houses where it takes a little while before movements and facial expressions reach the audience high up and far away on the third balcony. A smiling dancer has to allow some time for the audience to react to the smile, before moving on to the next step. In classical ballet, crucial turns of events are explained through mime such as when the Prince in Swan Lake lifts his right arm high up in front of him with two fingers pointing upward meaning 'I promise and swear to always love you!' On video and television, dancers' movements and facial expressions have to be adjusted to the smaller screen, and are thus more delicate and nuanced. For the camera is merciless, registering unbecoming details in costume and make-up, as well as sweat and panting that, however, can be edited later (cf. Wulff 1999).

Another aesthetic circumstance in screen dance is that not every dancer with a renowned stage personality comes across as forcefully on screen as on stage. There seems to be a photogenic quality, like looking good in a photograph, about being able to communicate via a screen. And among those dancers who have this quality, there are some who turn out to be very bleak on stage. On a bad day, in a small role, it is possible to hide on stage. This is out of the question when a dancer is being filmed for a video or television. Still, making dance for video or television entails the option to repeat the filming a number of times if things are unsatisfactory, whereas live dance performances cannot be stopped and restarted while in progress. From the dancers' point of view this is an advantage of screen dance over live dance, just as the possibility to film a long sequence during a number of short cuts that later are put together. There are, however, often longer periods of time in between the dancing during filming than in between entrances in the theatre. Such long waits interrupt the acting process as well as dancers' concern about keeping warm in order to avoid injury. All of a sudden a dancer is expected to get into a role or a feeling again, while in the theatre dancers are more or less inside a role all evening. Another aspect of dancing in television studios is that the floors are often too hard for dancing, which is yet another risk of causing injury (cf. Wulff 1998 on injuries, 1999).

Making Dance for the Screen

The most widely used choreography computer software is *Lifeforms*, which many choreographers work with as they start new productions (Wulff 1999). They take notes, so to speak, by drafting steps on the screen, and then have real dancers in a studio doing the steps. Based on what that looks like, the choreographer then makes changes on the screen, and tries these out on the real dancers again. This can go on for a while. When English choreographer Mark Baldwin works with *Lifeforms* he has the dancers videoed together with a footage of his own improvisations, which he then edits and shows to his dancers with the aim of inspiring them in their improvisations. Elizabeth Charman (1995) has discussed how Baldwin makes use of technological accidents especially when there is a shaky passage between sections in the movement flow. To make aesthetic points out of such 'accidents' has in fact been something of a style among choreographers with an interest in technology. A spin-off of making choreography on software is that this has also produced a new dance form: the little dance figures in the software are printed out as animated stills that are enlarged and exhibited in art galleries. Importantly, these stills can portray animated dancers turning and twisting their bodies in ways real dancers cannot.

As American dance historian and critic Joan Cass (1993) has noted, the pioneers of dance on television and video, choreographers such as Merce Cunningham and Twyla Tharp, have declared that they do not want to have 'a repertory' (e.g. revive their productions time after another), they strive to move on to new ideas. Paradoxically perhaps, the video dances of Cunningham and Twarp will be preserved, they will be there to watch for anyone over time.

Dance videos are broadcast on television, stage dance is filmed for television, and dance is choreographed for television and recorded in a studio. Stage dance can also be rechoreographed for television filming. Video dance and dance on television tend to feature double exposures, slow motion, close-ups, changing camera angles. What used to be a two-dimensional technology now includes a third dimension, depth. This is created by way of chromakey technique which offers a change and choice of background such as from the studio to a mountain landscape via a city centre and then on to a kitchen. Dancers can be edited to move through all these places.

Swedish choreographer Birgit Cullberg (1992), who was among the pioneers in television choreography (the most famous pieces are probably *Miss Julie* and *Medea*), wrote about the aesthetic consequences of the fact that the television screen is small and rectangular. Inspired by how movement was created through contrast inside rectangular frames in Renaissance art and modern paintings, Cullberg saw how the enclosed television screen released new choreographic form. Cullberg worked with the whole screen, and had dancers moving toward the camera in close-ups. She arranged platforms at different levels for the dancers to move on, some of them in the foreground, others in the background. Cullberg also experimented with the law of gravity, especially different ways to disregard it by having dancers making entrances from above or below, and inserting a foot or a hand from the side (Wulff 1999).

In a review of choreographer Kenneth Kvarnström's television dance *5 danser*, dance scholar and critic Cecilia Olsson (1995) has described how Kvarnström works with slow motion and moves out of the usual television format by creating a cinematic mailbox format:

> ... it is the camera which creates dynamics: cuts, close-ups, dissolves, double exposures and slow camera movements, connect, rhythmize, and give the dance a form. Time and space are manipulated in ways that are impossible on stage.

Riverdance: Technology in the Global Marketplace

It was on 30 April 1994 that seven minutes of traditional Irish dancing dressed up in glamour during the interval of the Eurovision Song Contest mesmerized millions[6] of television viewers. Surfing on the economic boom, the so-called Celtic Tiger, which was still making progress in the Republic of Ireland at the time, *Riverdance* became a symbol for Irish modernity, confidence and prosperity. The show also became a target of Irish debate, however, raising questions about authenticity and representation such as: who has the right to represent Ireland abroad, and what should this representation look like?

The success in the Eurovision Song Contest spurred producers Moya Doherty and John McColgan to build the seven minutes of Irish step dancing into a full-length show lasting for two hours. They were aiming for an Irish show which would feature elements of crossover and in this spirit they added a flamenco dancer, a troupe of Russian folk ballet, African-American tap dancers and gospel with an Irish choir to the Irish dancing. Taking its departure in 'our ancestors ... and their bond with the place they called home' (Riverdance The Show Official Programme 1998: 30), i.e. Ireland, the story unfolds celebrating the Irish land, tradition and mythology. Act two begins with a total change of mood: it portrays the pain of emigration, the arrival to the New World in the United States and a tour around the globe. This is where the crossover comes in. Then there is a happy ending with a homecoming to Ireland. The dancing is mixed with poetry read by a male voice. The show is accompanied by Irish music played on stage, but also by sections of prerecorded step sound, so-called 'support sound' which has been one point of controversy about the show. It was the dancers who first told me about these tapes. To them, the prerecorded step sound was helpful, for if someone forgets a step or makes a mistake, it is less visible, less obvious because the step sound from the tapes 'evens out' irregularities in the dancers' execution. So the visual appearance of remarkable physical co-ordination of the troupe is in fact partly created through a sonorous manipulation. Yet the composer Bill Whelan explained to me that this 'support sound' was crucial for coming across in the huge sport arenas and theatre houses where *Riverdance* is performed. This is also why the leading dancers are 'miked' – they carry tiny microphones on the back of their shoes in order to amplify the sound of their steps. This focus on the sound of dance goes back to the centrality of the sound of dance, the *clicks*, in traditional competitive Irish dancing, the dance form that *Riverdance* evolved from.

The producers Doherty and McColgan did have some problems with the funding of the full-length show, 'because no one really believed in the project!' as set designer Robert Ballagh commented to me in an interview. In fact, Doherty and McColgan were putting a major sum of their private money at stake (Smyth 1996). It would not take long, however, before financial worries were a memory of the past: soon they were to make more money than they could possibly ever have dreamed of.

As *Riverdance* graduated into a full-length show with its mind set on foreign tours, it was time for marketing strategies. One such strategy was to do the show as a part of Irish festivals abroad. Another, even more important, marketing strategy has involved technology: *Riverdance* became an instant hit on television, and this is the medium that has been the most effective in reaching the vast number of people who now remember having caught a glimpse on television of the long Chorus Line of Irish dancers pounding out their intricate steps at high speed in the signature section of the show. Documentary programmes have contextualized the show backstage, on tours and also in Ireland. Every time *Riverdance* comes on tour to another country, and often when the show comes back, one of the television programmes has been broadcast as a trailer to the live show. But, again, the scope of the fame of *Riverdance* was produced by the television appearances. According to the Media Information Pack from 1998, the number of people who had been touched by *Riverdance* on television was even higher than the already remarkable figure of 5 million people who had come to the live show. The figure of 'in excess of 1 billion people' (ibid.: 5) watching *Riverdance* certainly makes the head spin. It does not come with any specifications, however, such as the same fans watching as many times as they can, or the geographical distribution of this watching. The Media Information Pack moreover presents sales figures for the four videos: more than 6 million copies sold between 1994 and 1998. The composer Bill Whelan won a Grammy Award for the CD record with the music in 1997.

Television, video and CD records have thus been central marketing technologies for *Riverdance* spreading the whole show, sections of it as well as documentaries about it. But the use of technology in the show such as the prerecorded step sound has also been important for the force of the performance. The large size of the live show is a part of the concept: the set is huge and the technological equipment with flashing lights backstage, computers and mixing tables is massive in order to create blazing rock-show lighting on stage.

In his book about the making of *Riverdance*, Irish journalist Sam Smyth (1996) reports on the opening night of the full-length show which took place at the Point Theatre in Dublin in 1995. The show ended with a standing ovation that went on for nearly half an hour. There was a British agent in the audience the next night, and he offered *Riverdance* to do ten performances at the Labatt's Apollo Theatre in London. They stayed for one hundred and fifty-one performances! This was when conflicts began over control of the show and the choreographic rights, says Smyth. The stars of the show had made most of the choreography, but who had done what sections? Who, for instance, was the brain behind the long line of thirty-two Irish dancers? It was probably this formation that sparked the entire success of *Riverdance*. There had been lines before in competitive Irish dancing, but not this long, which produces a very powerful effect when the dancers move at an accelerating speed in total unison toward the audience. The choreographic rights were difficult to settle since the choreography is not notated. As the show shot to new levels of success this became more of an issue than it had been before. The choreographers are acknowledged in the *Riverdance* programme, but it is quite remarkable that the advertisements for this dance show credit the composer, the producer and the director – but no choreographer.

Conclusions: Social Virtuality in Dance Technoscapes

Has dance then finally been caught? The elusive nature of dance, often called 'the art of the moment', is now set on all kinds of screen to be viewed over and over again. This chapter has discussed the changing technoscapes of dance, how dancers work and watch dance. Global collaborations in dance were exemplified in the beginning by the dance production *Ghosts and Astronauts*, which was performed in London and California at the same time via the Internet's video-conference link. This is only one among many ways to use this link, which connects artistic, scholarly and political conferences and meetings globally.[7]

Combining Benjamin's (1969 [1936]) classic idea about the political equality potential of 'mechanical reproduction' of art, Sorell's (1981: 399) exclamation about 'the triumph of technology' for the arts, and Hanna's (1988) report on a survey about the increase in dance performance audiences after dance was introduced on television in the United States, I have suggested that dance on television and video have contributed to a democratizing of dance. More people have been reached by dance through technology such as television, video and the

Internet than was the case before the advent of these technologies. Dance also appears in new arenas through technologies. Music videos often feature dance sections, for example, as do television commercials and technological art installations. Even though technology has been linked to dance as long as it has existed, digital technology has opened up an even greater awareness of dance. As dance writer Jennifer Dunning (1999: 10) summarizes:

> Today's computer technology can make important contributions to the inherently visual art of dance, and dance contributes to the evolution of the technology, as it did with film.

In discussions about whether new technology has revolutionized social life or not, I am taking the stance that in dance it certainly has. Not only has new technology revolutionized dance as an art form, i.e. the aesthetics, but it has also entailed major changes in the work practice. For even though the Euro-American dance world has always been transnational (cf. Wulff 1998), global and transnational connections and collaborations have increased dramatically with new technology. It has also entailed that choreographers and dancers work with new categories of people such as sound designers, movie directors and video artists. The Irish dance show *Riverdance* is one of the dance forms to which this applies. I have analysed *Riverdance* in terms of a commercial enterprise in the global marketplace. Technology, especially television trailers, but also videos and CD records, have been the principal points in the marketing and thus in the global success of the show. There is also technology in the performance: rock-show lighting and sound, and of course the debated prerecorded step sound.

New technology has, moreover, evoked a discussion about reality versus virtuality, and body versus machine, as if these entities were completely separate. Based on my ethnographic experience of dance and new technology I would like to suggest that bodies and machines can be closely connected in a type of social relationship. This is in agreement with Miller and Slater (2000: 6–8) who argue that life on-line is a part of everyday life off-line. Virtuality is as real and social as any life form (cf. the Introduction to this volume).

There is a traditional distrust among Euro-American dance people of recorded representations of their dance, and this is still lingering on in relation to new technologies and screen dance. It is seen as less real, and unable to convey the excitement and closeness of live dance. Swedish dancer and choreographer Åsa Unander-Scharin once described for me what it is like to be filmed in a studio:

> without an audience, you don't know who you're communicating with. You lose the sense of the spatial. On stage you relate to the entire room, but when you're being filmed, there's only one angle.

This obviously makes the dancing different. An unease with technology, and its representations of reality, is admittedly not confined to the dance world, but is still a part of social life. Many computer users have experienced an initial euphoria, a trance-like state when the whole world seems to be within reach through the Internet, but this phase gradually disappears. For even though technology is everywhere around us, and definitely here to stay, there has recently been something of a backlash when it comes to using technology in dance (cf. Parry 1998/1999, Rubidge 1999). Choreographers often run out of technological-imagination steam. Those who work and experiment with new technology tend not to stop creating technological dance, however, but after an intense period with technology, it is common that they refrain from it for a while. This does not mean that they go back to the state before technology, however. Because of the impact technology has had, its absence is noticed. This is when dance becomes unplugged.

Acknowledgements

This article draws on studies funded by the Swedish Research Council for the Humanities and Social Sciences and the Bank of Sweden Tercentenary Foundation.

Notes

1. Telematics is a technology that connects distant places in various ways, but basically through image and sound. Before making *Ghosts and Astronauts*, Kozel (1998a) set up a telematic performance link for a piece titled *Multi-Medea: Exiles* between Vancouver and London. In Vancouver, Kozel was dancing at midnight with another dancer who was in London at dawn. This technique was also used by Wayne McGregor who was dancing in London with Australian dancers in Melbourne in the transcontinental performance called *Trial by Video* (Parry 1998/1999). In 2002, another piece by McGregor, titled *Phase space*, was performed by ten dancers in Stockholm and ten dancers in Suffolk, England. While the Stockholm dancers were being filmed from the wings and this footage simultaneously was projected on a screen in England for the English dancers, the latter appeared on a transparent screen in Stockholm doing the same steps and dressed in the same costumes as the Swedish dancers. The dancers did not really interact across the North Sea, however, at least not from the Stockholm point of view, according to which the screen with dancers was more like a film on a backdrop (Ångström 2002).
2. See Sally Banes (in preparation) for a discussion of the problems of choreo-

graphic copyright in the United States. See also Acocella (2001) on the ten-year conflict over Martha Graham's dance estate. This conflict was finally settled through a court decision in 2002 when Martha Graham Centre won the the ownership of ten dances created by Graham (Prodance News 2002).

3. It is important for dancers to put rosin on their soles since that will give them a good grip. If a dancer slips, it often causes injury.

4. Despite digital experiments with viewer participation in interactive dance installations on CD-ROM where viewers are asked to select and combine dance sections, there is obviously no physical touch through the screen. Touching the screen does not mean touching another human body.

5. For even though there is always the risk that technology such as television sets and VCRs break down, or videotapes get stuck, video dance does imply that there is a recording of a dance piece from beginning to end. During the course of live dance, many things can go wrong, a performance may have to be interrupted and even stopped in the middle because a leading dancer gets injured, for example (Wulff 1998a, 1998b).

6. Riverdance Media Information Pack (1998: 5) reports that an estimated 300 million viewers were watching *Riverdance* breaking through. *Riverdance* is included as one dance form in my current study of dance and culture in Ireland and questions of social memory, modernity and place. The other dance forms are dance theatre, traditional and competitive dancing (see Wulff 2002a, 2003).

7. The videoconference link on the Internet is also used for emergency medical consultations across vast distances.

References

Acocella, Joan (2001), 'The Flame: the Battle over Martha Graham's Dances', *The New Yorker*, 19 and 26 February: 180–95.

Ångström, Anna (2002), 'Hisnande idé – blek konst', *Svenska Dagbladet*, 30 April.

Appadurai, Arjun (1996), *Modernity at Large: Cultural Dimensions of Globalization*, Minneapolis: University of Minnesota Press.

Banes, Sally (in preparation), 'Homage, Plagiarism, Allusion, Comments, Quotation: Negotiating Choreographic Appropriation'.

Banks, Marcus (1997), 'Representing the Bodies of the Jains', in M. Banks and H. Morphy (eds), *Rethinking Visual Anthropology*, New Haven: Yale University Press.

Banks, Marcus and Morphy, Howard (1997), 'Introduction: Rethinking Visual Anthropology', in M. Banks and H. Morphy (eds), *Rethinking Visual Anthropology*, New Haven: Yale University Press.

Benjamin, Walter (1969 [1936]), 'The Work of Art in the Age of Mechanical Reproduction', in *Illuminations*, New York: Schocken.

Born, Georgina (1997), 'Computer Software as a Medium: Textuality, Orality and Sociality in an Artificial Intelligence Research Culture', in M. Banks and H. Morphy (eds), *Rethinking Visual Anthropology*, New Haven: Yale University Press

Cass, Joan (1993), *Dancing through History*, Englewood Cliffs, NJ: Prentice Hall.

Charman, Elizabeth (1995), 'Dances from Cyberspace', *Dance Now*, 4(4): 63–5.

Cullberg, Birgit (1992), 'Television Ballet', in W. Sorell (ed.), *The Dance Has Many Faces*, Pennington, NJ: a capella books.

Dafova, Marina (1999), 'Cunningham's Ghost Dancers: Motion Capture', *Ballett International*, 10: 55.

Dunning, Jennifer (1999), 'Choreographers and the Computer: It's a Pas de Deux', *International Herald Tribune*, 25 February.

Edwards, Elizabeth (1997), 'Beyond the Boundary: a Consideration of the Expressive in Photography and Anthropology', in M. Banks and H. Morphy (eds), *Rethinking Visual Anthropology*, New Haven: Yale University Press.

Ginsburg, Gaye (1998), 'Institutionalizing the Unruly: Charting a Future for Visual Anthropology', *Ethnos*, 63(2): 173–201.

Grimshaw, Anna (2001), *The Ethnographer's Eye: Ways of Seeing in Modern Anthropology*, Cambridge: Cambridge University Press.

Hanna, Judith Lynne (1988), *Dance, Sex and Gender: Signs of Identity, Dominance, Defiance and Desire*, Chicago: University of Chicago Press.

Hendry, Joy (1997), 'Pine, Ponds and Pebbles: Gardens and Visual Culture', in M. Banks and H. Morphy (eds), *Rethinking Visual Anthropology*, New Haven: Yale University Press.

Hughes-Freeland, Felicia (1997), 'Balinese on Television: Representation and Response', in M. Banks and H. Morphy (eds), *Rethinking Visual Anthropology*, New Haven: Yale University Press.

Kozel, Susan (1998a), 'Exiles, Ghosts and Astronauts', *Aura*, IV(1): 83–90.

—— (1998b [1996]), 'Spacemaking: Experiences of a Virtual Body', in A. Carter (ed.), *The Routledge Dance Studies Reader*, London: Routledge.

MacDougall, David (1997), 'The Visual in Anthropology', in M. Banks and H. Morphy (eds), *Rethinking Visual Anthropology*, New Haven: Yale University Press.

—— (1998), *Transcultural Cinema*, Princeton, NJ: Princeton University Press.

Media Information Pack. Riverdance The Show (1998), Unpublished brochure.

Miller, Daniel and Slater, Don (2000), *The Internet: an Ethnographic Approach*, Oxford: Berg.

Olsson, Cecilia (1995), 'Flöde av laddad energi: Kameran skapar dynamiken i TV-rutan'. *Dagens Nyheter*, 16 November.

Parry, Jann (1998/1999), 'Site-Seeing Tour', *Dance Now*, 7(4): 9–14.

Penman, Robert (1993), 'Ballet and Contemporary Dance on British Television', in S. Jordan and D. Allen (eds), *Parallel Lines*, London: John Libbey.

Prodance News (2002), The Assocation of Professional Dancers in Ireland, November, unpublished brochure.

Riverdance The Show Official Programme (1998), Unpublished brochure.

Rubidge, Sarah (1993), 'Recent Dance Made for Television', in S. Jordan and D. Allen (eds), *Parallel Lines*, London: John Libbey.

—— (1999), 'Defining Digital Dance', *DanceTheatreJournal*, 14(4): 41–5.

Smyth, Sam (1996), *Riverdance: The Story*, London: André Deutsch.

Sorell, Walter (1981), *Dance in Its Time*, New York: Columbia University Press.

Thomas, Nicholas (1997), 'Collectivity and Nationality in the Anthropology of Art', in M. Banks and H. Morphy (eds), *Rethinking Visual Anthropology*, New Haven: Yale University Press.

Williams, Raymond (1975), *Television*, New York: Schocken.

Wulff, Helena (1998a), *Ballet across Borders: Career and Culture in the World of Dancers*, Oxford: Berg.

—— (1998b), 'Perspectives toward Ballet Performance: Exploring, Repairing and Maintaining Frames', in F. Hughes-Freeland (ed.), *Ritual, Performance, Media,* London: Routledge.

—— (1999), 'Representing and Creating Dance: A Social Organization of New Technology and Aesthetics', *Antropologiska Studier*, 62–3: 33–41.

—— (2001), 'Dance, anthropology of', in N.J. Smelser and P.B. Baltes (eds), *International Encyclopedia of the Social and Behavioral Sciences*, Oxford: Pergamon/Elsevier Science, pp. 3209–12.

—— (2002a), 'Yo-yo Fieldwork: Mobility and Time in a Multi-Local Study of Dance in Ireland', *Anthropological Journal on European Cultures*, issue on Shifting Grounds: Experiments in Doing Ethnography, 11: 117–36.

—— (2002b), 'Shooting the Dancer: Photography, Market and Aesthetics', Paper for workshop on 'Art, Aesthetics and Artists: Renegotiating Collective Representations, Agency, and Visualization' at 7th Biennal EASA Conference, Copenhagen, 14–17 August.

—— (2003), 'The Irish Body in Motion: Moral Politics, National Identity and Dance', in E.P. Archetti and N. Dyck (eds), *Sport, Dance and Embodied Identities*, Oxford: Berg.

Screening the Classroom: Students, Teachers and Computers in an Urban American School

William Washabaugh, Catherine Washabaugh, Mary Roffers, and Kira Kaufmann

Introduction

Ethnographies are traditionally impartial accounts. This one is not. They usually spring from participant observation, with more emphasis placed on observation than on participation. Here the reverse is the case. We confess to being partial and biased in our descriptions of the social life and learning practices of an urban American high school classroom. Moreover, we emphasize our participation in the lives of the high school teachers and students whose activities we describe. We are pursuing this line because we are not only describing the results of observations in classrooms, but also reporting on the impact of our attempts to intervene and promote innovative teaching above and beyond traditional methods of lecture and textbook.

This chapter outlines the successes and failures of a specialized high school teaching team created to address the needs of students identified as 'at risk'. These 'at-risk' students fit the profile of those who have high rates of academic failure, of absenteeism and of dropping out. This particular team formed a school-within-a-school to tackle these problems and to increase their students' success in a post-secondary-school education or career. Additionally, this chapter reports on the social and academic changes that took place as a result of our efforts to introduce computers and to integrate computer use into a small number of classes at Riverside University High School, Milwaukee, Wisconsin. We took advantage of information technology to reorganize classroom activities around research on the Internet and to facilitate the creation by students of multimedia digital reports. Whereas traditional methods attract the attention of only certain types of learners, such as reading and aural learners, teaching with technology engages a wide array of learners, such as those who are visual or kinetic learners.

Among the authors, Catherine is one of the teachers on this special high school team, and William is a professor of Anthropology who has been helping to develop computer-assisted learning practices at UWM for the past decade.

The Setting

We worked in three classrooms at Riverside University High School (RUHS) in Milwaukee, Wisconsin. It is an old and hallowed institution located on the 'East Side' of the city. Revered as one of the city's first high schools, it has recently enjoyed newfound prominence – and a revised name – as the result of an alliance with a local university.

We observed the behaviour of four teachers and an aide as they worked with about eighty students who circulated between their classes in this small school-within-a-school unit. While the rest of the school population is somewhat more evenly distributed, more than 90 per cent of the students in this 'at risk' group are African American and Hispanic. Less than 10 per cent come from the white majority who live in the largely white, university-dominated 'East Side' community. This unusual demography is explained by the social and political history of the school and of the school district.[1]

A brief description of the physical situation at RUHS will help one understand the behaviour we observed. The school building dates from 1915. The corridors are a dozen feet wide, and the ceilings reach eleven and twelve feet. The terrazzo stairs are hollowed from decades of use. The hardwood floors are bronzed and resonant and scarred by the permanent seating that was long ago replaced by moveable desks and tables.

Classroom size varies; from 700 to 900 square feet. In most rooms, a bank of windows forms one wall. The original windows were nine feet high but, in the 1970s they were retrofitted with opaque hardboard insulating sheets that cover two-thirds of the original window area. The one-third-sized windows that remain are glazed with polycarbonate that yellows over time, becoming milky and translucent. Only two of these small window panels can be opened for fresh air. Steam-heated radiators stand under the windows. The school has no air-conditioning.

The student body arrives at 7:25 a.m. The boys generally wear sneakers and baggy pants slung low to offer just a glimpse of colourful boxer shorts beneath. Shirts are fashionably baggy, or simply T-shirts. The boys' hair is usually short or braided in corn rows. A few boys sport long hair. Girls wear close-fitting pants, tight T-shirts, high square-heeled shoes or sneakers or sandals. Boys as well as girls wear necklaces, but girls adorn themselves with more accessories, such as finger rings, multiple earrings, piercings and facial jewelry. The girls' hair is variously and often quite creatively styled.

Prior to the sounding of the bell that signals the beginning of a class, students jostle in the hallways. They run at, and dodge, each other, yelling and laughing, hugging and punching. The pandemonium eventually subsides after the bell, but not immediately. At the beginning of each teaching hour, the teachers in this group face the uphill challenge of quelling student noise and focusing their attention. Often these teachers are forced to remove disruptive individuals from the room. Periodically in each day, and then day after day and week after week, this scenario leaves teachers frustrated and students resentful. Worse, these students often end their high school years ill-prepared to operate as intelligent adults. They leave without the skills and knowledge they will need to shoulder the responsibilities of employment and citizenship in their later years.

The source of the problem is decades of poverty in a society where wealth is inequitably distributed, as Jonathan Kozol has explained (1991). The children of the poor in Milwaukee grow up in families where scholarship often cannot be pursued as the first priority and where education is not always highly valued. These are some of the children that come to RUHS. Some of their disruptive behaviour springs from the fact that they – or at least many – are 'at-risk' students in need of special attention. Their learning disabilities are emotional and cognitive, but not unrelated to the raft of deeply rooted and highly publicized social problems that lie beyond the school's influence, as indicated above. Still the teachers and staff at RUHS are doing all they can within the limits of time and funding to fit them out with learning skills and critical-thinking practices.

In the year 2000, with support from the University of Wisconsin System Administration and from the Cultures and Communities Program at UWM, we began an initiative aimed at preparing teachers with the knowledge and skills necessary for marrying teaching practices with information technology in their classrooms. We provided teachers with the knowledge and skills necessary for developing innovative teaching practices that involve the use of computers in the classroom. During the 2001/02 academic year, with support from the Carl Perkins Grant for education (http://www.dpi.state.wi.us/dpi/dlsis/let/cpgrant.html), we were able to deploy a mobile system of twenty-one laptop computers with wireless Internet connections to be used in project-based learning modules by the three cohorts of 'at-risk' students at RUHS. The intervention then proceeded into the 2002/03 academic year. Two anthropology graduate students, Ms. Mary Roffers and Ms. Kira Kaufmann, assisted in the project. They coached teachers and students, made observations and recorded the changes in classroom social life. They provided immediate at-the-elbow guidance to students as they learned to use the Internet. They coached on issues such as critical inspection of resources, evaluation of websites, assessment of biases, and techniques for creating digital reports. Together, we introduced new kinds of learning practices to about 75 students during the spring semester of 2002. In broad terms, they learned the meaning of self-directed assignments, self-review, group commentaries on assignments, project-editing, critical thinking, justifications for decisions about student work, and computer-competency skills. Finally, we observed the changes in their behaviour that followed in the wake of these introductions.

The Project

The aim of our intervention was to introduce teachers and students to learning practices that are computer-assisted, discipline-integrating, project-based, all the while emphasizing visual literacy as a complement to textual literacy. The aim of this chapter is to report on the impact of our intervention into the school lives of teachers and students. In order for readers to appreciate the impact of this intervention, one must first appreciate the substance and content of the intervention itself. To this end, we will explain each of the four aspects of the programme.

First, we encourage teachers to devise computer-assisted learning assignments. The advantages are multiple. Obviously, students learn marketable computer skills. The medium of their learning is brought into line with the media of interaction they will face as adults, where finding a library book, filing taxes or ordering concert tickets will all require some computer literacy. Even more importantly, computer-assisted learning makes it possible to shift the classroom spotlight away from teachers and to place it on students. With well-designed learning projects, the students' particular needs and skills, as well as the students' preferences and penchants, play a direct and immediate role in lessons they learn. As a result, student motivation for learning is enhanced. Finally, the Internet makes it possible for teachers and students to supplement classroom and school resources with those available on the World Wide Web, thereby effectively transcending the boundaries of the classroom and the walls of the school.

In computer-assisted learning, the Internet often assumes a significant role as a learning resource in the classroom. In this role, it is promising, but fraught with dangers that teachers and school administrators have been quick to point out. First and most obviously, many websites advance erroneous, hateful and obscene material. Such sites constitute a danger to young and impressionable students, a danger that is only partly mitigated by the filters that constrain all Internet activities within the school. But secondly, and less often mentioned, the Internet is dangerous because it presents students with a virtual tsunami of information, an onrush of data that begs for, but rarely receives, selective attention, careful discernment and critical reflection. One particularly problematic aspect of this onrush of information is its speed. Words and images come pouring forth onto the screen and are replaced with the touch of a button by more words and more images.

In the face of this dangerously rapid information turnover, we encourage teachers to develop lesson plans that include measures to slow down the outpouring of information, plans that encourage the students to pause over images and to pore over pictures rather than glancing at them momentarily. Students need to avoid aimless, saltatory explorations of the Internet, and must instead focus their attention if they are to take full advantage of the disciplinary integration that our intervention includes.

This second dimension, disciplinary integration, was already well developed in this small cohort of RUHS teachers during the years prior to our intervention. These teachers recognized the importance of integrating studies of literature, history, art, mathematics, cultural studies and career skills. It is not just because these disciplines complement each other that they warrant integration. More importantly, integration is warranted by the fact that the most profound forms of learning are those that arise as students reflect on ideas and facts in diverse contexts. For example, female sexual surgery can be described anatomically with some profit, but students gain a more profound understanding of it when they consider it with an eye to cultural studies (as an enforced practice in many African societies), literary studies (as compared to the suffering of women in writings as diverse as those of Maya Angelou and Kamala Markandaya) and its bearing on health and hygiene. David Perkins and his collaborators (1991) have recommended that teachers embrace a pedagogical goal of 'inside under-standing', fostering learning that is flexible, malleable and endlessly productive. Such inside understanding is one of the benefits of drawing knowledge from one experience and then applying it in different ways to other experiences. In other words, 'inside understanding' is a result and benefit of well-designed interdisciplinary studies.

Inside understanding is not something that teachers can force down the throats of students. It only comes when the students make their own learning leaps. Consequently, our intervention has emphasized student-centred and project-based learning. 'Although the teacher may have considerable responsibility in facilitating investigative and discovery activities, it is expected that the students will gradually take responsibility for their own learning' (Glasgow 1997: 34). 'Problem-based learning supports the integration of content, process, and concept learning through the engagement of students in realistic problems' (Boyce et al. 1997: 374).

Twenty-one Internet-ready laptops can turn a conventional classroom into a project laboratory instantaneously, and such a transformation can be promising and exciting. However, an unfortunate consequence that we observed is that students can easily slip into a highly focused solipsistic mode of project-development. They 'zone out', ignoring peers, teachers, distractions and advice as they immerse themselves in projects of their own design. As some educators have observed, project-based learner-centred activities sends an implicit message that 'collaboration and interaction with peers is not central, nor even necessary ... learning [becomes] a highly individualistic, autonomous, non-social activity' (Gifford and Enyedy, 1999). We worked to avoid such exaggerated individuation and self-isolation by creating teams of students who would either collaborate in producing a single project or assist each other in the production of multiple projects.

Finally, and perhaps most importantly, our intervention places an emphasis on visual literacy as a complement to the textual literacy that drives much of the curriculum in contemporary schools. The warrant for this emphasis is straight-forward: the ability to discern, analyse and construct visual images relies on cognitive operations that are at least as sophisticated as those needed to read, analyse and write texts. Moreover, the operations involved in the former rein-force those involved in the latter. Given that visual media are approachable and appealing, we argue that the visual deserves a stronger place in school curricula in our own day, even as it was emphasized in European education until the end of the eighteenth century. Our views of the benefits to be realized from empha-sizing visual literacy are echoed in the writings of Barbara Stafford:

> Public education is in a shambles … Students and educators alike perceive schools as ineffectual and boring. Instead of attempting futilely to retrieve nineteenth-century ideals and standards of textual literacy, it might be helpful to focus on the other side of the historical story … High-order thinking was taught [in the 18th c.] in the construc-tion of visual patterns, and optical technology often boosted the learning process of difficult abstractions (Stafford 1994: xxiii).

In order to enhance the visual literacy skills of students as they pursue proj-ects and explore the Internet, we encourage teachers to introduce elementary concepts of figure, ground, pattern and juxtaposition, and to direct student atten-tion to visual aesthetics and to the role of contrast, simplicity and co-ordination in image construction. For example, students in Ms Washabaugh's classes began studying visual experience by mapping on paper the colours and fonts appro-priate for presenting *The Raven* by Edgar Allan Poe. Only later did they experi-ment with background colour, font colour, font type and size as they developed digital reports (on Microsoft WORD documents) on Harlem-Renaissance artists they had selected for another project.

The Changing Life of an Urban High School Classroom

We began to make use of laptop computers in the freshman English class at RUHS in January of 2002. As we took the first steps, we were acutely aware of the behavioural track record that had been accumulated by the 75 students between September and December. To say that the students were disruptive would be an understatement. Absenteeism was high. When students did come to school, they arrived late to class. When they did arrive, they refused to sit down and attend the teacher. They regularly talked to each other about personal issues before and then during class, often loudly. It was a monumental achievement when teachers were able to gather the attention of a whole group of twenty students, but this achievement was rarely sustained for any lengthy period. If a teacher tried to advance a classroom discussion by posing an open-ended question to the group, the response was a barrage of remarks designed more clearly to make impressions on other students than to advance the discussion intended by the teacher.

When computers were introduced into the classrooms for the first time, the teachers, graduate-student assistants and project director were more than a little nervous in the face of this track record. The technical support specialist in the school added to the anxiety by raising concerns about the strong possibility that the machines would be damaged during classroom use. He, like us, could see that these freshmen classrooms had developed a carnivalesque atmosphere in which computers might as well be used for basketball as for word-processing and web-supported projects.

To alter this atmosphere, we walked students through a series of procedures for withdrawing computers from the mobile storage cart, for powering them up, for shutting them down and for returning them to their original place. We reinforced our instructions with a short film that illustrated these steps. We required that students proceed singly to the storage cart, that they sign in and sign out, that they keep two hands on the laptop computers when moving, and that they remain with the computers while they are in operation. By enforcing these procedures, we hoped to promote a temperate level of energy and activity in the classrooms.

These steps, which we enforced as evenly and consistently as we could, did help to moderate the classroom atmosphere at the same time as the new computer-centred activities helped to focus students' interest. However, they inadvertently created a new problem. Some students came to the classroom with some computer skills, and others with none at all. Some of the former complained that they were being treated like babies:

A student named Daisy gets Ms Washabaugh's attention, exclaiming 'I am a 3.8 student. I know how to use this computer. Ms Washabaugh, you are treating us like babies. We have had a computer class with Ms Garrity. We know how to do this.'
Ms Washabaugh asks the class, 'Do you think you know how to do this, to get the computers out carefully and turn them on? Can you do this on your own? Raise your hand if you think you can?'
Most of the class raises their hands. Ms Washabaugh says, 'Okay, go ahead. Let's give it a try.'

Thereafter, the students persistently test the limits of this newly relaxed atmosphere. For example, Daisy breaks the rule about leaving a laptop unattended while she tries to help a friend with a software problem. Remembering Ms Washabaugh's initial advice to hold students to compliance with a rule against leaving a laptop unattended, Ms Roffers reminds Daisy about the rule, and then moves her to a seat where the two students work together. The following day, Daisy complains to Ms Washabaugh, saying that she was offended by Ms Roffers's intervention on the previous day. Ms Roffers comes over to the huddle that had formed in the back of the classroom, and explains that she had to treat Daisy the same as everyone else in the classroom. Still, since Daisy demonstrated both some competence with computers and a willingness to coach other students, the best way to handle the situation was to move her seat so she could help her friend. Daisy backs down a bit.

Ms Roffers and Daisy continue their conversation. Ms Roffers tells her that she, Daisy, seems to be an advocate for much of the rest of her class. 'I admire that, but with that comes the responsibility not to stir up the class in the process.' Daisy says she understands and agrees to work closely with Ms Roffers toward the goal of advancing the skills of the whole class.

Daisy and some other students felt themselves more advanced than their peers. Such a sense of advancement, real or imagined, figures prominently in activities that involve computer use. A student's ability to manipulate software is demonstrated to others immediately, and the gap between those who know and those who do not can be gauged quickly by observing the senders and receivers of a question such as, 'How do you do X?' Just one day of laptop use was enough to light a fire under Daisy because she felt that she, being an advanced user, was stifled by rules that were apt for novices. At the same time, many other students began the project with far less computer preparation or interest. Nancy's case is indicative:

Nancy is a student who began the project with few skills and no motivation to advance. She typed with one finger at a time, the whole time resting her head on the other hand. To make matters worse she has long fingernails that get in her way. She kept knocking two keys at once, or brushing the keys with her jacket sleeve. She was totally disinterested. She told Ms Roffers, 'I don't want to do this anyway.'

Nancy was more than just apathetic. She harbored hostilities and resentments that boiled up regularly when the other students provoked her even slightly. Not uncommonly, she would become embroiled in physical conflicts with others and would have to be removed from the classroom. She rejected help and advice from everyone, and made it clear that she wanted to be left alone. Ms Roffers noted that 'there were times when I simply avoided the area where she sat so as not to aggravate her and to keep peace in the classroom. At the same time, I had the sense that if she could master one simple skill, she might have a chance at getting something, anything other than sleeping done in class'.

One of the first steps taken to get Nancy on board was to deal with her fingernails. Ms Kaufmann, drawing on personal experience, coached Nancy on techniques for keyboarding with nails. Initially, the coaching seemed to have no impact on Nancy's behavior. However, over the course of weeks, during which students progressed from computer-assisted projects on the Harlem Renaissance, to Greek Gods, to studies of European social life, Nancy gradually warmed to the tasks. At one point, Ms Roffers was surprised by Nancy's request to help her find an image for her illustrated report on France and food. Thereafter, she would repeatedly call me over to help her saying, 'I have to get this done!'

Ms Roffer's comments on Nancy's oral presentation of her PowerPoint report on France at food are revealing: 'Nancy is pumped up and ready to do her presentation. Is this the same young woman who lay on her sleeve while typing last February? She is animated and speaks confidently about her project. Her fellow students tease her as she begins. Instead of getting ready to punch them as she would have earlier in the semester, she simply returns the tease. By academic standards the project is far from perfect. However, recollecting where she was in the beginning of the project, I consider her one of the project's major successes.'

The development of Daisy and Nancy attest to the potential of our intervention to serve the needs of students with different interests and talents. But it also reminds us of the important role that is played by coaches. It is not incidental to the success of this programme that two students from the university were on hand for most of these class sessions. They interacted with the freshmen in ways that differed from the familiar student-staff interactions. Perhaps the university students were impartial voices that, for the freshmen, seemed less intimidating and less invested in the institution, and therefore more approachable. For the academic year, 2002/03, it was anticipated that four more university students would begin working as intern-coaches at RUHS. The outcome of their efforts will enable us to evaluate more clearly the importance of such impartial voices for the success of the intervention.

While university coaches seemed to be significant for the success of both Daisy and Nancy, peer-coaching contributed significantly to the successes of others. The students often learned by teaching peers some of their new-found skills. Ms Kaufmann's description of RUHS classroom's midway through the semester is telling:

Students' eyes stay on the laptop screen or other students when the laptops are in use. Students often glance over at other students to see what they were doing and then sometimes ask, 'How did you do that?' or 'How did you get there?' or 'How did you find that?'

Interestingly, as Kaufmann's notes suggest, students attend to other students before they attend to teachers or university coaches. This is 'because learning with computer-support is not a spectator activity. The students are always talking about what they discover as they experiment with searching or design sites. The laptops give them prompt feedback. If something is not working, they know it immediately. This learning environment differs from conventional school practices where students get feedback only after they have turned in their work and the teacher has returned it with comments and a grade.'

One way to describe this shift in general terms is to say that classroom activities became less teacher-centred.

Classroom activities also became less confined, and we found this to be both promising and dangerous. Let us explain. During the periods of the semester when students were involved in studies of the Harlem Renaissance, Greek gods and goddesses, and European social life, they spent equal time exploring the World Wide Web for information and drawing on that information to create multi-media projects of their own. During the time when they were exploring the World Wide Web, they were subject to the distractions that inevitably pop up for all web users. Internet filters that modify web-searches launched through the RUHS server prevent contact with obscene websites. However, embarrassing pop-ups can still occur. For example, one young student was exploring a link on a practice page about sport fishing that we had recommended, and found herself confronting a pop-up advertisement for Viagra. The teaching potential of the moment was not lost, however. Ms Roffers coached the student to a clearer understanding of the use of demographics in targeting advertisements, marketing surveys and the profitability of pop-up advertisements on web pages.

On another occasion, the source of the distraction was car stereo systems. As the semester was just beginning, Ms Roffers discovered two boys in the corner looking at a magazine that was filled with articles about car stereo systems. Later on in the semester, she found the same two boys looking at car stereo systems on the web. Repeatedly, she found them turning to sites on car stereos, and, each time, she advised them to return to their assignments. But, as she watched them, she could see that, in the course of researching car stereos, they had acquired an extraordinary facility with the web. They learned to navigate more efficiently than most of their classmates. These same boys were independently described by Ms Kaufmann as they completed their projects at the end of the semester:

> By the end of the semester, Bernardo and Steven had learned to add graphics, to change colours and backgrounds to achieve specific aesthetic objectives, and to perform other improvements on their history PowerPoint presentation. They were able to explain why they had used particular fonts, and why they had selected particular font colours and background hues. They had improved their problem-solving and web-searching skills. They were also able to use their critical thinking skills to explain why certain websites were 'better' or more authoritative than others.

The strides that Bernardo and Steven made during the semester forced us to rethink the experiences that we started out calling web-distractions. Their 'distractions' turned out to be significant learning experiences. This is a hard lesson for teachers to learn and even harder to take advantage of in the midst of a classroom that is all abuzz with Internet activity. It is usually assumed that classroom activities will pivot around the teacher's focus and the text's content. But after working with students on the Internet for a semester, we can see that it is not always best for students to march to the rhythm set by the teacher. Sometimes they are able to hone skills by other methods that are not teacher-centred. While we still agree that the curricular content should flow from the teacher and the text, some abilities are best refined with off-topic activities. Exploring car stereo sites, for Bernardo and Steven, was as effective a skill-builder as any we have seen. While their attention to such sites may have diverted their attention away from the curricular content of gods and goddesses, it taught them how to search for information and to make judgements about the information that they uncovered. Strange as it may seem, researching car stereos on the web was a profitable preparation for learning about Greek gods and European social life. We were particularly impressed by their ability to explain their reasons for selecting particular images, fonts styles and colours, because such explanations and justifications constitute an important part of what we mean by visual literacy.

Teaching visual literacy skills has turned out to be one of the most challenging aspects of this whole collaborative project. The nub of the problem is speed: images are flashed in front of students and then replaced by new images at a high rate of speed. Students react favourably to this rapid replacement. To them, it is exciting and energizing. However, it also thwarts critical reflection. Where image-replacement is rapid, students do not have time to discern multiple meanings and hidden agendas. Nor can they explore the ramifications in polysemous images. As a result, they fall back on superficial image-reading. They come away with just a fraction of the story that an image presents to them. Intelligent viewing proceeds best at a slow pace, allowing the eye to range over the figure and the ground. Critical viewing requires time to appreciate the role of internal structures and of external information in image-interpretation (see for example the exercises available at http://www.uwm.edu/People/wash/Objects/lookset.htm).

RUHS students are generally reluctant to pause and dally over images. We asked one student, for example, why he illustrated the waterways of Denmark by using a photo showing cars caught in a muddy river at flood stage. His response was that this was the only image of Danish rivers he had time to find. The implications of his explanation seem to seem to have been lost on him. Another young student was frantically searching for photographs of Marian Anderson to adorn her report on this famous operatic figure. She proudly displayed images that she had copied from a web-based album of photos taken during the 1999 wedding of a young white Texas couple. Coincidentally, the bride's name was Marian Anderson. The discomfiting lesson here is that speed kills understanding of visual images.

Conclusion

During this past semester, at least once – and usually many times – during each class session of every school day, a teacher would tell students to hurry. Not that such an admonition would not have been heard in traditional classrooms, but it is heard more frequently when learning is supported by computers. The reason for the hurry is that learning by way of computers takes vastly more time than learning from books due, in part, to the choices that students make, choices they have to make – and want to make.[2] The unlimited range of choices that are offered on the World Wide Web are both a curse and a blessing. On the one hand, students want to take advantage of the choices, clicking on as many hyperlinks as they can. Their choices are self-empowering. As they click away, here and there, they feel themselves in charge. They sense themselves exercising their own initiatives in matters of what to learn and how. But on the other hand, each click is a tick on the clock, and the time is always limited. As a result, on the web, the hearts of students and teachers alike beat faster and breathing accelerates; everyone is psyched and hyped. Such a condition of metabolic acceleration can be advantageous in the classroom – it is more difficult to fall asleep over a web-screen than over a hard-cover edition of *The Tale of Two Cities* – but it can also lead students down a path toward superficiality.

Unlike the days when white paper formed the background for just about every report, backgrounds today can be any of a thousand colours; and each student wants to exercise a choice over the matter. Backgrounds can be coloured spectrally or in gradient style. They can be textured or watermarked or illustrated, and each of these choices takes time. Font styles are equally numerous – we could not dissuade a freshman from using the font called Script in her PowerPoint presentation; she clung to it because she said it was cool despite the fact that it was illegible in a PowerPoint display. As this example suggests, students feel compelled to make the choices, to become personally involved in their choices, often ignoring the needs of those who view and read their work. Above all, students want to take the time that such personal choices require.

Generally speaking, then, when learning is computer-assisted, pacing and time-management become primary classroom concerns. You can feel it from the very first moments of a session, as students line up at the mobile storage cart, anxious to get their machines. Some of their urgency is due to the fact that our particular machines require unusually long boot-up times, due in part to on-board security and Internet-connection devices. But some anxiety is also due to students' eagerness to wade into the attractive choices they are forced to make as they explore sites and create projects.

Ironically, computers have been touted as time savers, and not a few of our own students at RUHS have said as much: 'When we work on laptops, we don't have to spend all that time roaming around the library. It's all right there in front of you.' But it is clear to anyone who looks at the situation that the pace of class-room-life is accelerated when students use computers.

Perhaps, one might say, this choice-making is a sign of schools coming of age, of catching up to commercial enterprises where the individual's choice has long reigned supreme. Department stores offer hundreds of fragrances, innumerable styles of blouse and endless shelves of bibelots. Restaurants are constantly trying to stretch their menus to include more choices. Buying a car, or a computer, or a house is all about making choices to fit one's individual needs. With computers in hand, students are now studying their lessons in the same way that they have been shopping – that is, by making choices.

In the past, teaching was often done in a one-size-fits-all manner. When we were freshmen in high school, we all had to read *A Tale of Two Cities*, and everyone had to write a report on the same topic. We all faced tests with the same questions, and wrote our answers on the same kind of paper with the same kind of pencil.

Clearly, such lockstep education failed to consider the multiple learning styles that individuals brought to their task. The response of many – some of us included – was to fall asleep over our books. With computer-assisted learning, students spend much less time daydreaming. More positively, they find ways to engage in a variety of topics in a variety of ways that may well match their learning styles. It is promising that even the most challenging students find this engagement attractive and satisfying. (If there is any one thing that these Milwaukee urban high school freshmen need for their learning to get on track, it is involvement; they need to be emotionally involved in their studies, and computers have helped to bring that about.) However, as in all Faustian bargains, the benefits are purchased with dangerous coins. The very devices that can involve students in their studies show great potential for trapping them into habits of haste that can work against what is needed for insight and understanding. We do not yet have an answer for the problem of pace, but we can see that it will be essential to slow students down if they are to achieve the goal of understanding, and ultimately to arrive at the kind of intelligence that is required of citizens in a democracy.

Notes

1. Ethnographies that report on ethnographers' interventions are not without precedent. Fifty years ago, Allan Holmberg (1950) described the results of

the changes he introduced into the lives of the Siriono, changes that resulted from his introduction of guns to replace the longbows that hunters traditionally used. As he himself acknowledged, the consequences of the changes he introduced were tragic. Consequently, 'ethnographic interventions' since Holmberg's day have been viewed with suspicion to say the least. It is not that anthropologists have lost the desire to intervene, but only that we fear the unfortunate consequences of intervening unwisely. As Nancy Scheper-Hughes argues, 'the anthropologist is always straddling a dichotomy between believing that reflection and understanding is in the nature of an intervention itself, and at times wanting to see a more direct impact on human life'. But most of the time anthropologists have resolved their concerns about this dichotomy by concluding that 'the witnessing itself and the writing are maybe the best we can do in terms of an intervention, and [we] leave the applications to others perhaps more suited to do that than ourselves' (Scheper-Hughes, 2000).

We acknowledge the dichotomy that Scheper-Hughes describes, but we have not limited ourselves to merely witnessing and writing. In line with Paul Bohannan's admonition (1979) that anthropologists 'cannot do nothing' in the face of the social conflicts that unfold before them, we have attempted an intervention in an urban high school, attempting to ameliorate a problematic situation at the same time as describing it. The high school, Riverside University High School (RUHS), is one that has enjoyed a stellar reputation in Milwaukee Public Schools system. Currently, it is challenged by demographic changes afoot since the mid-1980s.

RUHS was begun as Milwaukee High School in 1868, the first institution of secondary public education in this fast-growing city in the upper midwestern state of Wisconsin. It underwent a move and a name-change to East Division High School before being rebuilt in its current location as Riverside High School in 1915. It was renamed again in 1984 to reflect its partnership with The University of Wisconsin Milwaukee (UWM), located about four city blocks to its north-east.

This partnership and the name change were responses to the extraordinary social upheaval that had been rocking the city for a number of years. The most dramatic phase of this upheaval began with a 1976 court ruling that required the integration of Milwaukee public schools. During the years following this ruling – even to the present day – children were bused to schools of their choice rather than being required to attend their neighbourhood schools, because those neighbourhood schools were frequently marked by sharp demographic contrasts, that is, by de facto segregation. In the wake of the 1976 court ruling, many wealthy whites fled to the suburbs. As a result, the student population, formerly elite, was gradually replaced by one that was considerably poorer. The Milwaukee School Board attempted to staunch the flight of the well-to-do by creating 'magnet schools', specialty schools of high quality that would attract elites as well as the poor. Consistent with these developments, the UWM-RUHS partnership was launched in 1984.

Well-intentioned as the partnership plan was, UWM's contributions to the partnership dwindled as years passed. Moreover, with this same passage of time, students at RUHS became increasingly poorer and less well prepared for the college-bound programme that the high school continued to offer. The results at RUHS have been mixed. The high expectations of teachers and students in 1984 gave way to frustration and discontent with the lack of resources and funding necessary to meet these high aspirations. Instead of enjoying the benefits of an intimate collaboration with a neighbouring university, RUHS found itself suffering 'downturns' along with the rest of the schools in the Milwaukee Public School District.

Milwaukee's local newspaper put these 'downturns' into stunning statistical perspective in a series of reports published in 2001 and 2002. These reports show that, compared to other American states, Wisconsin ranks first in graduating high school students to college, but it ranks fiftieth – that is, last in the nation – in graduating minority students. Of all the states in the nation, Wisconsin has the highest per capita incarceration rate for African Americans. Compared to fifty large cities in the nation, Milwaukee, Wisconsin has the second largest income gap between African American and mainstream populations, and the highest rate of rejection of mortgage loan applications by African Americans.

These numbers notwithstanding, the administrators, teachers and students at Riverside University High School have forged ahead to make it a school that works. It offers a challenging academic curriculum, and a rigorous university-preparatory programme. Honours classes are offered in ninth and tenth grades, and Advanced Placement classes are offered in the upper grades. In fact, Riverside is the only high school in Wisconsin recognized by Jay Matthews (1998) as one of the top public high schools in the United States when economic and demographic conditions are taken into consideration. It ranked sixth of all public high schools in the Milwaukee area in a survey from the May 2002 *Milwaukee Magazine*.

Still, not all students who enter Riverside fit the profile of the high-achieving student, and, while the entrance process emphasizes commitment to academics, it does not ensure it. As a result, students entering Riverside come from wide-ranging social, economic and academic circumstances.

In an era when schools must do more with less, the RUHS staff and community continue to work to meet the needs of all the students regardless of preparation, skill-level or motivation. But, understandably, the work is frustrating. It is this frustration at RUHS that prompted our intervention: an experiment that involved the introduction of 21 laptops computers into some of the classrooms at RUHS with the neediest students.

2. A second explanation of the pressures felt by teachers and students when studying from the World Wide Web is the fact that they must screen and filter their own information. Traditionally and conventionally, textbook publishers shouldered that task for both teachers and students. They, along with teams of scholars, combed through textual information and graphic imagery, selecting and culling and arriving at carefully packaged ensembles of descriptions and illustrations for students to use in their studies.

On the World Wide Web, however, there is no such advance-filtering process that prepares materials for students, except perhaps the crude Internet filters that screen out obscene material from school computers. The whole world of information is out there for students to use, and they must be taught to use it and, at the same time, to screen it and filter it for themselves. This all takes a great deal of time.

Still, we regard it as well worth the time. In this teaching experiment, students were empowered to act as their own filtering force. They learned to take on to themselves the responsibility of evaluating the vast sets of information available on the WWW. They learned how to set the parameters of their filters to get the appropriate information for their projects, and then to cull again in order to create presentations that were reasonably sized and appropriate for their audiences.

References

Bohannan, P. (1979), 'You Can't Do Nothing', *American Anthropologist*, 82: 508–24.

Boyce, L.N., Van Tassel-Baska, J., Burruss, J.D. Sher, B.T. and Johnson, D.T. (1997), 'Problem-based Curriculum: Parallel Learning Opportunities for Students and Teachers', *Journal for the Education of the Gifted*, 20(4): 363–79.

Gifford, B. and Enyedy, N. (1999), 'Activity Centered Design: Towards a Theoretical Framework for CSCL', in C. Hoadley and J. Roschelle (eds), *Proceedings of the Computer Support for Collaborative Learning (CSCL) 1999 Conference*, December 12–15, Stanford University, Palo Alto, California, Mahwah, NJ: Lawrence Erlbaum Associates, http://www.ciltkn.org/cscl99/A22/A22.htm.

Glasgow, N. (1997), *New Curriculum for New Times: a Guide to Student-Centered, Problem-Based Learning*, Thousand Oaks, CA: Corwin.

Holmberg, A. (1950), *Nomads of the Long Bow: the Siriono of Eastern Bolivia*,

Washington, DC, U.S. Government Printing Office.

Kozol, J. (1991), *Savage Inequalities: Children in America's Schools,* New York: Crown.

Matthews, J. (1998), *Class Struggle: What's Wrong (and Right) with America's Best Public High Schools,* New York: Times Books.

Perkins, D., Crismond, D., Simmons, R. and Unger, C. (1991), 'Inside Understanding,' in D. Perkins, J. Schwartz, M. Maxwell West and M. Stone Wiske (eds), *Software Goes to School: Teaching for Understanding with New Technologies*, New York: Oxford University Press, 70–8.

Scheper-Hughes, N. (2000), 'Studying the Human Condition: Habits of a Militant Anthropologist: Conversation with Nancy Scheper-Hughes', http://globetrotter.berkeley.edu/people/Scheper-Hughes/sh-con6.html#between.

Stafford, B. (1994), *Artful Science: Enlightenment Entertainment and the Eclipse of Visual Education,* Cambridge, MA: MIT Press.

−11−

Open Source Software Development as Gift Culture: Work and Identity Formation in an Internet Community

Magnus Bergquist

The Kwakiutl Indians of the Pacific Northwest once flourished with their potlatch (or gift) economy, but other Americans have had little experience with the idea of prospering by giving wealth away instead of hoarding it. No wonder, then, that we're uncertain about how to label open source: whether as animal or vegetable, politics or theology. Open source pits the virtues of collaboration and participation against the habits of consolidation and control – and, as far as the development of software infrastructure goes, it works. Still, how much cultural significance can be bundled into a software package? (Blume 1999)

Open source is a phenomenon that has lead many thinkers, columnists, business analysts and researchers to scratch their heads. In the quote above, Internet columnist Harvey Blume does not seem to be sure whether to define open source as a political or a theological occurrence, whether 'animal or vegetable'. And whether it is work or leisure, one might add. Software is produced and then given away. Software developers are not organized according to market-economy business models. Instead they form some kind of gift culture and have created a 'gift economy' based on its own logic: collaboration instead of competition; openness instead of proprietary rights and trade secrets; quality code instead of profitability. And still, new companies based on this gift-economy model emerge and thrive.

In the recent years an increasing academic interest in open-source software development can be noted (see e.g. Feller and Fitzgerald 2002, von Hippel 2001, Tuomi 2000). Areas covered include software engineering, systems-development methods and the rise of new business models. However, there is not much attention paid to open source as a cultural phenomenon. In this chapter I wish to address the question posed by Harvey Blume concerning the cultural significance of open-source software. How is actually cultural significance bundled into a software package and the practices evolving around it?

Open source points to a new form of work context that differs from software development as work in software companies. Conventional business values and motivations are rejected or turned upside-down. This is done within an organizational form that often is described as 'community-based' and kept together with the help of norms, values and practices that are partially created on the Internet and communicated in different on-line environments regularly visited by open-source developers. In the following I will describe the basics of open-source community management and outline a theoretical framework for understanding gift giving as social glue and a way of managing identity among community members. The chapter is outlined as follows.

Work, collaboration and sharing of knowledge in open-source communities are culturally organized around the concept of gift giving. Gift giving creates flows of knowledge and makes it possible to innovate and refine software-development processes on a global scale. The importance of gift giving and the way it is socially organized in open-source communities can be explained on the one hand by the character of digital information, which can be reproduced an infinite number of times without being reduced in number or quality, and on the other hand by the Internet as a global arena for cooperative work.

Living in a society dominated by commodity transactions, open-source activists have to be socialized into the specific culture of gift giving embraced by the community. I will use some examples to show how the basic norms and values are taught to newcomers (so called 'newbies').

Gift giving is in this context also a way of creating and maintaining relationships of power between groups and individuals. Open-source gift giving transforms these relationships to interdependencies based on the idea of reputation. Practices have evolved to assure that the best code produced is integrated into the software distributions. Classic theories of gift economies do not clarify how gifts can be treated as parts of quality-assessment processes. Here, I will relate open-source gift giving to another kind of gift economy – the academic society – and suggest a model for how gift giving and peer-review systems relate to the concept of reputation in open-source communities.

What is Open Source Anyway?

Open source means, in short, to let the source code of a software program become public, so that others can use and modify it. The people who are active in the open-source community are highly skilled programmers who collectively develop software, often of a quality that outperforms commercial proprietary software, and then gives it away for others to use, improve or manipulate. Open-source software development is done in networks where people mainly interact through web pages, news groups, discussion lists and mailing lists. In this way a community of experienced and motivated programmers is created.

Open-source-like software-development activities can be traced back to the programming practices that evolved in university milieus during the 1960s and 1970s at MIT and similar computer-technology research labs (e.g. Bell Labs and Xerox Parc).

The development of the computer programming language C and the operating system Unix created an infrastructure upon which a plethora of computer-related activities would arise. The simplicity and portability of C and Unix revolutionized computer-programming and usage, and became widely popular within computer programming communities (Moody 2001, Raymond 1999). Since there was little or no monetary compensation involved in systems and computer programs in these environments a culture of knowledge sharing, continuous improving and sharing of software became common, which has become closely related with the term *hacker* as a kind of ethic for very skilful programmers (Feller and Fitzgerald 2002).

Gradually companies began to understand the commercial potential of developing software-package solutions for different contexts. Companies like Microsoft (1975) and Apple (1977) grew and realized that systems and software were business opportunities that gradually lead to software becoming copyright-protected and source code a proprietary commodity (Levy 1994, Moody 2001). The kind of free knowledge sharing and gift giving that had characterized software development in the 1960s and 1970s continued, however, in universities and research labs.

Richard Stallman was one of the hackers at MIT AI Lab who felt that the hacker culture seemed to be withering away. To ensure the openness and knowledge sharing in software-development projects Stallman founded the Free Software Foundation (FSF) in 1984. The purpose of FSF was to develop and distribute software under the General Public License (GPL), or 'copyleft', which prevented software from becoming proprietary. Stallman also took an active part in developing components for a completely free operating system (Levy 1994, Moody 2001).

But the perhaps most famous and groundbreaking example of open-source software development is the operating system Linux, which was developed by a Helsinki University student by the name of Linus Torvalds in 1991 (Torvalds and Diamond 2001). Linux was developed as a Unix-like system for the Intel platform, which meant that it could be used on any ordinary PC. Torvalds put the code on the Internet and made it free for the community of programmers to use and comment on and of course also to improve. This resulted in a huge base of users around the world who have contributed to the development of Torvalds's original ideas into a complete operating system (Raymond 1999, Moody 2001). It is estimated that Linux has a user-base of millions of people around the globe, of which several thousands are programmers who contribute to the development of Linux. The impact of Linux has been so huge that it has been appointed an important threat against Microsoft's market dominance in the field of operating systems for PCs.

The Organization of Open-Source Projects

Open-source projects can best be described as a special kind of organization of roles and activities. A typical open-source project starts when a user/programmer 'scratches a personal itch' in terms of a problem occurring on his own computer or in his network domain (Feller and Fitzgerald 2002, Ljungberg 2000, Raymond 1999). He starts to construct a solution for the problem and publishes the source code on the Internet. Other programmers find the solution and realize that they have the same itch and that they like the basic idea of the solution. Users start to develop the original idea and post bug reports, patches and improvements to the original author who now is being recognized as the owner of the project.

This is a common scenario for how open-source software projects are launched and socially organized. It is typical that open-source projects start with a single programmer solving a small problem affecting his own work. For example, the origin of WWW was the work by Tim Berners-Lee to help high-energy physicists to share their work. Another example is Larry Wall who wrote the script language Perl to solve problems in systems administration (O'Reilly, 1999). When open-source solutions turn out to be significant and attract other users, different roles arise. The following roles are frequently occurring.

The *owner* of an open-source project is the person (or group) who is recognized by the community as the one who originally started the project. The owner has the exclusive right to make decisions about what modifications should be included in the next release of the software. Basically there seem to be three ways to acquire ownership of an open-source project: to found it, to have it handed over by a former owner, or to volunteer to take over a dying project if the former owner has lost his interest (Raymond 1999). As the owner attracts contributors, i.e. people that discover the software and want to contribute to its development, the owner becomes more of a co-ordinator and project leader than an actual code writer.

In large and complex projects it is common that a group of *core developers* write most of the code concerning new functionality, review submitted code from other users, and make decisions about releases together with the project owner (Mockus et al. 2000). This procedure could be of a more formal nature as in the Apache web server core-development group, where frequent contributors might be nominated as new members to the community and approved by anonymous voting by the group members. This means that almost all the new functionality is implemented and maintained by a small group of core developers (Mockus et al. 2000, Ghosh and Prakash 2000).

Other roles include *defect repair* that involves a much wider development community than the core group. *Problem reporters* are an even wider group. The *user support* seems to be mainly performed by users who voluntarily provide answers to questions from other users (Lakhani and von Hippel 2000). *Documentation* has a similar organization.

Today there are a huge number of *users* of open-source software who are not actively contributing to its development. By using the software these actors are, however, important contributors. Creating a critical mass of users is important both for the usability of a system or software and for the construction of the symbolic attraction surrounding open-source development style. Similarly *commercial business* tied to open-source projects provide additional resources for developing the free components of the software, but even more importantly it helps to promote open source by legitimating it as an alternative to commercial mainstream software (Osterhout 1999). Companies have arisen around open-source software projects to make money out of open-source software by selling it as so called *distributions*, which are compilations of different open-source software that has been tested and bundled together with an installation program (O'Reilly 1998). Some of the more popular distributions (in the form of open-source companies) are Red Hat, SuSe and Mandrake. It is, however, important to note that these companies also have free copies of their open-source software for downloading as well as the source code. CDs are sold as a convenience for users who cannot download via the Internet or who want the accompanying manual and installation instructions. The companies also sell services in the form of maintenance, individual business solutions and adaptations of existing open-source software. It seems important for commercial actors to behave in a way that they do not interfere with the communities' norms and values for gift giving in the form of source code if they want to continue being recognized as part of the community.

Open Source as a Gift Culture

Based on the kind of arguments presented in the opening quote by Harvey Blume it has been argued that, since there often is no monetary compensation to be expected for efforts conducted in open-source projects, the will to contribute to the community cannot be explained by traditional market-economy business models. For the majority of code submitters, open-source software development is not paid work. Here the idea of the open source being a *gift culture* has been proposed (Raymond 1999). Gift cultures are based on an organizational form where social relations are not regulated by the possession or exchange of money or commodities, but on the exchange of gifts in various forms.

Howard Rheingold (1995) is often attributed with having developed discussions around the custom in virtual communities to give away pointers, texts, advice or, as is common in open-source communities, source code, as a special 'gift culture'. This connects the inhabitants of Internet communities in what Rheingold describes as 'a marriage of altruism and self-interest' (Rheingold 1995: 58).

Rheingold also separates two kinds of information-sharing practice. The first can be found among people who are interested in new cultural phenomena that have led them to explore different virtual worlds. They share information about almost everything. But sharing can also mean emotional support. The second consists of professionals who rely on having information constantly at their disposal. This kind of giving-away is based on a hunger for intellectual companionship, initially most commonly found among professionals who work more or less on their own, e.g. journalists, freelance artists and designers, programmers, etc. (Rheingold 1995: 56). Besides a need for social stimulation they have a shared and immediate demand for accessing relevant information that otherwise would be difficult to reach to the extent that is required. By creating a network of contacts the plausible chance of getting to relevant information sources increases dramatically. At the same time social relationships are continually developed, creating a kind of social contract in the particular community that arises around a certain type of professional activity. These early adopters have been followed by others, some of them networking only for social reasons, such as many of the inhabitants in the WELL, an on-line community analysed by Rheingold:

> If, in my wanderings through information space, I come across items that don't interest me but I know would interest one of my worldwide affinity group of online friends, I send the appropriate friend a pointer or simply forward the entire text (one of the new powers of CMC is the ability to publish and converse via the same medium). In some cases I can put the information in exactly the right place for ten thousand people I don't know, but who are intensely interested in that specific topic, to find it when they need it. And sometimes, one of the ten thousand people I don't know does the same thing for me (Rheingold 1995: 57).

When gift giving is not more than one click away and people are motivated to share for pleasure or for the benefit of their professional conduct, a culture of sharing can arise.

But gifts can be of different kinds and given or received for different reasons. Gift-giving relations can also range from the gratuitous gift at one extreme to the exploitative relationship on the other (Sahlins 1972, Godbout 1998, Godelier 1999). The classic analysis of the social and cultural context of gift giving is Marcel Mauss' *The Gift* (1990 [1950]) where he describes a gift as the transaction of objects co-ordinated by a system of rules. The rules are in fact symbolic translations of the social structure in a society or a group of members. Mauss does not provide us with a romantic view of gift giving. On the contrary, he argues that giving a gift brings forth a demand for returning a gift, either another object or, in a more symbolic fashion, a token symbolizing the object. Gift giving therefore creates social interdependencies and becomes a web upon which social structure is organized.

However, it is important to distinguish the general idea of gifts and the habit of giving gifts in the kind of societies described by Mauss compared to the highly technological and to some extent virtual societies in which the open-source community is located. First of all, the presence of and access to the Internet must be important for understanding how gifts in the form of information and software can be transferred around the globe. The Internet promotes the possibility that people with the same interests and the same 'itches to scratch' will encounter and become aware of each other.

Also important is the character of digital gifts. Peter Kollock (1999) has discussed the character of digital information storage as an explanation for the intensive sharing of work, social experiences and other forms of knowledge between members of the community by focusing on the possibility of producing 'an infinite number of perfect copies of a piece of information, whether that be a computer program, a multimedia presentation, or the archives of a long e-mail discussion' (Kollock 1999: 223). The contributor can give away an infinite number of copies of a document or software without losing it or diminishing its value (which is the case with material objects). The Internet also provides an easy way to distribute large amounts of information. The cost of providing one person some information is not a greater effort than providing ten million people the same information, no matter where in the world the consignees are. And from the receivers' point of view: the transaction cost of downloading a document is almost the same irrespective of where in the world it is originally posted.

With this in mind, Mauss's discussion of gifts can be seen differently. His argument about the social character of gifts is based on how gifts are perceived and handled in a world of material objects. The scarcity of material objects and the costs associated with transactions are important for how the value of gifts and the giving of gifts are experienced. Information and executable software in combination with the Internet radically transforms the context for how we should understand this relationship. But is the social character of gifts disappearing, then, when anyone can give anything to anybody with a transaction cost hitting almost zero? The answer to this is no, but this does not mean that gifts are used and experienced the same way in virtual communities as in the kind of societies Mauss described.

Two tendencies can be spotted. The almost total reduction of scarcity problems concerning the dissemination of information has intensified the awareness in the community of the presence of other forms of scarcities, which has led to the development of different practices aimed at decreasing time cycles of innovation and development, and scarcities inherent in the organization of cooperation and co-ordination. Further, the community is primarily a loosely coupled network of individuals with no organizational powers in terms of economy or management that can force other individuals to behave in a certain way. Mauss argues that gifts express but also create power relations between people. One of the norms of gift giving is the rule to accept gifts. Hereby the receiver becomes subordinate to the giver. In the open-source community this can be the fact. But the opposite is also important. Refusing to accept a gift can in some situations be a way to show superiority.

Rationales for Gift Giving: Reducing Scarcity and Increasing Speed of Development and Quality of Code

Sharing digital goods creates an abundance of available resources for individuals within and outside the community. Digital information thereby disarms one fundamental characteristic of material goods and its relation to space. Because a material good cannot be shared without someone losing it and somebody else gaining it, material objects are subjected to the rules of scarcity. The cost of transferring material objects is a proportional one related to the distance over which it is conveyed. Digital information is not subject to any of these constraints.

Still there are other types of scarcity that have to be managed. One gets the impression that the insight into the mechanisms of digital information makes domains of scarcity even more unbearable. One of the most fundamental and difficult to cope with is the scarcity of time. It is not possible to compress, rationalize, extend or share time. There is no way to manipulate time, no matter how sophisticated a technology there is available; no matter how transparent and far-reaching an information network there is. From the individual's point of view this becomes a question of how to allocate resources bounded by the course of life. Since the individual's life span is impossible to scale up, clone or manipulate in the way digital information can be manipulated, the collective effort of the community has to be interlaced and synchronized. The collectively reached outcome supersedes all individual exertions but also makes it possible for an individual to surpass himself beyond what is possible for one person to create on his own. The result becomes greater than the sum of the parts. Linus Torvalds's creation of the Linux kernel could probably never have reached the size and complexity of a whole operating system had he not involved other programmers by making the code accessible on the Internet.

Open-source culture is therefore devoted to compressing time-consuming activities in order to speed up work, information dissemination and learning processes. All overheads measured in time must be reduced as much as possible. The habit of mirroring sites worldwide in order to diminish time for downloading due to network constraints, and thereby increasing the amount of information a person can be exposed to during a given space of time, is the perhaps most widely spread practice even outside the community.

Efforts are made to ensure that work is intensified. It is seen as very important that hackers speed up work by building on previous efforts as much as possible. Raymond (1999) points out that one of the most important things for a hacker to do when launching a new project is to search for existing attempts to solve the problem one is currently working on. The chance that one will find something similar that at least can function as food for thought is likely to arise. Because time is a scarce resource it is seen as extremely important not to 'reinvent the wheel' over and over again.

Yet another scarcity dilemma addressed is the one concerning how the community learns. In order to develop software for new and interesting fields of application, it is seen as extremely important that learning cycles are reduced in time. For this purpose many on-line services have developed in the community. One widely used is Usenet News Groups subscription. News Groups are typically divided into areas of interest (programming language, operating system, miscellaneous, etc.) and members are encouraged to subscribe to News Groups covering their fields of interest in order to get as much input as possible to their current work. Normally a question is posted and answers are threaded so that readers can easily follow how questions, answers and arguments are presented. The motivation for answering is the common need for relevant information as well as the social stimulation in the form of intellectual companionship discussed above. News Groups are often equipped with FAQs (Frequently Asked Questions), collections of questions and answers often posed. It is an established custom to take part of the information gathered in the FAQ before raising questions in News Groups or to the project-owner team. FAQs can also come in the form of Digests, which are summaries of discussions about a certain topic, or summaries of the discussions that have taken place in different News Groups during a given period. Such resources are ways to condense time by making series of questions and answers, mistakes and successes available packed in a concentrated form. It is easy to access worldwide and also cheap: because the community relies on community focus rather than cost-intensive mass advertisement, learning and information dissemination becomes an integrated practice of the community.

Learning to Become a Gift Giver

Open-source communities are in constant need of new users with high competence. Newcomers are called 'newbies', which also is a definition of their position in the community. Newbies can be seen as problems because they take up space in News Groups and block out the important questions. Experienced programmers tend to treat newbies in a rather rude way, flaming them with nasty comments if they occupy News Groups with questions found in the FAQ (Bergquist and Ljungberg 2001). But at the same time newbies are important for the survival and development of the community. An important activity is therefore to foster newbies to the community-netiquette in the form of norms and behaviours for a certain kind of communication and cooperation practice and the culture of gift giving. Here resources in the form of Internet *portals* have been created to facilitate this process. Newbies have created portals of their own, like linuxnewbie.org, where newcomers can learn the basics of open-source practices before attending the established forums. Another portal is Freshmeat.net that hosts an index of Unix and cross-platform software. Here new applications, released under an open-source license, are launched to a wider audience. Freshmeat offers content on technical, social and political aspects of software and programming. A comment board is attached to each article and column, providing users the possibility to add their experiences, comments, bug reports, technical support, questions or critique.

Portals such as Freshmeat work as an instrument for socializing new users into the community. Users are taught the basic ideas, e.g. expanding on previous attempts, sharing knowledge between users, giving away solutions for others to improve. This process is very much done with guidance based on real world cases. An example shows the principles for how this is achieved. On 4 May 2002 Ingmar Schuster, a Freshmeat writer, published an article entitled 'Those Messy True Types' on Freshmeat.net. Using and organizing type fonts is a well-known source for problems on the Linux platform among experienced users. In the article Schuster shares some experiences about this by explaining some of the problems with fonts ordinary users will stumble upon. Licensing is one complication since many fonts are 'sharefonts' which are supposed to be erased by the user after a limited time:

> I'm supposed to erase them after a certain number of days of use. I'd do that (I have enough fonts to choose from now), but I don't know which those fonts are and how long I'm allowed to try them. The site does not provide any information regarding copyright, creator, or license. Even if it did, it'd be troublesome to get it. I didn't download all those fonts manually, of course; I used wget. Such information should be stored in the font itself, so you don't need to ask the creator 'What was the license again?' (if you even know who the creator was) (http://freshmeat.net/articles/view/442/).

Here some basic principles of open-source problem solving and gift giving are wrapped in a discussion about problems concerning the handling of fonts on

Linux computer systems. Schuster tells the reader where to get free fonts, which serves as geographical guidance to open-source clusters and affiliates around the world that are resources for open-source developers. It is problematic to organize fonts if the user has access to several thousands of fonts on the computer. But this problem, which at the beginning is stated as a problem, is only a pseudo-problem that 'hides' the actual message. The common rule is that fonts are not free to download and use. The real problem is that fonts are copyright protected. The optimization of TrueType rendering has been stalled by patents that hinder people from legally using optimization that is provided with the font file itself. If the users only had access to the 'source code' of type fonts, there would be no problems. Or more correctly: members of the community would soon solve the problems. The solution suggested is to define a patent-free format for font files, which becomes the actual mission in the article.

About two hours after the article was published comments start to arrive. 'Matt' suggests that the solution is to create a 'font book': 'That's what you get when you buy commercial fonts. You look through the font book to see which one you want. They are organized by serif, sans-serif, decorative and symbol. Sometimes you'll see more categorization.' 'Goose' sends a reply suggesting that the font-selection dialogue should act as a font book and Yazz replies that gfontview, an existing tool, can be used as a font book, but 'it would be neat if you were able to rearrange the listing to fit your needs right from the tool'.

Sharing thoughts and ideas and giving critique to bad suggestions serve as a kind of verbal prototyping that speeds up the innovation phase. The quote above shows what can be regarded as the cultural kernel of the open-source approach to software development that is seldom explicitly stated. The 'ideology' of open-source software development is usually codified into symbolic practices (Bergquist and Szczepanska 2002). However, there seem to be an evolving need to formulate the guiding principles more clearly. Eric S. Raymond's *The Cathedral and the Bazaar* (1999) is generally seen as the official manifesto for the open-source community. Other important publications are Linus Torvalds's *Just for Fun* (Torvalds and Diamond 2001) and Robert Young's (CEO of Red Hat, Inc.) *Under the Radar* (Young and Goldman Rohm 1999). Here the ethos of open-source software development is given a shape from which newbies and members of the community can learn and become motivated.

Giving and Receiving as Power

Sharing of gifts in on-line communities seems to create a very friendly and unselfish environment for work. But this does not mean that social stratification and struggles over power cease to exist. When giving is easy and gifts become non-reducible, dependencies are reshaped and transformed to new kinds of relationships. Software is often not given to anyone in particular. It is made public (on web pages) and thereby made available to anyone who cares to make use of it. An application or some information does not really become a gift because someone finds it and use it. However, if a giver manages to get attention from the receiver, people will turn the things offered into gifts, which means that a social bond is created between the giver and the user. Since gifts do not imply a monetary compensation, virtual-community gift giving is managed through acknowledgement: the giver is 'paid' by the community by receiving a certain amount of fame and respect.

The difference between gift giving and commodity transactions is that the giving of gifts should not involve explicit bargaining. In bargaining no obligation exists after the exchange is accomplished. Where commodities are exchangeable, gifts are unique. A commodity that is purchased, and then given as a present, is transformed from a product to an obligation. By giving away the giver shows superiority and the receiver becomes dependent. There is an obligation to repay the gift in the future. As Mauss argued, a gift can be a way of showing social status. The giving of artefacts creates asymmetrical social relationships, especially if the gift never can be refunded and the giver knows it. Cheal therefore talks about gift giving as based on a moral economy (Cheal 1988).

On the Internet, however, the receiver is often unknown to the giver (Kollock 1999). Anybody can download a piece of information or an executable file and use it for various purposes. The focus for the production of meaning in the gift economy on the Internet therefore has to be tied to the open-source communities where people share the context of what a gift is and how it should be treated. In these communities the value of the gifts is dependent on the amount of attention the giver gets from the receivers that choose to make use of the gift.

Becoming an owner of a project that becomes successful gives the owner the right to decide who should be entitled to give back and who should not. The more attention an open-source project owner gets from the members of the community, the more status and reputation the owner achieves. And the more a project gets attention, the more users would like to contribute to it and become a part of the project, and as a result of this, get some of the attention (Raymond 1999). Attention in the context of open source is not about being bold and loud, but to be recognized or 'seen' as a good programmer and contributor to the community. The power structure, compared to gift giving in a world of artefacts, is therefore restructured according to the logic of how reputation is formed in the community. A person who has achieved a good reputation by, for example, founding a successful project will be able to execute power over people who want to contribute to the project and thereby become recognized as competent hackers. 'Hacker' is, according to the hacker ethics, not something a person calls himself. It is a title ascribed to the person by others. Reputation is about being recognized as a person of importance for accomplishing the community's goals.

It has been argued that the openness of the open-source movement is over-stated. Practices like flaming are not only used to exclude people who overrule the core values of the community. In the following example the author of the posting claims that it is also used to exercise power over those who want to contribute to the community by delivering code to different projects:

Giving Back

siberian – April 01st 1999, 21:31 EST

More then once I have had the urge to begin contributing to the community. I have written code, documented it and gained authorization for its release. But at the last minute I always hesitate and then stop. Why? I think I fear the fangs of the community. At this point, everywhere I turn it's a big flamefest and getting quite tiresome. Its gotten to the point where it seems one has to be some sort of Jedi Master level coder to contribute. On more then a few mailing lists I have seen contributors flamed for their contributions! Flaming someone for GIVING something away. It's incredible (http://freshmeat.net/articles/view/128/).

There is on the one hand a message of openness, not only when it comes to source code, but also that openness is a fundamental feature of open source as an organizational entity. And indeed there is openness, in the sense that everything that is shared among the community members is on display on web pages and discussion lists. But on the other hand does the honouring of the successful projects and the heroes behind them create boundaries of in-groups and out-groups?

Virtual collaboration puts high demands on people having trust in one another. Giving away the best piece of code a person has produced demands strong social ties between the giver and the receiver. The receiver has to present himself and act in a trustworthy way, otherwise the giver will not give away his code. At the same time, the demands for high-quality source code give the project owner the moral right to judge whether a contribution is of high enough quality to be considered as a part of the final distribution. It becomes important for the receiver to present himself as trustworthy in the eyes of the givers. Virtual collaborative work in open-source communities must thus be based on trust in order to make criticism regarded as something that can contribute to the overall quality of the software.

A problem with the openness of the Internet and the open-source community is that anyone can comment, even if not really serious, about the matter in question. A strategy proposed in some postings is to develop an ability to be indulgent toward weirdos, overlook 'script kiddie'-critique, shrug one's shoulders and move on. Good critique should be taken into account, because it is dangerous to ignore critique since good development is dependent on review processes. One has to fight against the 'reinventing-the-wheel' syndrome that seems to be lurking in the virtual bushes. The two strategies proposed are 'trust', if the critique is good, and 'ignorance', if not serious. Talking about a certain kind of critique as 'flaming' creates a mental distance that becomes a resource for the individual in this highly exposed environment.

The harsh and sometimes crude critique serves the social purpose of maintaining the ground-principles of reducing scarcities of time and securing the quality of the code. The critique against those who feel that their attempts to give to the community have been ignored is brought back to the fundamental principles of the community. The only reason to deny or refuse a contribution is the ambition to maintain and develop the good quality of open-source software development, which also is the core argument for spending time developing such software.

Peer Review as Quality Assessment Procedure

A recurrent theme in the open-source community is, as we have seen, the question of why gift giving is important in order to support open-source software development. Values and norms surrounding quality assurance and the sharing of knowledge therefore become an important topic for understanding the open-source community's cultural foundations. Here, comparisons with basic principles in academic research practices seem to have much resemblance to a gift culture such as open source. For instance, both Raymond (1999) and Bezroukov (1999) have noticed the similarities between gift giving in open-source communities and research communities in academia. As stated by Raymond:

> I suspect academia and the hacker culture share adaptive patterns not because they're genetically related, but because they've both evolved to be the most optimal social organization for what they're trying to do, given the laws of nature and the instinctive wiring of human beings. The verdict of history seems to be that free-market capitalism is the globally optimal way to cooperate for economic efficiency; perhaps, in a similar way, the reputation-game gift culture is the globally optimal way to cooperate for generating (and checking!) high-quality creative work (Raymond 1999: 132).

Connecting open-source to academia in this way is not accidental. Many open-source projects originate from university contexts. What Raymond more specifically seems to aim at is the particular practice of academic peer-review processes. If we view open source from the perspective of peer review, we could gain a more in-depth understanding both of the quality aspect of open-source software development and of how the power relations are socially organized.

In academic communities knowledge is given away, not only because researchers are altruistic but because that's the way careers progress within the academic field. Knowledge and information is shared and given away in return for status and reputation. The acceptance of a gift by a community implies recognition of the status of the donor. Scientific contributions can be understood as gifts since publication normally does not result in direct monetary compensation. Publications with the explicit purpose of being put on the market (e.g. textbooks) are usually held in much lower esteem than a paper published in a journal or in peer-reviewed conference proceedings (Hagstrom, 1982). Just as a research community rates journals and conferences, open-source projects are rated as more or less important and influential.

By sharing knowledge and being open about results and methods, the results can be justified and replicated. Others can give contributions by responding, or by continuing on the published work, pushing the scientific frontier forward. By writing and publishing papers and by being referred to by others, not only is knowledge being shared, but one is also becoming visible in the academic community. The reputation is secured by the rule that one can use knowledge produced by somebody else, but it must always be clear from whom the idea originates. The more other researchers will quote an author's work, the more the author's reputation will grow.

Here peer review is recognized as the main principle for handling and evaluating contributions to the scientific community. Peer review has its origins in the establishment of a referee system in the first scientific journals in seventeenth- and eighteenth-century Europe (Ziman 1968, Chubin and Hackett 1990). It is by now a fairly established academic practice for determining the scientific quality of a piece of work, for assigning a candidate to a position or for approving or rejecting a research proposal. All established researchers are more or less involved in peer-review processes, as reviewers of others' articles, project proposals or CVs, or by being reviewed by others themselves.

The peer-review system makes it possible to let a community judge if contributions are good enough to enter the field. Among many contributions the best ones are chosen. When people make selections they try to be reasonable in their selections. But what seems reasonable for one person is not always reasonable for another. There are no objective criteria for what counts as 'relevant', 'interesting' or 'new' research. Peer review is thus a social mechanism through which a discipline's experts or the core members of a community maintain control over new knowledge entering the field (Merton and Zuckerman 1973, Chubin and Hacket 1990). Peer review can therefore be seen as a way of organizing relationships of power within a given community or in relation to other fields of activity.

The open-source communities are driven by similar norms. A programmer provides a project within the community with a piece of software. The contribution is peer-reviewed by the owners of a software-development project, and if it is good enough, the project owners will give credits by letting the contribution become a part of the project. The result (i.e. the code) is also visible to members of the community to use and learn from. There is an interesting relationship between how usable an idea is and how much attention it can get. In the academic society a good theory seem to be more tradable than a partial analysis. Theories can potentially be of general benefit for large parts of the research community. There seems to be a similar relationship concerning the rules for how ideas are valued in the open-source community. A generally applicable service such as Linus Torvalds's Linux operating system becomes, like a theory in the academic society, a general base for others to act upon. This makes Linux famous and Torvalds a respected member of the community. Writing a driver for an application is similar to, let's say, doing an empirical study where a theory is used.

Conclusion

Open source is gaining more and more attention from media, business and researchers as a new kind of work environment, business model and cultural phenomenon. In this chapter I have discussed the culture of gift giving in the open-source community as an important system for the organization and performance of software development.

It seems to be true that the Internet and the increasing use and importance of digital information is changing the working environment for software development and developers, and to some extent other knowledge-intensive activities where innovation, cooperation and quality assessment are important. This seems to put new demands on mastering gift giving as a social activity. Living in a society dominated by commodity transactions, open-source activists have to be socialized into the gift culture by learning a set of basic norms and values.

Giving away ideas and source code is the base for different kind of activities in the open-source community, which also becomes fundamental for the creation of culture. However, gift giving does not mean that people are unable to execute power or make a career. Hierarchies are created based on the principles of gift giving in digital domains and become a question of giving or receiving more or less attraction. The giver-receiver relationship must be understood as a dynamic process with no fixed dependencies. It is facilitated through the process of peer review which has the purpose of guarding the quality of the code produced. Making the source code open for inspection by peers is regarded as a guarantee of the high quality of the code. Practices have evolved to assure that the best code produced is integrated into the software distributions. This is important because producing high-quality source code is the key motivator for members, but also for legitimating the open-source community as a social actor in society. The system of giving credits to the ones that the community thinks deserve it is therefore accepted and even favoured among the community members. One could understand this as a kind of amalgamation of collectivism and individualism: giving to the community is what makes the individual a hero in the eyes of others. Heroes are important influences but also powerful leaders. Their presence is important as a way to converge different values and goals in this heterogeneous context, focusing on common goals, but also legitimating the asymmetries in power relationships.

Acknowledgements

I wish to thank my colleagues Jan Ljungberg and Anna Maria Szczepanska in *The Open Source Project*, a research project at the Viktoria institute, Göteborg, Sweden. I would also like to thank Brian Fitzgerald and Joe Feller for inspiring discussions, workshops and seminars.

References

Bergquist, M. and Ljungberg, J. (2001), 'The Power of Gifts: Organizing Social Relationships in Open Source Communities', *Information Systems Journal: Special Issue on Open Source,* No. 11, London: Blackwell Science.

Bergquist, M. and Szczepanska, A.M. (2002), 'Creating a Common Ground: Developing Discursive Practices as Means for Aligning Systems Development Projects in Open Source Communities', *Proceedings from IRIS 25*, Conference on Information Systems Research in Scandinavia, Copenhagen: Copenhagen Business School.

Bezroukov, N. (1999), 'Open Source Software Development as a Special Type of Academic Research (Critique of Vulgar Raymondism)', *First Monday*, 4(10). Available online at http://firstmonday.org/issues/issue4_10/bezroukov/index.html.

Blume, H. (1999), 'Exquisite Source', *Atlantic Unbound*. Available online at http://www.theatlantic.com/unbound/digicult/dc990812.htm.

Chalmers, R. (1999), 'The Original Upstart', *Linux World*. Available online at http://www.softpanorama.org/OSS/postulates.html.

Cheal, D. (1988), *The Gift Economy*, London: Routledge.

Chubin, D.E. and Hackett, E.J. (1990), *Peerless Science: Peer Review and U.S. Science Policy*, Albany: State University of New York Press.

Feller, J. and Fitzgerald, B. (2002), *Understanding Open Source Software Development*, London: Addison Wesley.

Fielding, R.T. (1999), 'Shared Leadership in the Apache Project', *Communications of the ACM*, 42(4).

Ghosh, R. and Prakash, V.V. (2000), 'The Orbiten Free Software Survey', *First Monday*, Issue 7, July. Available online at http://www.firstmonday.org/issues/issue5_7/ghosh/index.html.

Godbout, J.T. (1998), *The World of the Gift*. London: McGill-Queen's University Press.

Godelier, M. (1999), *The Enigma of the Gift*, Cambridge: Polity.

Hagstrom, W. (1982), 'Gift Giving as an Organizing Principle in Science', in B. Barnes and D. Edge (eds), *Science in Context*, Stoney, Stratford: Open University Press.

von Hippel, E. (2001) 'Innovation by User Communities: Learning from Open-Source Software', *MIT Sloan Management Review*, 42(4).

Kollock, P. (1999), 'The Economies of Online Cooperation', in M. Smith and P. Kollock (eds), *Communities in Cyberspace*, London: Routledge.

Lakhani, K. and von Hippel, E. (2000), *How Open Source Software Works: 'Free' User-to-user Assistance*, MIT Sloan School of Management Working Paper #4117.

Levy, S. (1994 [1984]), *Hackers*, London: Penguin.

Ljungberg, J. (2000), 'Open Source Movements as a Model for Organizing'. *European Journal of Information Systems*, 9(4), December.

Mauss, M. (1990 [1950]) *The Gift: the Form and Reason for Exchange in Archaic Societies*, London: Routledge.

Merton, R.K. and Zuckerman, H. (1973), 'Institutionalized Patterns of Evaluation in Science', in R.K. Merton (ed.), *The Sociology of Science*, Chicago: University of Chicago Press.

Millen, D. (2000) 'Community Portals and Collective Goods: Conversation Archives as an Information Resource', in *Proceedings of HICSS 33*.

Mockus, A., Fielding, R. and Hersleb, J. (2000), 'A Case Study of Open Source Software Development: the Apache Server', in *Proceedings of International Conference on Software Engineering (ICSE) 2000*, Limerick, Ireland.

Moody, G. (2001), *Rebel Code: How Linus Torvalds and the Open Source Movement are Outmastering Microsoft*, London: Allen Lane.

O'Reilly, T. (1998), *The Open Source Revolution. Release 1.0, Esther Dyson's Monthly Report*. Available online at http://www.edventure.com/release1/1198.html.

—— (1999), 'Lessons from Open Source Development', *Communications of the ACM*, 42(4).

Osterhout, J. (1999), 'Free Software Needs Profit', *Communications of the ACM*, 42(4).

Raymond, E.S. (1999), *The Cathedral and the Bazaar: Musings on Linux and*

Open Source by an Accidental Revolutionary, Sebastopol: O'Reilly.

Rheingold, H. (1995), *The Virtual Community: Finding Connection in a Computerized World*, London: Minerva.

Sahlins, M. (1972), *Stone Age Economics*, Chicago: Aldine-Atherton.

Torvalds, L. and Diamond, D, (2001), *Just for Fun: The Story of an Accidental Revolutionary*, London: Texere.

Tuomi, I. (2000), 'Internet, Innovation, and Open Source: Actors in the Network', *First Monday*. Available online at http://www.firstmonday.org/issues/issue6_1/tuomi/index.html.

Young, R. and Goldman Rohm, W. (1999), *Under the Radar: How Red Hat Changed the Software Business – and took Microsoft by Surprise*, Scottsdale: Coriolis.

Ziman, J.M. (1968), Public Knowledge: an Essay Concerning the Social Dimension of Science, Cambridge: Cambridge University Press.

Index

aesthetics, 18, 19, 188, 192, 194, 195, 195, 200, 214
Agre, P.E., 171
America Online (AOL), 174
Appadurai, A., 2, 40, 135, 155, 161, 188
Apple Computer, 17, 123, 125, 154, 165, 168, 169, 173, 177, 182, 225
culture, 167
AppleLink, 165
architects, 14, 91–108 passim
ARPANET, 146–7, 173, 178, 180
audio links, 76, 77, 82

Baldwin, M., 196
Bangeman Report, 54–5
Banks, M., 4, 194
Bauman, Z., 183
Benjamin, W., 3, 190, 199
Berg, P. O., 121, 133
Bergquist, M., 134, 139n14, 232, 233
Bezroukov, N., 236
Biped, 190–1
Blume, H., 223, 227
body (bodily), 18, 19, 42, 57, 109, 191, 193, 194
and mind, 2
expressions, 193
parts, 43n2, 193
versus machine, 192–4, 200
Borsook, P., 171, 172

Bourdieu, P., 15
Boyce, L.N., 209
British Government, 11–12, 45, 46, 50, 54, 55
broadband, 131
Bruegger, U, 75, 83, 84
Brunsson, N., 182
Burruss, J.D., 209
business, anthropology of, 12

Calhoun, C., 77, 184n3
Campbell, C., 134
capitalism, 9, 12, 56, 75
free-market, 236
Carrier, J. G., 80
Cass, J., 190, 196
Castells, M., 2, 13, 69, 73, 74, 75, 81, 84, 87n5, 109, 129, 160, 168, 170
CDs (CD-ROM, records), 10, 33, 34, 35, 188, 198, 200, 227
installation, 136
Charman, E., 196
Cheal, D., 234
choreographers, 195, 196, 201
chromakey, 193, 196
Chubin, D.E., 237
Comaroff, J., 84
Comaroff, J.L., 84
computer, computing 3, 4, 10, 15, 16, 20, 25, 26, 27, 28, 31, 34, 38, 39, 40, 41, 42, 45, 46, 47, 50, 52, 61,

70, 75, 91, 96, 106, 107, 108, 124, 126, 127, 136, 148, 165, 181, 188
competency skills, 208, 211
course, 29, 46, 47
data organizer, 27
desktop, 94, 106, 122, 123, 126
equipment, 125, 128
game, 17, 27, 34
   playstation, 35
hyperlinks, 123, 130, 216
in the classroom, 205–17 passim
know-how, 27, 29, 30
laptops, 18, 92–, 92, 94, 95, 102, 106, 107, 108, 148, 149, 207, 209, 210, 211, 212, 213, 214, 217
matériel, 30, 32, 35
PC (personal computer), 34, 126, 225, 226
PowerPoint presentations, 72, 214, 216
   non-use of, 149, 159
   report, 213
practices, 120, 121, 128, 138
programming, 224, 225
supercomputers, 125
upgrading, 135–7
computerization and the work place, 1–2, 27, 43, 122, 126
conceptual congruity, 15, 121–4, 137
consumption, 19, 41, 42
control, 10, 26, 41, 76, 102
   see also transnational panoptical environment
cosmopolitanism, 16, 17, 146, 160
crackers, 172–4
Cullberg, B., 196
Cunningham, M., 190, 196
cybercafés, 10
cybersex, 17, 193
cyberspace, 56, 158, 165, 175–183
   passim, 193, 194

Dafova, M., 190
dance, 18–19, 187–201 passim
   and democracy, 189–191, 199–200
dancers, 19, 188, 191, 194–5, 197, 199
Delio, M., 173
Dery, M., 175
designers, office 14, 21, 94–112 passim
Developing Countries Networking Symposium, 145
Diamond, D., 241, 233
Dilley, R., 77
Dodge, M., 182
dot.com
   boom, 55
   bubble, 7, 9, 11
   fiasco, 7, 9, 11
Downey, G. L., 2, 56, 77
Dubinskas, F., 2
Dumit, J., 2, 56, 77
Dunning, J., 200
DVD, 34

e-commerce, 4
economy, 9, 11, 54, 55, 57, 60, 104, 112, 230
   gift, 223, 234
   global, 73–5, 119
   information, 93
   market, 223, 227
   moral, 234
   network, 119
   new, 119,120, 121, 122, 124, 137
e-greeting card, 17
Elias, N., 169
e-mail, 3, 4, 28, 47, 50, 51, 72, 76, 91, 107, 108, 127, 129, 148, 149, 150, 153, 157, 158, 170, 174, 175, 177, 181, 229
   Microsoft Hotmail, 174

SPAM, 175
  Yahoo Mail, 174
emoticons, 176–178
  smileys, 176–178
  on SMS, 177
Enyedy, N., 210
Eriksen, T.H., 79, 85
Escobar, A., 147, 154
ethnographic approch, 2, 22
European Union, 46, 48, 49, 50, 54,
  55
Evans, P. B., 119

Feller, J., 223, 226
Ferguson, J., 160
Fielding, R., 226
film, 189, 190, 191, 211
financial analysts, 69–85 passim
financial brokers, 12, 69–85 passim
financial traders, 69–85 passim
Fitzgerald, B., 223, 226
flexibility, 101–104, 106–108, 112
  flexible, 11, 48, 51, 53, 55, 62, 64,
    65, 93, 101–11, 113, 170, 209
Foucault, M., 42
Framfab, 120, 121, 122, 123, 124,
  133, 135, 137, 138
Free Software Foundation (FSF),
  225
future, 4, 5, 7–18 passim, 27, 46, 60,
  72, 119–138 passim
  and S-curve, 15, 124–5, 133
  and time, 4
  see vaporware

Gaffin, A., 176
Garsten, C., 2, 4, 82, 85, 113n18, 130,
  154, 160, 168
gender, 28, 167
Ghosts and Astronauts, 187, 188, 189,
  199

Gifford, B., 210
Gilson-Ellis, J., 191–192
globalization, globality, 1, 2, 16, 54,
  57, 69, 73, 75, 93, 104, 109, 146,
  152, 159, 160, 167, 182, 187, 188,
  193, 224
  fragmented, 82–6
Glasgow, N., 220
Godbout, J.T., 228
Godelier, M., 228
Goffman, E., 19
Goldman Rohm, W., 233
Ghosh, R., 226
Green, S., 45
Grimshaw, A., 194
Gusterson, H., 4, 157

hackers, 172–3, 181, 225, 231, 234
Hacket, E. J., 237
Hagstrom, W, 237
Hakken, D., 2, 4, 147
Hambridge, S., 181
Hanna, J. L., 189, 190, 199
Hannerz, U., 2, 4, 85, 146, 148, 150,
  151, 152, 154, 158, 160
Haraway, D., 2, 56, 57
Harvey, P., 45
Hasselström, A., 80
Haythornthwaite, C., 183
Heelas, P., 167
Heitkötter, J., 185
Hersleb, J., 226
von Hippel, E., 223, 227
Hirsch, E., 41
history, 9
home, 77, 102
  and computers, 15, 122, 126, 129,
    130, 131, 149
  renegotiations of, 1
  within the office, 99, 100
  work from, 1, 15

home page, 4
Hoxmeier, J. A., 132, 133

IBM, 17, 169
ICANN, 155
ICT (information and
    communications technologies),
    11, 46, 47, 54–61 passim
see technologies
ideals, 7–22 passim, 48
ideology, 13
INET (International Networking), 149
Intel, 132
Internet, 2, 3, 4, 5, 11, 16, 20, 31, 32,
    33, 35, 37, 43, 45, 47, 49, 55, 120,
    123, 124, 125, 129, 130, 145, 146,
    148, 149, 150, 152, 154, 155, 156,
    157, 158, 168, 170, 171, 172, 187,
    188, 190, 201, 209, 215, 216, 223,
    224, 226, 227, 229, 230, 234, 235
and social interaction, 167, 182
and the developing world, 152–7,
    160
community, 145–161 passim, 171,
    228
filters, 208, 214
governance, 155
informalization, 165–183 passim,
    182
pioneers, 145–161 passim
portals, 232
regulation, 165–183 passim, 182
Society (ISOC), 145, 146, 148,
    151, 153, 154, 156, 157, 160
annual conference of, INET, 145,
    146, 148, 149, 150, 151, 152,
    153, 154, 155, 156, 157, 158,
    160
web site, 149
standardization, 168, 170, 178, 180,
    182

videoconference link, 187, 199
Internet Engineering Task Force
    (IETF), 168, 178–181
Intranet, 87n7, 106, 165
Irish dancing, 197–199
IT (information technologies), 46, 50,
    124, 125, 127, 132, 133, 136, 137,
    138, 156
see technologies

Jacobsson, B., 182
Johansson, M., 125
Johnson, D.T., 209
Johnson, S., 135

Kamiya, G., 171
Kelly, K., 1, 119, 121
Kiesler, S., 170
Kisselgoff, A., 189
Kitchin, R., 182
Knorr Cetina, K., 75, 83, 84
Kollock, P., 229, 234
Kozel, S., 187, 188, 192, 193
Kozol, J., 207
Kvarnström, K., 197

Lakhani, K., 227
Lally, E., 15
Latour, B., 147, 161
Lave, J., 78
Learndirect, 45
learning, 20, 47, 205, 215, 230, 231
    computer assisted, 206, 208,
        213–14, 216, 216, 217
    Internet-based, 20
    lifelong, 11, 45, 48, 51
    practices, 207
Lerdell, D., 168
Levy, S., 172, 181, 225
Linux, 225–26, 230, 233, 238
Ljungberg, J., 226, 232

Luddite, 17, 59, 172
  neo-Luddite approach, 172

Malkin, G., 178
Manchester Women´s Electronic
  Village Hall (WEVH), 45, 46,
  47, 48, 49–54 passim, 60
Manovich, L., 121, 123, 130
Manuel, P., 3
Marcus, G. E., 4, 158, 159
market, 9, 13, 30, 31, 33, 40, 48,
  69–87 passim, 124, 132, 134, 154,
  188, 237
  black, 32, 33, 34, 35, 36, 37, 40
marketplace, global, 197–9, 200
materiality, 14, 16, 18
material objects (goods), 229, 230
Mauss, M., 228–9, 234
media, digital, 121, 122
  new, 18, 48, 61, 122, 169
Merton, R.K, 237
methodological approaches, 4
  intervention, 205–17 passim,
    217–220n1
  interviews, 4
  mobile field studies, 4
  multi-sited field studies, 4, 157,
    158, 159
  on-line (e-mail, e-mailing lists,
    discussion groups, websites), 4,
    158, 168
  participant observation, 4
  polymorphous engagements, 4,
    157, 158
  transnational field studies, 4
Miller, D., 2, 3, 4, 5, 8, 10, 16, 18, 40,
  41, 56, 80, 147, 160, 168, 200
Microsoft, 132, 133, 225, 226
  MSN Chat, 176
  Windows 98, 126, 136
  Word, 16, 128

Misztal, B. A., 169, 170
Mitchell, W., 110
mobile phones, 1, 3, 26, 28, 30, 32,
  91, 94, 95, 106, 107
mobility, renegotiations of, 1,
  101–104, 106–108, 112
  hypermobility, 73, 74, 75, 81
  see work place
Mockus, A., 226
modems, 1, 129, 130–1
Moody, G., 225
morality, 10
Morphy, H., 4, 194
motion capture computer technology,
  190
MUDs, 181, 183–4n2

NAIS Report, 155
National Grid for Learning, 45
netiquette, 17, 165, 174–6, 183, 232
  USENET, 174–5
netizens, 178–181, 183
network society, 73–4, 120, 122, 124,
  137, 160
newbies, 21, 181, 224, 231, 232, 233
Nielsen, J., 127, 130
Norberg, P., 77, 79, 84, 86n3
Norman, D. A., 126, 127, 128, 136

objectification, 16
office,
  alternative, 93–94
  flexibility, 14, 101–4, 105, 106,
    107, 109, 110, 111
  mobile, 91–112 passim
  virtual, 93
off-line, (world), 2, 16, 17, 18, 168,
  181
Olsson, C., 197
on-line, (world, community), 2, 4, 11,
  16, 17, 18, 45, 50, 54, 55, 56, 59,

60, 61, 110, 149, 167, 168, 181,
182, 224, 228, 231, 233
cyber networks, 69
message services 77, 81, 82, 83
news, 71, 78
social interaction, communication
146, 148, 177
trading 77, 84
open-source technology, 20–2,
223–239 passim
flaming, 232, 235, 236
fonts, 233
O'Reilly, T., 226, 227
organizational culture, 1
Osterhout, J., 227
Overing, J., 42

pager, 26
Parry, J., 201
Penman, R., 189
Perkins, D., 209
Pfaffenberger, B., 2, 147, 168
photography, 189
place, 2, 75–81 passim, 92–3, 107,
109–12
placebound, 85
Platt, C., 181
pornography, 10, 17
porters (hospital) 10–11, 13, 20, 22,
25–43 passim
Povall, R., 191
Prakash, V.V., 226
prerecorded step sound, 197–8, 199,
200
property rights, 223, 225
and dance, 189, 199

Rapport, N., 38, 41, 42
Raymond, E.S., 173, 225, 226, 227,
231, 233, 234, 236
regulation, 17, 18, 21, 26, 48, 75, 165,

167, 169, 182
anti-regulation, 169, 171, 174
deregulation, 73, 75
reregulation, 75
self-regulation, 155
revolution
and dance technology, 200
and television, 3
computer, 4, 127
information, 46, 48, 54–61 passim
Rheingold, H., 228
Ribbing, M., 175
Riverdance, 19, 189, 194, 197–9, 200
Riverside University High School
(RUHS), 205–17 passim
Robertson, R., 160
Roszak, T., 172
Rubidge, S., 190, 201

Saffo, P., 186
Sahlins, M., 228
Salaf, J., 183
Sale, K., 172
Sassen, S., 75
Schneider, M. A., 169
Schwarz, H., 112n1, 114n30
Scott, J., C., 42
screens, 1, 3, 12, 19, 25, 56, 70, 71,
76, 77, 82, 84, 91, 96, 127, 188–9,
191, 194, 195, 199, 200, 208, 216
cinema, 188
making dance for, 196
sexuality, exceptional, 36, 37, 38
Shea, V., 175, 181
Sher, B.T., 209
Slater, D., 2, 3, 4, 5, 10, 16, 18, 40,
56, 80, 147, 160, 168, 200
SMS, 177
Smyth, S., 198, 199
socially excluded, 11, 46, 47, 48, 54,
58, 59, 60

social exclusion, 11, 48, 52, 54, 55, 56, 58, 59, 60
social welfare, 11, 53, 54
socio-technical systems, 2
Sorell, W., 190, 190, 199
soundscape, 192
space, 1, 74, 75, 80, 85
  in dance, 188, 192
  work (office), 92–93, 96, 97, 98, 100, 101, 102, 103, 104, 106, 108, 109–12
speaker systems, 71, 76, 77, 81, 82
speed, 15, 16, 20, 58, 77, 79, 82, 85, 119–138 passim, 149, 188, 193, 198, 208, 215, 216, 230–1, 233
Sproull, L., 170
Stafford, B., 221
Strannegård, L., 120
Strathern, M., 41, 42
students at risk, 205, 206, 207
subversion, 10, 20, 22, 38, 40, 41
support sound, 197–8
Szczepanska, A.M., 233

Tamm Hallström, K., 180
teachers, 20, 205, 206, 207, 208, 209, 211, 213, 214, 215, 216
technolibertarianism, 170–2
technologies
  and locality, 2
  and office, 106–12
  and women, 53
  and work practice, 1, 7
  commodification of, 7, 10, 13, 22
  communications, 1, 2, 3, 4, 8, 25, 41, 50, 56, 60, 73, 79, 110
  digital, 123, 188, 200
  information, 1, 2, 3, 4, 13, 25, 27, 41, 50, 56, 60, 69, 73, 76, 77, 79, 81, 83, 85, 110, 205
  myth of origin, 9,10,11,12, 13, 22

new, 2,8, 9, 10, 13, 16, 17, 18, 19, 21, 22, 40, 42, 57, 92, 124, 126, 131, 133, 134, 188, 189, 191, 200
power of, 41
portable, 94, 107, 108, 131
technoscapes, 188, 199–201
Telematic Dreaming, 192–194
telephone, 10,11, 25–26, 32, 70, 76, 77, 81, 92, 106, 157
telepresence technology, 187, 192
television, 19, 76, 127, 158, 188, 189, 190, 191, 195, 196, 197, 198, 199, 200
text messaging, 32
Tharp, T., 196
The Secret Project, 191–2
Thrift, N., 80, 127, 138
time, renegotiations of, 1, 4, 15, 74, 75–81 passim, 83, 84, 85, 230, 231, 236
  and waiting, 126–9, 130
  management, 216
  real-time, 69, 76, 77, 78, 82, 83, 84, 85
  savers, 217
  temporal cycles and financial flows, 78–9
  temporal immediacy, 129
  see also future
Torvalds, L., 225, 230, 233, 238
transnational anthropology, 158
transnationality, 2, 85, 86, 146, 152, 154, 155, 187, 200
transnational panoptical environment, 76
transparency, 112, 128
  transparent, 78, 230, (screen), 188, 201
Traweek, S., 2
Trouillot, M.-R., 74, 86

Tuomi, I., 223
Turkle, S., 42

Uimonen, P., 4, 145, 146, 147, 155, 156, 158, 160
Unander-Scharin, Å., 200
United Nations, 54
Usenet News Groups, 231, 232

Van Tassel-Baska, J., 209
vaporware, 15, 132–3, 138
videos, 33, 34, 188, 190, 191, 192, 194, 195, 196, 198, 199, 200
    cameras, 192, 193
    links 76, 77, 82
virtual, 19, 40
    collaboration, 235
    communities, 229, 234
    interaction, 192, 193
    sex, 193
    societies, 229
virtualism, 8
virtuality, social, 2, 80–7 passim, 168, 182–183, 194, 199–201
    and social life, 2, 74
visual anthropology, 4, 194
visualization, visuality, the visual 4, 188, 194
    and graphical interface of hierarchical file system, 123
    and work practices, 4
    in schools, 210
    new anthropology of, 4
visual literacy, 208, 210, 215

voluntary organizations, 11, 46,47, 48, 49, 53, 55, 59, 60,154

Wagner, P., 169
web browsers, 130
    Internet Explorer, 130
    Netscape Navigator, 130
web pages, 3, 130, 214, 235
    see also home page
websites, 4, 129, 130, 207, 208, 217
    chat rooms, 4
discussion groups (lists), 4, 235
Wellman, B., 183
Wenger, E., 78
Whelan, B., 198
Williams, R., 3, 190
Willim, R., 120, 138n2, 139n13
women´s groups, 11, 13, 50, 52
Woolgar, S., 8, 16
work place, 22, 91–112 passim
work practice, 1, 5, 7, 8, 41, 188, 189, 200
    see technologies
World Wide web (the Web, WWW), 31, 36, 37, 38, 123, 129, 130, 148, 157, 167, 181, 183, 208, 211, 214, 216, 226
Wulff, H., 4, 40, 79, 80, 188, 195, 196, 197, 200, 202n5
Wurster, T. S., 119

Young, R., 233

Ziman, J.M., 237
Zuckerman, H., 237